GENDER VIOLENCE AND THE TRANSNATIONAL POLITICS OF THE HONOR CRIME

GENDER VIOLENCE AND THE TRANSNATIONAL POLITICS OF THE HONOR CRIME

Dana M. Olwan

THE OHIO STATE UNIVERSITY PRESS
COLUMBUS

Library of Congress Cataloging-in-Publication Data
Names: Olwan, Dana M., 1981– author.
Title: Gender violence and the transnational politics of the honor crime / Dana M. Olwan.
Description: Columbus : The Ohio State University Press, [2021] | Includes bibliographical references and index. | Summary: "A transnational feminist examination of how responses to gender-based violence known as the 'honor crime' become entangled in national debates about belonging and citizenship in legal, political, and literary genres, across the United States, Canada, Jordan, and Palestine"—Provided by publisher.
Identifiers: LCCN 2020034294 | ISBN 9780814214664 (cloth) | ISBN 0814214665 (cloth) | ISBN 9780814281024 (ebook) | ISBN 0814281028 (ebook)
Subjects: LCSH: Women—Violence against. | Honor killings.
Classification: LCC HV6250.4.W65 O46 2021 | DDC 364.152/3—dc23
LC record available at https://lccn.loc.gov/2020034294

Cover design by Derek Thornton
Cover image by Lena Merhej
Text design by Juliet Williams
Type set in Adobe Minion Pro

∞ The paper used in this publication meets the minimum requirements of the American National Standard for Information Sciences—Permanence of Paper for Printed Library Materials. ANSI Z39.48-1992.

CONTENTS

ILLUSTRATIONS

ACKNOWLEDGMENTS

THIS BOOK has journeyed with me over multiple geographies and homes for over a decade. Its completion is owed in large part to so many people and communities who helped me recognize its importance and encouraged me to pursue the difficult intellectual and political questions that I wanted to ask and tried to answer here.

My work was made possible through a number of generous grants and scholarships that helped support this project. A Future Minority Studies postdoctoral fellowship informed the shape of the project in profound ways, connecting me with Chandra Talpade Mohanty, who has supported my work from day one. Her brilliant scholarship resonates through many of the pages in this work. Thanks are due to the Simone de Beauvoir Institute, which granted me the Lilian Robinson Scholar Award and hosted me at Concordia University as I was completing my research on honor crime discourses in Canada. A Palestinian American Research Council grant helped me better understand contestations of gender violence in Palestine. Thanks are due also to the College of Arts and Sciences at Syracuse University for its generous support of my research and the production of this book.

I am thankful to the members of the Department of Women's and Gender Studies at Syracuse University (SU). My colleagues in the department, Himika Bhattacharya, Pedro DiPietro, Eunjung Kim, Vivian May, Danika Medak-Saltzman, Gwendolyn Pough, Robin Riley, and Chandra Talpade Mohanty, are all incredible scholars whose commitments to feminist scholarship and pedagogy have inspired my own in so many ways. I also am grateful for the crucial administrative assistance and support of Susann DeMocker-Shedd and Alice Loomis. At SU, I have had the pleasure of working with brilliant students and activists from whom I have learned so much. Special thanks are owed to Laura Jaffee, Pamela Sertzen, and Nicole Tanquary for sharing their feminist pedagogies, their labor, and their support. My students in my undergraduate classes and senior students in the feminist solidary seminar have challenged and transformed how I understand the world.

Transnational feminist scholarship has framed and inspired my analysis throughout this work. The works of Lila Abu-Lughod, Elora Halim Chowdhury, Yasmin Jiwani, Nadine Naber, Sherene Razack, Chandra Talpade Mohanty, and Sunera Thobani have indelibly shaped my own. I thank Elora Halim Chowdhury for her support of the project. Thanks to Nayrouz Abu Hatoum, Sophia Azeb, Lisa Bhungalia, Chandni Desai, Keith Feldman, Mali Golomb-Leavitt, Saleem Haddad, Emilie Cameron, Chris Churchill, Michelle Hartman, Tamara Isaak, Jimmy Johnson, Vani Kannan, Marcy Knopf-Newman, Natalie Kouri-Towe, Haneen Maikey, Eli Manning, Corinne Mason, Emily Mitchell-Eaton, Scott Morgensen, Jennifer Moghannam, Shaista Patel, Randa Serhan, Mejduline Shomali, Gohar Siddiqui, Heather Turcotte, Ariana Vigil, and Suzy Zepeda for their friendship, guidance, and support throughout this journey. Dima Ayoub's love and laughter have carried me through multiple moves across many borders. Mari Spira's fierce intellect and our sustained connection for many years have transformed my understanding of feminist praxis.

The following colleagues and friends read and offered generous and incisive feedback on parts of this manuscript and different iterations of my work. Allison Brown provided editorial development that helped reshape the trajectory of this project. Vani Kannan offered important research work that helped guide my chapter on US honor crime discourses. Christine Abbott provided vital editorial assistance. Wahiba Abu-Ras offered helpful and encouraging advice. Many thanks are owed to Chris Eng, Amy Kallander, Margaret Little, Corinne Mason, Margaret Pappano, Shaista Patel, Sophie Richter-Devroe, Robin Riley, Mari Spira, and Chandra Talpade Mohanty for their intellectual insights, their advice, and their work in reading and reviewing parts of my manuscript. Carol Fadda has labored over every single part of this manuscript and cheered me to the finish line. Across the Syracuse University campus, a number of colleagues have become mentors and friends whose compassion, commitment, and kindness have made the academy a more livable place. I thank Barbara Applebaum for supporting my work from the moment I arrived at the SU campus. Thanks also to Mike Gill, Kara Herold,

Margaret Himley, and Charlotte Sharp for supporting me in various stages of this process.

I am thankful to friends from Canada who made me feel remembered and loved in spite of the distance and borders between settler colonial states. I thank them for crossing these borders when I could not cross them. Molly Kraft and Eliane Mazzawi made one of the first visits to Syracuse when I moved here. Our hikes in Ithaca and incessant laughter still ring in my ears many years after that fun-filled trip. Raneem Azzam is a dear and constant friend. Trina Zeimbekis embodies a type of love, care, friendship that I aspire to. I thank her for the baklava-making nights and for making me see what I often miss. With Aruna Boodram, Yasmeen Abdelhadi, Wren Pragg, and Nanky Rai, I took a road trip to New Orleans that healed my heart and reminded me of the power of friendships born of trust.

Sunera Thobani's fierce and brilliant feminist politics have provided a compass for my own. I am grateful for the deep commitment and love she has shown me since the day I met her. Harsha Walia invited me into her radical activist world and helped me connect the dots between and across so many struggles. I thank her and Nassim Elbardouh for the type of love that distance cannot unmake. I thank Elena Ismail for many great meals and her thoughtful company. Özlem Sensoy became a friend and mentor in Vancouver, and I owe much to her. Many thanks are also due to Abdullah Khalifeh, a kind friend. Margaret Pappano and Adnan Husain treated me like family when I lived in Kingston, breaking fast together during Ramadan and sustaining the connection between our worlds when we no longer shared the same spaces. Ariel Salzmann was always generous with her time. Laith Marouf and Gretchen King generously hosted me in Montreal countless times. Margaret Little's heart and feminist politics have been an inspiration for more than a decade. I am so grateful for her friendship and care. I am thankful for the rekindled connection with David Thompson. Amidst a global pandemic, he reminds me of the power of words to heal and transform.

Between 2015 and 2018 I spent three formative years at the Doha Institute for Graduate Studies (DI). There I was welcomed by Ayat Hamdan and Inaam Charaf, who generously helped me navigate a new academic space and learn to write, think, and teach in Arabic once more. I was lucky to have the opportunity to coteach a class on Arab feminisms with Sophie Richter-Devroe, who quickly became a cherished friend. I thank my students who taught me so much about the diverse and intertwined social and political struggles of people from across the region. In Doha, Jad Kawtharani, Dana Kawtharani, Ayhab Saad, and Ahlam Saad opened their homes and hearts to me from the moment we met. Both families welcomed my bonds and friendships with their daughters, Joud and Salma. I thank Paolo D'Urbano and Laura Treglia for their continued friendship and support. Eyas Hmouz became a trusted friend. Maram Kabbara's friendship, heart, and wit made leaving Doha a very difficult decision. I am grateful for our continuing and growing friendship.

In Jordan, the lifelong friendships of Rand Al Jammal, Nour Abu Ragheb, and Dima Zannouneh have been so central to my growth. I thank Dima Zannouneh for her love and support and the many memories we have shared together since our days at Yarmouk University. Abeer Dababneh was a generous host at the Center for Women's Studies of the University of Jordan. My friendship with Farah Al-Haddad has traveled with us through our moves from Jordan and the US. In Palestine, Ayhab and Ahlam Saad were generous hosts in Ramallah. Haneen Maikey's friendship and love have transformed my time in Palestine.

My return to Syracuse and the US after a long absence was made easier with new and renewed friendships that shortened the Syracuse winters and helped me make a new home in the US. Christine Abbott's constant love has spanned two decades of life in the US and many unforgettable road trips and travels. Amy Kallander, George Kallander, and their daughters, Mona and Sabrina, have provided support and laughter when things were hard. I thank Amy for nourishing our friendship with late-night calls, check-in emails, and run encouragements and for being there for me from the moment I set foot in this city and on this campus. Farha Ternikar's kindness and friendship have been a gift for many years. Robin Riley has stood by me through many ups and downs. Many thanks are owed to Jessie Nissim, who is a model of compassionate love and care. Thanks also to Gretchen Purser for many chats and coffees. Rashmi Gangamma and I arrived at Syracuse at the same time, and we have been friends since our orientation. Hannah Ehrenreich welcome me into her home in Syracuse, making me see this city in a way no one else has. Nikeeta Slade's politics and insights have inspired and transformed my analysis so often. Thanks also to Pedram Magsoud-Nia for political discussions that redefined our friendship. I thank Laura Jaffee for her ginger cookies and care. Laila Kobrossy Audi's kind heart and genuineness are what authentic friendships are made of. Fahimeh Zaheri's fierce sisterly love and support have helped me navigate many difficult life decisions and moments. Siham Doughman's kindness and positive outlook on the world are an inspiration. While I was completing this manuscript, the sharing of laughs and growing friendships with Su Nam and Susan Thomas were a much-needed gift. Thank you to each and every one of you for all the delicious food we have shared and the many more memories we will create.

Taralee Cyphers believed in my project from the moment I met her. I thank her for the valuable advice, care, and efficiency with which she has championed my work. Many thanks are owed to her, Laurie Avery, Rebecca Bostock, Kristen Ebert-Wagner, Kristina Wheeler, and the entire editorial team at The Ohio State University Press for supporting this book. I am also thankful for the generative feedback of the anonymous reviewers of this manuscript whose comments helped me refine many of the arguments made throughout this work. Sections of chapter 1 are revised versions of previously published work: "Pinkwashing the 'Honor Crime': Murdered Muslim Women and the Politics of Posthumous Solidarities," *Signs: Journal of Women in Culture and Society* 44, no. 4 (2019): 905–30; and "'No Place in Canada': Triumphant Discourses, Murdered Women, and the 'Honor Crime,'" in *In the Name of 'Honor': Responding to Violence Against Women from Socio-legal and Policing Perspectives,* edited by Aisha Gill, Karl Roberts, and Carolyn Strange (London: Palgrave Macmillan, 2013), 218–36. I thank Sharif Mosa, Samar Dudin, Majd Sidawi, and the Jordanian National Commission for Women for allowing me to include their work and images in my book. I am grateful for their kindness and generosity. I thank Lena Merhej for designing the inspirational and moving cover of this book and for emphasizing themes of feminist resistance in her art.

Through the long writing process, messages from my family members, dispersed across the world, reminded me that I had so many people rooting for me. My aunt Hala Al Aruri and my uncle Musa Al Aruri made Jordan home again with delicious meals and love. I am thankful to my cousins Ahlam Abed, Diana Olwan, Zaineb Olwan, and Maha Zibdawi, who took time out of their worlds to encourage me to keep moving forward. Their supportive messages helped me feel connected and cared for always. Hana Al Aruri's strength and resilience inspire me. I am thankful for the sisterly love that we grew and our bond and connection, which go far beyond biology.

I would be lost without Carol Fadda's love, friendship, and sisterhood. The completion of this book is owed in large part to her critical and meticulous feedback, her unwavering support, and her generous intellect. From the moment we met, Carol welcomed me into her life unconditionally, making me a part of her family both in Syracuse and in Beirut. Nada, Wadad, and Nahi, Carol's late father, made Lebanon a second home. Sean Conrey's kindness, compassion, and care are what radical love is made of. I thank all of them for the countless calls, meals, walks, and runs that have sustained and deepened our connections for many years now. Carol, Sean, and their daughters, Mira and Emily, are my home away from home and my family.

My deepest gratitude goes to my nieces and nephews: Emily, Mira, Omar, Jenna, Faris, and Layla. Having the privilege of being a part of their magical worlds and seeing them grow into strong and thoughtful beings has been a privilege and a gift. My siblings, Rami, Rana, and Omar, have supported me throughout this journey and have stood by me when my life took strange and unexpected turns. Rana's tough-love approach has helped me in more ways than she knows. I am in awe of her no-nonsense views on the world and her unwavering love for me. Thanks to Kate Azima for her loving heart and gentle kindness. Thanks to Lina Sarie for the supportive messages and the virtual calls. In Mohamed Chaaban, I have a true brother. His goodness shines through always.

My final thanks go to my parents, Mohammed Olwan and Hiyam Abudhais, whose love and care for me is boundless. My father's intellect and integrity inspire and ground me. My mother's intuition and wisdom are my guide. I thank them both for modeling strength and resilience in the face of life's certain uncertainties.

This book is dedicated to people struggling against gender violence and fighting to bring an end to it in all its formations.

INTRODUCTION

Genealogies of the "Honor Crime"

IN 2000 the United Nations Population Fund (UNFPA) published "Lives Together, Worlds Apart: Men and Women in a Time of Change" as part of the yearly State of the World Population report. The eighty-four-page study, published at the turn of the century, focused on gender inequalities between men and women, arguing for the importance of "bringing gender inequality fully into the light and treating it as a matter of urgency affecting both human rights and development priorities" (2). The document combines country-based reports with research and analysis about the role of states and nongovernment organizations in creating safe and healthy environments for their communities. Nestled within the document is a section that discusses violence against girls and women as a human rights violation that negatively impacts their health and well-being. In this section, the document specifically names sex trafficking and "'honour' killings" as two forms of violence that are on the rise and that affect a growing number of children, girls, and women worldwide (29). In its discussion of the honor crime, the report estimates that "throughout the world, perhaps as many as 5,000 women and girls a year are murdered by members of their own families, many of them for the 'dishonour' of having been raped" (29).[1] The report attributes this form of violence to "the community's or the family's demand for sexual chastity and virginity" (29), suggesting that these crimes take place all around "but tend to be more prevalent in, but are not limited to, countries with a majority Muslim population" (30).

Since its publication in the UNFPA report, this estimate has become one of the most cited numbers on the phenomenon of gender violence known as the "honor crime"—often losing its initial reference point or citational origin. Frequently appearing in a broad array of nongovernment reports, news media articles, and academic texts, the UN-endorsed number serves to give a name to a specific and distinct form of gender-based violence. This statistic also raises the alarm about the honor crime's impact on girls and women and the crime's abrogation of their right to life, safety, and human dignity. Astonishingly, the UN report provides no information on the methods and strategies used to arrive at this estimate but provides the qualification of "perhaps" to note that the number it cites may, in fact, be an underestimate of the crime's scale or its rate of occurrence. More than a figure that measures the number of women murdered in the name of honor, the UN estimate disseminates and constructs its own truths about the magnitude and scope of this phenomenon, which is today speculated to claim the lives of almost 12,000 women per year (Gill 2018). As a numerical figure that draws its power from the authority of its nongovernment purveyors and their stated investment in gender equality and women's rights, this number has become a definitive measure for honor-related violence and its annual rates of occurrence. Stripped of historical and geographic specificity, it operates as a free-floating signifier that produces transnational circuitries of knowledge about a social problem of macabre global proportions.

Knowledge about the honor crime has sought to reveal both the global magnitude of this form of gender-based violence and its specific features or identifying traits. Citations of the UN figure do not always acknowledge their original source, but they are often accompanied by notes about its limitations. In the statistical data section of the Honor Based Violence Network, for example, the UN number is included with an introductory note that states that "these figures are considered estimates and are widely believed to be severe underestimates. Due to lack of focused reporting and recording of Honour Killings internationally very little is known about the true extent of HBV worldwide."[2] Such remarks do not question the methodology or validity of the collected data but point, instead, to their shortcomings and their potential underestimation of the phenomenon of honor-related violence. Similarly, an article on honor-based violence published in National Geographic alludes to the difficulties of counting honor crimes but nevertheless claims that "hundreds, if not thousands, of women are murdered by their families each year in the name of family 'honor.' It's difficult to get precise numbers on the phenomenon of honor killing; the murders frequently go unreported, the perpetrators unpunished, and the concept of family honor justifies the act in the eyes of some societies" (Mayell 2002). Oscillating between a figure that estimates hundreds and possibly thousands of killings, the author emphasizes the lack of accuracy around this form of violence which is attributed to underreporting.

In other coverage of the crime and its occurrence in the US, Gregg Zoroya (2016) of *USA Today* acknowledges that "no one really knows" how common honor-related violence is but states that the "the practice appears to be getting worse, although it's unclear whether the higher numbers stem from better reporting or greater frequency. The Internet appears to play a crucial role, both in learning more information about the violence and in creating more opportunity for families to track down inappropriate behavior by relatives." Increased knowledge about honor-related violence is here linked to modern forms of information collection and reporting through the internet, but the author concedes that it is not clear whether the internet generates what we know about this violence or whether it simply documents actual higher incidences and rates of occurrence. In other words, even in reports that insist on the pervasiveness of honor-related violence, there remains an unresolved tension between the claimed figures and the methods used to procure and disseminate them.

Global efforts to end the phenomenon of gender and sexual violence have predominantly employed two strategies: the first relates to the work of "quantifying" the social problem of gender and sexual violence. Typically, this includes the production of a measure of the problem or the collecting of data and information, which is then translated into numerical evidence. This evidence is then combined with qualitative knowledge (some explicitly stated and some implicitly drawn) that is then used to shed light on the magnitude or scale of the social issue under study. The second pertains to producing policies, procedures, and indicators that can help mitigate or end the numerically identified social problem. The quantification of gender-based violence has a long history, one that has been codified in the various reports, documents, and fact sheets produced by the United Nations, nongovernment organizations such as Amnesty International and Human Rights Watch, and a large body of qualitative academic literature. The need to track gender-based violence emanates from a recognition of its global impact and the belief that producing numerical knowledge about the problem can assist in efforts to contest and end it. Work to quantitatively study gender-based violence draws its legitimacy from the power of numbers or the belief that numbers reflect, rather than construct, uncontested and scientifically collected bare facts about the world. Writing on the practices of measuring and quantifying gender violence,

Sally Engle Merry argues that numbers "convey an aura of objective truth and scientific authority despite the extensive interpretive work that goes into their construction" (2016, 1). Merry's work explores the links between numerical information and the processes of creating indicators or measures of complex and not readily traceable or easily calculable phenomenon like human rights, gender violence, and sex trafficking. Providing a cautionary note about the "seductions of quantification," Merry's study reveals that the ability to produce numerical figures about such issues operates under the assumption that they are, in fact, not only knowable but also quantifiable social phenomenon.

Critical scrutiny of the numerical edifice that surrounds the honor crime has been expressed by anthropologist Lila Abu-Lughod who, in her groundbreaking work on the subject, has stated that "reports regularly note that honor crimes are on the increase; however, no evidence or explanation is given of how the figures are derived" (2011, 38). Abu-Lughod questions the terms of classification on which honor-based violence is identified and then counted. She argues that such work requires the disappearance of the context and the specificities of these crimes. Drawing attention to the disputable methodologies that inform the nascent claim that twenty-three to twenty-seven honor killings occur in the US per year, Leti Volpp (2019) has carefully shown how data about the honor crime work in tandem with assumptions about the nature of this form of gender violence and assumptions about the backgrounds of their perpetrators.[3] As Volpp states, "Of course, data has its own magic, carrying with it the notions of objectivity, science, and truth. Yet there is also a willing belief in the prevalence of 'honor killings' among Muslims that aligns with longstanding narratives of the dangerous Muslim man and the imperiled Muslim woman" (167–68).[4] Despite the important scholarly interventions surrounding available numerical data, quantitative information continues to converge with a set of structuring, essentialist, and generalized narratives about the form of this violence and its perpetrators in order to produce the phenomenon that is known as the "honor killing" or the "honor crime." Although no definitional consensus about what constitutes an honor crime exists today, data about honor killings produced by the UN and other nongovernment organizations, government reports, media accounts, and activist interventions against honor-based violence, combined with a bevy of scholarly and academic literature on the subject, coalesce to create powerful discourses surrounding honor-related violence, its staggering rates of occurrence, and its far-reaching scope.[5]

Apprehension surrounding the contemporary constructions, deployments, and circulations of knowledge about gender violence known as the honor crime gives shape to some of the central concerns of this book. This apprehension is not animated by a questioning of the existence of gender-based violence that is motivated by and carried out in the name of "honor"; nor is it compelled by a desire to disavow such forms of violence as unassociated with the religion of Islam and therefore un-Islamic.[6] Rather, this apprehension is informed by a commitment to trace the appearance of this discourse and its political, social, and cultural workings in this historical conjuncture and understand its power. By discourse, I refer not only to the language that is used to identify the honor crime but also to the reports, policies, and practices that are produced in and enacted under its name. Following the work of Elizabeth Bernstein in providing an ethnography of the sex trafficking discourse, I understand discourse to "signal a constellation of words, materialities, and practices as they coalesce in historically and culturally situated ways, constructing the empirical object under consideration and the social locations in which it is manifest" (2018, 25).

I am therefore interested in mapping a set of stories and narratives that honor crime discourses elicit and produce. In this book, I trace how these discourses enact particular and multiple modes of knowing gender violence and how, ultimately, they structure and delimit horizons of antiviolence contestations. In paying attention to what now constitute honor crime and honor killing discourses, I seek to better understand the various forms of gender-based violence that the honor crime describes, invokes, and encompasses. Before delving into this discourse and its workings, it is important to note a distinction between the "honor killing" as the act of murder and the "honor crime," a term that invokes a broad range of violence, including death and murder, that are enacted under the name of honor or rationalized through its invocation. In using the term honor crime, I am also pointing to efforts to enact laws and regulations that construct this violence, in its various manifestations, as a criminal act. When possible, I have used the term honor crime over honor killing unless a text specifically refers to the act of killing or murder. In describing the honor crime, I am primarily referring to forms of gender violence recognized to operate under the logic of honor that is attached to "communities defined by their alien difference from us" and subsequently unmoored from an understanding of a broader continuum of gender violence (Abu-Lughod 2013, 128). Throughout this book, my use of the term seeks to problematize it, offering a genealogy of its construction, appearance, and circulation.[7]

Gender Violence and the Transnational Politics of the Honor Crime is invested in thinking about the ways in which discourses surrounding the honor crime operate: how they work in tandem with or separately from a range of linguistic, literary, political, and metaphorical texts and contexts; and how, through their uneven proliferation, they construct particular material realities. Discourses around the honor crime are of course not singular, uniform, fixed, or unchanging, and they do not operate uniformly across different geographic contexts. The discourses surrounding the honor crime appear in both hegemonic and dominant forms, and they can also be replicated, circulated, and disrupted. Dominant and mainstream discourses surrounding the honor crime continuously insist on its singularity, specificity, separateness, and distinctiveness from other forms of gender violence. As this book will show, honor crime discourses that construct this form of violence in this singularized way work in complicated ways, distributing meanings unevenly and unpredictably. Their appearance, however, is neither sudden or coincidental but historically specific and contingent. Tracking the contemporary movements, productions, and deployments of these discourses illuminates the unstable and ungovernable means by which they appear to circulate. To better understand their tractions and uptakes, I follow multiple and wide-ranging narratives and stories about the honor crime, showing how they proliferate between and within nation-states. I refer to discourses in the plural in order to highlight the multiple texts and contexts that construct the honor crime as it is today understood. Through the following chapters, I unpack how these narratives become tied to interconnected and overlapping forms of governance, state power, sexual control, and border management.

This project therefore analyzes a broad range of texts that span legal, political, and literary genres and that inform normative and critical understandings and confrontations of gender-based violence known as honor crimes. I understand hegemonic honor crime discourses as sets of signs, symbols, and rhetorical, discursive, and political practices that appear to describe a unique and distinct form of gender violence. While this form of violence is understood to target the lives of both men and women, in this book I primarily focus on cases related to violence against women. The cases, sites, and narratives I focus on do not purport to exhaust the wide range of available materials on the phenomenon of the honor crime or the specific contexts in which gender violence takes place. Rather, I explore a certain set of narratives to examine the knowledge they produce about gender-based violence in general and the honor crime in particular. In following these knowledge constructions and narratives, I draw out the relations between the four separate but interconnected sites of Canada, the US, Jordan, and Palestine. Far from mere geographic proximity or geopolitical intimacies and entanglements, these sites are tied together through the nonlinear travels, maneuvers, and circulations of these discourses. In placing these sites side by side and analogously, the book asks the following questions: How have mainstream honor crime discourses emerged, and for what ends? What is their discursive currency, and how have the honor crime's meanings been constructed and transported from one context to another?

Although a number of critical studies now acknowledge the various complicated and interwoven mobilizations of honor crime discourses, relatively unexplored are the ways in which they travel across and between different geographies and contexts in multidirectional, uneven, and circular routes.[8] Through its focus on these disparate and interconnected sites and contexts, this book provides a transnational feminist examination of the movements of honor-related discourses and their shaping of community-based, state-sanctioned, and nongovernment responses to and activism against gender-based violence. At stake in the study of the intersections between political, legal, activist, and cultural discourses surrounding the honor crime is both their ascendancy and their regulation of notions and practices of modernity and citizenship today. My book demonstrates that the discursive severing of the honor crime from the broader continuum of gender violence does not emerge suddenly but has a genealogy or a contemporary and nascent history. In reading a broad array of texts together, I demonstrate that this discursive and textual move has broad political consequences for policies, practices, and the law. Throughout the work, I show how the honor crime functions as a signifier that governs and manages populations and how its meanings travel and circulate across and between separate and interconnected circuits of power and knowledge.

CIRCULAR DISCOURSES

In 2014 the Clarion Project produced a documentary called *Honor Diaries: Culture Is No Excuse for Abuse*. Coinciding in its release with International Women's Day, the documentary was promoted as the "the first film to break the silence on 'honor violence' against women and girls."[9] Bringing together nine "women's rights advocates with connections to Muslim-majority states who are engaged in a dialogue about gender equality," the documentary focuses on a broad range of topics associated with honor-related violence in Muslim-majority states, including murder in the name of honor, child and forced marriage, and female genital mutilation and cutting. Featuring individual and group interviews with the selected activists that are juxtaposed with scenes of suffering from around the world, the documentary covers a range of issues such as forced and compulsory veiling practices in Iran, the driving ban against Saudi women, and honor-related violence and legal statutes that offer perpetrators of such crimes lenient or reduced sentencing in Pakistan. It also discusses female genital mutilation and cutting in Sudan and Egypt and includes a television interview with an Egyptian cleric who endorses the practice and roots its origins in Islamic scripture and teachings. Due to the timing of its release, the documentary forays into a discussion of the incidences of sexual assault and violence against women protesters during the Arab uprisings. Connecting such a broad range of documentary priorities is the reality that these acts of violence occur in Muslim-majority states and the claim that they are inspired by an articulation of "honor" that is directly connected to the cultures most shaped by the religion of Islam.

The documentary made its debut at international film festivals and was screened in London in partnership with Amnesty International. Moreover, a copy of it was delivered to Navi Pillay, the former United Nations High Commissioner of Human Rights in Geneva (Prusher 2014). Soon after its release, the work was criticized by a number of organizations and Muslim women activists, who questioned the political motivations of its creators and its funders. The Clarion Project describes itself as "a non-profit organization that educates the public about the dangers of radical Islam." A central part of its education campaigns is the making and distribution of films about "how radical Islamists use terrorism, murder, subjugation of women, indoctrination of children, religious persecution, genocide of minorities, widespread human rights abuses, nuclear proliferation and cultural jihad—to threaten the West."[10] Critics of the film questioned the opportunistic uptake of Muslim women's rights in the documentary, making connections between some of the film's proclaimed experts, such as Ayaan Hirsi Ali, and right-wing organizations with anti-Muslim agendas.[11] Attempts to launch screenings of the film on US university campuses caused controversy, with some organizers either postponing or altogether cancelling scheduled screenings (De Bode 2014). The debate over the film also played out in the virtual world, where different factions impugned or defended the integrity of the filmmakers, the film's funders and promoters, and the various women activists who appeared in it. In their criticism of the film, Azeezah Kanji and a number of Muslim Canadian activists argued that the problem with the film is not its chosen focus on the violations of women's rights that occur in Muslim-majority states but rather the missing contexts of how, where, when, and why such forms of gender-based violence continue to take place. As they write, "*Honor Diaries* cherry-picks and decontextualizes statistics to bolster its narrative of virtually uniform Muslim oppression of women" (Kanji et al. 2014).

Controversies stirred by documentaries like *Honor Diaries* appear to unfold regularly and play out in predetermined and tediously familiar ways.

They often begin with the production and release of a cultural object, film, documentary, memoir, or novel that addresses the subject of gender-based violence or other violations of human rights.[12] The focus of the object is important, signaling an attempt to shed light on a social problem that spans a number of geopolitical and social contexts. Response to the work's engagement with the selected topic generally cleaves audiences across two positions. On the one hand, opponents of works like *Honor Diaries* call into question the ethics and politics of speaking on topics like gender violence in Muslim societies. To legitimate a singular focus on such topics in the eyes of opponents, the object must attend to the structural conditions that shape gender violence or demonstrate what Gillian Whitlock terms "communicative ethics" (2007, 47). That is, such critics demand reflective and thoughtful engagement with the politics of difference and its invocations, arguing that an engagement with topics such as gender violence requires attending to the specific contexts in which this violence occurs. Speaking on these topics in whatever chosen medium must be done responsibly, in a way that acknowledges the current anti-immigrant and anti-Muslim political contexts in which issues like honor-based violence are often highlighted or brought into view. Such positions are produced by a specific set of temporary and geographical constraints. They are informed by the recognition that contestations of gender-based violence are often appended to a set of discursive and political agendas that authorize militarized and securitized interventions domestically and transnationally as some of the chapters in this book will show.[13] And they are often also shaped by a fear that coverage of these highly charged topics would demonize or be used to demonize already marginalized groups and communities.

On the other side of the spectrum are those who unequivocally support the cultural object itself, arguing that the high rates of gender-based violence in Muslim communities warrant the singular and focused coverage it produces and receives. Adopting the rhetoric of free speech, they defend the right to speak, write, and present on these subjects regardless of the intentions of their creators or the potential political uses of the work. These audiences are situated as concerned citizens who wish to bring attention to atrocities that have been concealed, buried, or ignored and that disproportionately impact vulnerable populations of girls and women. They speak either from personal experience or because of a connection to the issues at stake or from a righteous motivation to act on behalf of the aggrieved and sometimes dead subjects of gender-based violence. In their frenzied defenses of the cultural object they support, make, fund, or endorse, they take on a mix of rhetorical and political positions that range from ardent support for freedom of speech and freedom of expression to staunch opposition of what they deem forms of political correctness, intimidation, and censorship.[14] Paradoxically, the raging debates disappear from view the phenomenon of gender violence they seek to describe and ultimately confront.

The two positions I discuss are reductive, not capable of fully representing the complicated operations of honor-related discourses in a variety of spaces and contexts or the varieties of positions they invoke and the range of actors they recruit. Certainly, there are overlaps between the stances I represent. Meanwhile, there are nuanced and informed viewpoints that cannot be captured by the rigid binaries that are set up in this exchange and that, in fact, far exceed and complicate them. I begin with this sketch, however, to lay bare the ubiquitous ways in which conversations, controversies, and debates about honor-related violence publicly unfold and how they appear to structure the contours of our knowledge about gender-based violence. Writing on public framings of honor killings in Germany, Katherine Pratt Ewing argues that "the concept 'honor killing' obscures the sources of actual, specific acts of violence against women by creating a simulacrum—a representation that bears an illusory and even deceptive resemblance to something that is claimed to be its original" (2013, 164).

In her discussion of the murder of Hatun Sürücü and its public framings, Ewing makes a clear distinction between the actual murder of women and the phenomenon of honor-based violence as it circulates in media representations. She thus works to "trace the points at which representations of the event diverge, are contested, and congeal into new forms" (165). Although the disjuncture between the honor killing as a rhetorically mediated and textualized event and the actual incidences of gender-based violence the term seeks to describe and confront has been identified by scholars like Ewing, the transnational emergence, turns, and circulations of the discourses have yet to be sufficiently examined. What has spurred the honor crime's surfacing? What are its enduring rhetorical and discursive characteristics and qualities? What forms of gender-based violence does the honor crime label contain and describe, and how does it travel from one place to another, and for what purposes? Reassessing the ideological assumptions and uses of honor is crucial to this task.

ARBITRATING HONOR

The honor crime began to appear in international discussions surrounding gender-based violence in the early 2000s. In December 2001 the United Nations passed Resolution 55/66, "Working towards the elimination of crimes against women committed in the name of honour" (United Nations General

Assembly 2001). The resolution called on member nation-states to fulfill their obligations to international human rights treaties and to develop specific and multidimensional strategies to "prevent and eliminate crimes against women committed in the name of honour" through legislative, educational, and social measures. It also called on member states and the international community to provide actual and potential victims of honor crimes "protection, safe shelter, counselling, legal aid, rehabilitation and reintegration into society" (2001, 3). The first UN resolution surrounding honor-based violence was spurred, in part, by the work of Radhika Coomaraswamy, former UN Special Rapporteur on Violence against Women (1994–2003), who began to report on honor-based violence as early as 1999.[15] Responding to accounts of rising rates of honor-related violence globally, Coomaraswamy expressed serious concern about this phenomenon and requested information on "such violence and measures that are being undertaken to combat it" (UN Economic and Social Council 1999, 7).

Coomaraswamy's initial reporting on honor-related violence identified it as a form of family violence that "comprises, *inter alia,* woman-battering, marital rape, incest, forced prostitution, violence against domestic workers, violence against girls, sex-selective abortions and female infanticide, traditional violent practices against women including forced marriage, son preference, female genital mutilation and honour crimes" (1999, 6–7; emphasis in original). In addition to identifying this violence as occurring within the domain of the family, Coomaraswamy sought to provide a definition of honor and its operations in relation to "traditional family ideology" (7). Her report showed how families enact the decision to execute a "female relative" who is deemed to have violated honor codes because of the belief or the assumption that she has engaged in "adultery, premarital relationships (which may or may not include sexual relations), rape and falling in love with an 'inappropriate' person" (para. 18, 7).

Coomaraswamy's subsequent coverage of honor-based violence described the phenomenon as one among a number of "practices in the family that are violent towards women and harmful to their health" (UN Economic and Social Council 2002, 2).[16] In a detailed report on "cultural practices in the family that violate women's rights," the former special rapporteur focused on the "dominant ideologies and structures within societies" that help perpetuate violence against women (3). The report amassed information on a number of harmful cultural practices, including female genital mutilation, witch hunting, forced marriage, marital rape, and honor killings. The section on honor killings provided a lengthy overview of the crime, delineating how it manifests differently and under many labels. Importantly, the UN report also listed "crimes of passion" as a form of honor-based violence that is enabled by the existence and codification of legislative loopholes that exonerate men who commit violence against women.[17] The report emphasizes, however, that these crimes share a common constitutive framework that utilizes honor "as a magic word, which can be used to cloak the most heinous of crimes. The concept of honor is especially powerful because it exists beyond reason and beyond analysis. But what masquerades as 'honour' is really men's need to control women's sexuality and their freedom. These murders are not based on religious beliefs but, rather, deeply rooted cultural ones" (13). Coomaraswamy's turn towards the recognition of honor-based violence as a harmful cultural practice echoes a shift in public discourse surrounding the links between culture and tradition, gender violence, and ongoing human rights violations. The report alludes to this shift in the introduction where it notes that certain forms of domestic violence have "avoided national and international scrutiny because they are seen as cultural practices that deserve tolerance and respect" (4). The report rejects the culturally relativist position that invokes culture as a legitimation for these crimes, a position that resonates with Article 4 of the "Declaration on the Elimination of Violence Against Women" (48/4) which insisted that "States should condemn violence against women and should not invoke any custom, tradition or religious consideration to avoid their obligations with respect to its elimination" (UN General Assembly 1993, 2). As Sally Engle Merry has noted in her study of UN resolutions surrounding gender-based violence, the shift in language was intentional, "paralleling a deepening critique of culture as an obstacle to human rights" (2006, 60).

Emphasizing the importance and broad influence of Coomaraswamy's reports and their shaping of the UN global agenda on gender-based violence, Merry also recounts the resistance that the discursive shift towards linking gender-based violence to harmful cultural practices provoked among member states, noting that "the discussion of honor killings was particularly contentious" (2006, 63). At stake in the debates surrounding the identification of honor killings as a form of gender violence and the assumed role that culture and tradition play in sanctioning or exacerbating these crimes is a tension between the desire of member states to condemn all forms of violence and a fear by some states that the first draft of the UN-level resolution, and its subsequent focus on honor crimes, had "associated crimes against women with Islam"[18] (UN General Assembly 2000b). Importantly, the press release on the adoption of the draft resolution on violence against women noted that some member states objected to a film that was shown prior to the presentation of the resolution and that they saw the language contained within the resolution as "non-objective" (UN General Assembly 2000b). The film in question was Shelley Saywell's *Crimes of Honour*, which received an Emmy Award for Outstanding Investigative Journalism. The film primarily focuses on cases of femicide from Jordan and the West Bank. In response to the perception that the film wrongfully linked Islam with certain forms of gender-based violence, the Organization of the Islamic Conference submitted a letter to the UN Secretary General stating that "the member states of the Organization of the Islamic Conference wish to reiterate that there is no linkage whatsoever between the killing of women and girls under any communal banner, including in the name of passion, honour or race, and the teachings, practices and values of Islam" (UN General Assembly 2000a, 2).[19]

This position is also well captured by the statement of the representatives of the two Muslim-majority states of Qatar and Jordan. The first statement, which was provided by Mr. Al-Mohannadi, the representative of the state of Qatar, argued the following:

> My delegation would like to offer its views on the draft resolution on crimes of passion against women. In Qatar, as in other Islamic countries, we try to protect women's rights, and we have always recognized full equality between men and women.
>
> My country believes that all crimes against men and women are equally reprehensible, and my country rejects these constant attacks against Islam, a religion that has more than 1.25 billion adherents. These crimes are not confined to any particular people or region. We believe that crimes called "crimes of honour" are crimes against people. Hence, we have reservations on the draft resolution entitled "Working towards the elimination of crimes against women committed in the name of honour," and we shall abstain in the voting. (UN General Assembly 2000, 6)

The Qatari representative's concern regarding the singling out of honor-based violence in the draft resolution captures a well-shared view that attempts to single out this crime were, in essence, thinly concealed attacks on the religion of Islam.[20] The Qatari representative thus carefully states his country's opposition to this resolution, dismissing the need for a specific resolution that condemns honor-based violence because all crimes against men and women are "equally reprehensible" in the eyes of the state of Qatar.[21]

Taking a different stance, the Jordanian representative argued that Jordan had abstained from voting on the resolution because the draft language would open up all states to the charge of human rights violations for "not having exercised due diligence to prevent the commission of such crimes" (UN General Assembly 2000c, 7).[22] The Jordanian representative argued that the draft law would need to distinguish between crimes committed in the name of honor and those committed in a fit of passion or "in a sudden state of rage," a difference that had been disappeared in the text of the resolution. The Jordanian representative's important point makes a distinction between premeditated crimes such as the honor killing and the passion crime or killing that occurs in a fit of fury, a difference that is central to the operations of the law in arbitrating cases of women killing. His country's opposition to the wording used in the draft registers a rejection of the potential charge that some states were providing impunity to those who murder women through the existence of codes in their legal systems that provide lesser or reduced sentencing for men who kill, a matter that I return to in more detail in chapter 4.

As Jane Connors reveals in her detailed discussion of the UN agenda and the crime of honor, the discussions that surrounded the adoption of the resolution made honor-related violence "a matter of human rights" (2005, 37). While this was an important political move that mandated that member nation-states fulfill their obligations to international treaties regarding exercising due diligence in preventing, investigating, and prosecuting these crimes, "the issue remain[ed] an uncomfortable one, with some delegations concerned that a focus on crimes against women committed in the name of honour is selective, rather than comprehensive in its treatment of violence against women" (37). With the elevation of honor-related violence to international and UN-level scrutiny, the crime became one of the most recognizable forms of violence against women. The UN resolution against honor-related violence and the debates that it invoked at the transnational level showcase the charged terrain surrounding discussions of gender-based violence and the world of policy making.

The tension between the positions outlined above elucidates a few paradigmatic and enduring qualities of discussions about honor-based violence. First, the debates delineated above chart what Merry names the "turbulent waters" of international efforts to produce effective legislation surrounding ending violence in general and the need to build momentum for efforts to end gender-based violence that have been associated with particular cultural practices (2006, x). As Merry makes clear, "Diminishing violence against women requires cultural transformation" and the remaking of the boundaries between acceptable and unacceptable forms of violence against women (25). This process is marked by tensions between those advocating for the change and those who are wary that such changes are fundamentally a challenge to their traditions, cultures, and religious practices or an attack on their social structures and orders. Second, the debates signal the growing anxieties around the singularized discourse of the honor crime and its linking to particular geographies of violence. Despite careful work, the honor crime remains invariably linked to specific sites, regions, and states, and it is thus attached to certain racialized bodies, publics, and communities. For example, in the *Special Rapporteur on Violence Against Women, Its Causes and Consequences,* Rashida Manjoo notes that "although honour crimes have occurred in the vast zone spreading from the Sahara to the Himalayas, it also occurs in other regions and countries with migrant communities" (UN General Assembly 2012, 12).[23] Despite the lack of specificity around what the honor crime is, the label nevertheless evokes rhetorical and geospatial connections between people and places and forms of gender-based violence identified as extreme. Third, the debates highlight the lingering ambiguities and definitional struggles that surround the honor crime as a specific form of gender-based violence. As Mark Cooney states, literature on the honor crime "conceptualizes honor violence variously: as a crime, as gendered violation, as a violation of human rights, as a discursive formation" (2014, 407). In other words, the term is immersed in imprecision not only because it describes a number of interconnected forms of gender-based violence but also because it is variously employed to criminalize violations of human rights and to bring attention to particular rhetorical and discursive positions, claims, and assumptions about a social problem. The explanatory power of the honor crime appears to be simultaneously limited and expansive, circulating knowledge that not only describes a phenomenon but also gives shape to it.

DEFINITIONAL HAZARDS

In January 2012, following an intense national discussion and debate on honor-related violence in Canada, the Canadian Council of Muslim Women (CCMW) issued a position paper that addresses the politics of naming gender-based violence or femicide. Titled "CCMW Position on Femicide [Not Honour Killing]," the paper lays out the organization's refusal to use the term honor killing to describe the phenomenon of the murder of women and girls:

> The Canadian Council of Muslim Women is strongly opposed to the use of the term "honour killing" to describe the murder of women and girls. Our argument is that no murder of a woman should be categorized by the rationale provided by the murderer, or by society itself, whether it be so called honour killing or crimes of passion.
>
> We urge that all murders/killings be identified as femicide—the killing of women and girls simply because they are females. This includes the killing of girls as infants—infanticide. This term does not separate women and girls

> into distinct groups based on race, culture or religion, and murders are the crimes committed against anyone of them.
>
> We hold that all forms of violence against women are regressive because somewhere in here lies misogyny and the lessened value of the lives of women and girls. (1)

The position outlined above by the CCMW is important because it captures the contours of the debate surrounding language used to describe the murder of women. CCMW's rejection of the language of honor in the naming of the murder of girls and women is further explained in the lengthy position paper. The authors claim that their stance is shaped by an unequivocal rejection of the contexts and rationales used to explain away this form of violence. It is also informed by a recognition that the language of "honor killing" is often divisive and that, when employed in Western contexts, it renders "these murders exotic, foreign, and alien" (1). CCMW's stance, however, is shaped not only by fears of how this label may be used to portray Muslim communities but by an awareness that the label can be utilized by perpetrators, allowing them to lay claim to culturally relativist arguments and explanations of their violence in social and legal settings. The CCMW's position, which can be seen as a religiously informed defense, refuses to name honor-based forms of gender violence by the label that its perpetrators give it because the group views such a discursive act as an acquiescence to the terms used to justify violence against girls and women (Mojab 2012). Rather than relying on the language of honor, the CCMW advocates for the use of the label femicide, which, they argue, "avoids inferences about the motives of the killers, and clearly states that violence is used as a tool against females and murders are the extreme end of the continuum of violence against women and girls" (2012, 3).

The issue of language is central in discussions of honor-based violence. In spite of various international, activist, and scholarly efforts, attempts to arrive at a singular definition of this form of violence have not been successful. Welchman and Hossain concede this definitional difficulty in their introduction to an important edited collection on honor crimes where they write, "Issues of definition and terminology come to the fore in the current international focus on 'crimes of honour' and their consequent perceived association with Muslim societies" (2005, 13). Similarly, Aisha Gill recognizes in her extensive work on honor crimes the long history of "discursive wrangling over the use of the term 'honour' in relation to VAW [Violence Against Women]" (2010, 218). In spite of the discursive disagreements around the term, definitions of the honor crime and honor killings abound in scholarly literature. In a key article on the honor crime in Turkey, Dicle Kogacioglu identifies the honor crime "as the murder of a woman by members of her family who do not approve of her sexual behaviour" (2004, 118).[24] Kogacioglu's analysis reveals how the honor crime terminology appears to evoke not only the killing of women but a range of violent practices that can also be motivated by notions of honor if the latter is understood to revolve around the regulation of sexual norms and behaviors. Thus, it is not uncommon for discussions of honor killings as an extreme form of violence to go hand in hand with discussions of female genital mutilation and other culturalized forms of gender-based violence.

Complicating the quest for academic and scholarly definitional consensus further are the various words that are associated with the concept of honor. For example, Diane E. King explores how "honor" can also be expressed through words like *namus* and *'ird* in the Kurdish communities in Iraq where the author conducted her study. King attends to the "set of ideas and practices associated with 'honor killings,'" arguing that an honor killing is a response to an affront to or breach of patrilineal sovereignty (2008, 318). King understands sovereignty as the ability of a "lineage and/or state to define its composition, to decide how it will utilize its resources, to define its boundaries, and to use violence" (318). The definition King provides shows how honor operates at the metaphorical and material levels and how infractions of honor, whether assumed, imagined, or real can have deadly consequences for girls and women in patrilineal societies.

In their study on cultures of honor in rural Turkey, Aysan Sev'er and Gökçeçiçek Yurdakul (2001) also note the variety of terms used to describe honor in the Turkish language, arguing that the existence of a range of expressions registers the importance of the concept of honor for Turkish society.[25] The authors argue that the violations of namus can have deadly consequences, "especially among the rural segments of the population where people are much more likely to be traditional, patriarchal, nonsecularly married at an early age, and illiterate or uneducated" (980).[26] While the authors advocate for a recognition of honor killing violence as a form of patriarchal violence, their analysis appears to reinforce a division between modern and traditional members of Turkish society, associating honor-based violence with rural as opposed to urban communities. This analysis reinscribes the modernity-versus-tradition framework often used to explain this form of violence which inheres patriarchal violence to traditional as opposed to modern worldviews and practices.

If the honor crime discourse works locally to produce distinctions between modernity and tradition, it is used in multicultural state contexts to both ethnicize and racialize the crime. In an article on the dangers of this discourse in the British context, Veena Meetoo and Heidi Safia Mirza argue that the appearance of "honour killings as a specific phenomena" is purposeful, with government and media applying this language "only among certain minority ethnic groups" (2007, 188). Meetoo and Mirza are critical of multicultural discourses that allow dominant societies to ignore the intersectional workings of power and violence within marginalized communities, arguing that "an overly sensitive multicultural approach" can rationalize the reluctant response from the state to investigate incidences of domestic violence within racialized and ethnicized communities (192). Within this context of relative state neglect of domestic violence incidences within racialized communities, the authors inquire why there remains a singularized focus on honor-related violence: "While we recognise that ethnic groups and communities do have specific religious and cultural traditions which they may themselves label as honour based, why, in the context of ethnicity, is domestic violence treated as a culturally specific honour crime by our wider organisations and institutions?" (188).

This tension between the politics of naming honor-based violence and efforts to include it in a more generalizable category like violence against women is well captured in a 2010 article by Rochelle Terman titled "To Specify or Single Out: Should We Use the Term 'Honor Killing'?" Published shortly after the highly publicized murders of Aqsa Parvez and Aasiya Hassan, Terman's article lays out the rhetorical and political positions of proponents and opponents of the term honor killings.[27] Informed by an understanding of the dangers of racism and Islamophobia, Terman's analysis seeks to develop a language that is both "anti-violence and anti-racist" (3). Terman thus charts the specifics of the term honor and the aspects that are recognized as the defining features of the honor killing, showing how a singularized focus on the crime in the West has helped animate the debate between those who are in favor of the term's use and those who are wary of its usages. While carefully charting the arguments for and against the use of the honor killing label to describe particular cases of violence against women, Terman concludes that the term cannot be avoided if we are to confront the specificities of this act of violence. As she states, "'Honor killing' is a categorization that helps us with a specific phenomenon that require specific strategies for redress elimination" (26). If the label offers a helpful categorization and framework for understanding this violence and developing efforts to combat violence against women, what, then, constitutes an honor killing?

In a much-cited definition of the honor crime which has informed dominant discourses surrounding honor-based violence, Human Rights Watch (HRW 2001) states that honor crimes are "acts of violence, usually murder, committed by male family members against female family members who are perceived to have brought dishonor upon the family." The short explanation provided by HRW does not enumerate what types of violence can be included in the definition or specify the particular social, political, and cultural contexts that give rise to such forms of violence; nevertheless, it suggests that honor-based violence is primarily committed against women who "are perceived to have brought dishonor" upon their families. The word perceived is important, signaling that women are murdered not for actual infractions of honor but because of assumptions that they have broken particular cultural or social codes. The definition takes for granted the meaning of honor, allowing readers to make causal connections between its infraction and acts of violence against women, including murder, that are enacted under its name. The brevity of HRW's definition accounts, in part, for its wide circulation and its acceptance by some scholars as a "neutral" definition.[28]

Aware of the conundrums that surround efforts to define honor-related violence, UN Women provides the following guidance to advocates and legal practitioners working to develop laws and policies that target the honor crime.[29] The drafting advice provided by the UN (2011) is worth citing at length here:

> Drafters are encouraged to use an expansive definition for "honour" crimes and killings. A definition must be broad enough to encompass "honour"-based violence in all its forms, such as murder, attempted murder, driving to suicide, rape, gang rape, torture, assault, virginity testing, kidnapping, forced marriage, forced eviction, harassment, threats, stove burnings, acid attacks and maiming. Legislation should clarify that the detailed list should not serve to exclude from sanctions some behavior that is not included.

The UN directive on definitions of honor-based violence and policies that confront this violence references both honor crimes and honor killings. While killings refer to acts of violence that intend to cause death or result in suicide or murder, honor crimes evoke a broader understanding of violence that includes both physical violence such as torture, forced marriage, stove burnings, acid attacks, and maiming, and sexual forms of violence such as rape and gang rape. Linking these distinct examples of violence is a broad and loose conception of "honor," which is again never explained or defined but is nevertheless cohered around different examples of gender violence. The document gestures towards the complexities of the concept by placing the word in quotation marks and to "imply the absence of 'honor' in these crimes." The UN guidance also makes clear that any list that provides examples of honor-based violence is not exhaustive and that other forms of violence, not here listed, can be included under this broad conceptualization of violence.

UN Women promotes the use of this language in spite of some of the discursive and political challenges it poses. As the site explains:

> Further, although some argue that designation of "honour" crimes as a distinct form of violence masks the universal nature of violence against women and risks demonizing cultures in which such crimes are more prevalent, the recognition of "honour" crimes as a particular, contextually-informed type of violence against women rightly acknowledges the unique characteristics of such crimes (such as their premeditated and collective nature). Acknowledging these features in turn facilitates the adoption of effective, targeted laws and policies to combat "honour" crimes. (2011)

The UN Women's directive on the work of defining honor-based violence serves as a reminder of the high stakes attached to the rhetorical act of naming violence. Labeling honor-related violence enables lawmakers to regulate this crime, to design laws that provide sanctions against this form of violence and, thus, seek to prevent its occurrence. To enable this regulatory mechanism, the law must make distinctions between different forms of violence, identifying its unique or distinguishing features such as premeditation and the collective familial or societal approval that precedes its occurrence. As texts that will determine the legal and criminal consequences for committing acts of violence, laws on honor-related crimes must be able to specify what, exactly, is unique and distinct about this form of violence.

Imbued in a discourse of singularity, the honor crime is arguably among the most internationally recognized acts of violence against women. While the debates over what actually constitutes honor-based violence have not produced a generally accepted or recognized definition of these crimes, proponents of the distinctiveness of honor-related violence from a broader continuum of gender violence maintain that three particular features render these crimes simultaneously distinct and particular:

1. Honor-based violence (HBV) is a premeditated act.
2. This gender violence occurs within a framework of collective family punishment and is motivated by a desire to control the sexual choices and social behavior of women.
3. Honor-based violence is often rewarded rather than punished.

These features can be summarized as relating to the crimes' original intent (Was the crime planned for? Did the perpetrator intend to kill? Or did the crime take place in a fit of fury or passion?), its form (Was the crime perpetrated by an individual actor, or was she or he aided and abetted by other members of their families or society?), and its consequence (Was the perpetrator of the crime ostracized by their family or society after the discovery of the crime? Was the perpetrator prosecuted, and, if so, was the sentence commensurate with the severity of the crime?) According to these three features, honor-related violence differs from other forms of violence against women (including intimate partner violence) because its victims are part of patriarchal cultures that see women as the property of men, where men and kin are encouraged to regulate the sexualities and social behaviors of women. When women act in ways that exceed cultural norms and expectations, they are punished for their behavior in order to protect the reputation and honor of their male kin. That this violence is premeditated and usually carried out by more than one member of the female's immediate and extended family (rather than by her husband) is taken as evidence that these crimes do not fit within the framework used to analyze other examples of gender violence, including intimate partner, domestic violence, or homicide, which are understood to be carried out by an individual male partner acting independently and out of his own accord and on impulse rather than with intent.[30] Noting the problems with this distinction, Sherene Razack argues that "the honour/passion distinction not only obscures the cultural and community approval so many crimes against women have in *majority* culture, but it reifies Muslims as stuck in premodernity while Westerners have progressed as fully rational subjects with the capacity to choose moral actions, even if the choice is a bad one" (2008, 128 ; emphasis in original).

In challenging arguments about the distinctiveness of the honor crime as a form of gender violence, opponents often focus their analysis on the ways in which the honor killing is rewarded in the social, legal, and cultural settings where they occur.[31] Certainly, codes that impugn crimes against women and that normalize heterosexual and patriarchal acts of gender violence, providing them both legal recourse and moral cover, are examples of legal rewards.[32] This position assumes a congruity between the letter of the law and its applications. Yet to only critique the plainly obvious and even explicit aspects of reward exhibited in some legal codes is to miss how manifestations of reward are also at work in Western legal and social systems for perpetrators of violence against women and violence against other marginalized subjects. More importantly, this narrow focus on legal codes ignores how tacit and implicit manifestations of reward operate both within and outside Western legal systems, sanctioning acts of violence against national subjects deemed unworthy and unnecessary and therefore deserving of state-sanctioned forms of violence.[33] In expanding conceptions of reward to include its mutually reinforcing manifestations within and outside the law, we begin to witness how certain acts of violence are facilitated, encouraged, and even rewarded by state silence, complicity, and inaction. This expanded framework reveals some of the difficulties that surround claims of the crime's specificity, distinction, and difference, especially when they are hinged on an analysis of the legal text and unmoored from the social and political and cultural worlds in which such texts become animated.

Writing on the specifics of honor-based violence, Shahrazad Mojab argues that "considerations of honour and its loss underlie the entire process of killings, allowing us to distinguish it from domestic violence" (2012, 129). Mojab's work, which draws on her extensive scholarship on honor killings and her experience as an expert witness in the trial for the Shafia murders in 2009,[34] presents a complex understanding of honor as a social institution.[35] As Mojab shows, honor is a central "regulator of gender relations," and its meanings are shaped by the interactions of a set of patriarchal, cultural, and religious institutions (129). Based on the social characteristics of honor, Mojab distinguishes between domestic violence and the honor killing, arguing that the former often occurs "without pressure from family, kin, or community," while the latter is often a response to a community or family expectation or demand to cleanse or restore honor that has been lost (130). Mojab's analysis insists on recognizing the particulars of the honor crime and the specific cultural contexts in which it occurs, suggesting that its confrontation requires "multi-dimensional, multi-disciplinary, and radical approaches" that do not fall into the traps of cultural relativism, nationalism, or racism (133).

Critical race feminist studies scholars have sought to contend with the ambiguities surrounding the honor crime. In a policy analysis document submitted to the Institute for Social Policy and Understanding in the aftermath of the murder of Aasiya Hassan (Zubair), Zareena Grewal explored some of the difficulties that surround the work of naming and contesting domestic violence in Muslim and communities of color. Grewal discusses how certain forms of violence are always already "culturalized," signaling to publics their distinct nature from a broader continuum of domestic violence or violence against women. Grewal (2009) offers practitioners strategies for speaking on violence against women; she contends that it is not possible to ignore the cultural aspects of gender-based violence, but, she asserts, "culture alone does not cause violence; however, the effects of violence are always cultural, as are the conditions that allow the abuse to persist" (13). Grewal's careful attempt to understand domestic violence beyond the binary of culturalism or racism serves as a reminder of the difficulties of speaking on and contesting these crimes in the often charged political and social contexts in which they occur.[36] It reveals how when a discourse is so imbued with an a-priori set of meanings and assumptions, it also becomes impossible to navigate outside of its charged, limited, and constraining discursive frames and referents. These efforts remind us that "words inevitably attain their actual understood meaning within contexts that animate specific connotations and references" (Alcoff 2018, 149). The honor crime, and the discursive terrains that surround it and which it helps shape, produces a complicated web of meanings that extends beyond the discursive realm into the social and political worlds that words animate and construct. In what follows, I do not seek to provide a singular definition of the honor crime or claim to resolve the tensions that surround its circulated and commonly accepted definitions. Rather, I explore its multiple meanings and deployments, offering instead a focus on its heterogenous evocations, usages, and deployments in multiple texts and contexts, showing how dominant discourses surrounding this crime work and the political worlds they animate.

METHODOLOGICAL AND ETHICAL CONSIDERATIONS

Researching a topic like honor-based violence is a challenging endeavor. As the previous sections have shown, honor crime discourses often trap scholars and activists between charges of cultural relativism and charges of racism. It is impossible to speak or write on honor-based violence without wading into the discursive complexities of the term, the various contestations surrounding both its usefulness and limitations. A discourse analysis of the honor crime necessarily requires assembling a wide array of texts that can help reveal how the language of the honor crime works in different contexts, how it neatly fits into or how it complicates or defies rhetorical and political expectations. In this work, and following the contribution of rhetorical studies scholars, "discourses are not seen as neutral ways of describing the world, but as ways of reproducing or challenging relations of power and dominance in society" (Bartolucci 2012, 564). Thus, my analysis of honor crime discourse attends to cultural, social, and political assumptions, desires, and goals of the word's conveyers. It seeks to reveal the web of politics and cultural workings that underpin the discourse's emergence and usage across national contexts. It attends to the worlds that the honor killing discourses construct and shape, acknowledging the varied and multiple meanings that they disseminate. I am invested in thinking about how the dominant rhetorics of the honor crime rely on the use of "the same set of words and linguistic constructions . . . reproduced and finally naturalised, eventually coming to be seen as commonsense" (563).

My goal in analyzing the linguistic formations that surround dominant honor crime discourses is to better understand their representation of this form of gender violence as singularized, distinct, and particular. By tracing the honor crime's appearance in a variety of texts and contexts, I reveal its powers to intervene in political, cultural, and social space. As rhetorical studies scholar Sara McKinnon (2014) notes, "This level of analysis focuses the analyst's eye on the function of discourse, or what it is doing within the organizations, institutions, and societies where they circulate. This level of analysis is the broadest level used by discourse analysts, and also perhaps the most important as discourse analysis *cannot* be discourse analysis without an examination of the sociocultural practice of the discourse" (8; emphasis in original). My investment in exploring the honor crime discourse emerges from a recognition that how we define things impact the strategies and policies that we develop to confront them.[37]

Definitions of social problems are never really static and are always in flux. They are shaped by competing interests and agendas and by the constant reshaping of public consensus about a social problem, its scale, and the urgency required to confront it. What we now recognize as the honor crime is discursively and rhetorically produced through policies, laws, media reports, and scholarly works and activism that aims to confront the social problem of gender-based violence. In what follows, I assemble varying texts to explore how different discursive materials such as policy, film, music, and the law construct the phenomenon of gender violence known as the honor crime. Drawing on a range of scholarly and interdisciplinary traditions, including critical literary analysis, transnational feminism, feminist rhetorical and discursive studies, and Middle East studies, this book analyzes the emergence of the honor crime as a severe form of gender violence and as a historically specific phenomenon, produced variably over time and space through a number of stories, narratives, ideas, and discourses. My work seeks to "make meaning of how these stories are created and re-created over time and with what consequences" (Chowdhury 2011, 15). By privileging the close reading of textual materials assembled from an array of sources and sites, *Gender Violence and the Transnational Politics of the Honor Crime* explores the constructions of the honor crime through a variety of textual, discursive, material, and practices. The book seeks to show how words shape our understanding of this phenomenon and how it manifests in public conversations and actions against gender violence. Rather than accepting these texts as reflections of knowledge about the honor crime, my work shows the active role that texts play in shaping knowledge about this phenomenon and efforts to end it.

By reading diverse textual materials in interconnected ways, my work shows the importance of critical reading practices and feminist discourse analysis that attend to the relationships between words and their social, historical, and political contexts. In refusing to attend to the singular manifestations of the honor crime discourse in specific geopolitical sites, my study employs a transnational analytic framework that identifies links and ruptures that trouble foreclosed boundaries of knowledge formations, inviting an analysis that engages how "texts participate in a field, and then in a set of fields, and thus in a social and political world" (McAlister 2001, 8). As the previous sections have demonstrated, the rise of honor crime discourse is tied to particular UN policies and activist efforts at a certain point in time when the agenda of women's rights as human rights was on the rise. But as the dominant discourses surrounding the honor crime began to take hold, certain complexities also came to the fore, fracturing some of the consensus surrounding the shape, form, and scale of this social problem. This work, then, maps some of these tensions and complexities, showing how these discourses ebb and flow, how they appear and disappear from view, and how, over time, they begin to cohere or alter.

The following chapters tell politicized stories about honor crime discourses and their unfolding in separate but interconnected transnational contexts. These stories attempt to reveal aspects of this discourse that are, at times, highlighted and those that are ignored, downplayed, or even normalized. Following the work of scholars like Yasmin Jiwani in her book *Discourses of Denial: Mediations of Race, Gender, and Violence,* I am interested in mapping how honor crime discourses get constructed and how their constructions overlap with "multiple and interweaving structures of domination" to define the parameters of a "particular subject matter in terms of how it is thought of and talked about" (2006, xii). By paying attention to both the everyday mundane and the spectacularized appearances of the honor crime in different textualities, this work explores the broader contexts and consequences of its mobilizations, showing how "separations between structural and more interpersonal forms of violence are maintained" (Jiwani 2006, xii). As James Ferguson (1994) has noted, "Discourse is a practice, it is structured, and it has real effects" (15). Exploring the varying intended and unintended effects of honor crime discourses is a central aim of this book.

Gender Violence and the Transnational Politics of the Honor Crime attends to the workings of this discourse in multiple spaces to reveal how it unfolds, moves, and travels. It thus brings into view the multiple, uneven, and varied consequences of this discourse. It shows the consistencies and inconsistencies surrounding its uptake in different geopolitical contexts, tracing the circular ways in which it moves from one place to another. Following the work of feminist scholars like Inderpal Grewal, I seek to reveal the continuities and breaks in discourses surrounding the honor crime and their transnational circulations. In her study of the movement of consumer culture across space, time, and place, Grewal argues that "it is only by examining the production and circulation of consumer culture and consumer goods within the context of biopolitics and geopolitics that we can see how identity politics operate at the complex nexus of political economy, national imaginaries, and related mobilizations of desire and individuality within liberal and neoliberal politics" (2005, 28). A transnational study of honor crime discourses thus requires analyzing not only the textual and discursive but also their productions, mobilizations, and circulations as disciplinary and regulatory scripts that produce particular positionalities and subjectivities. These multiple, varied, and overlapping circulations map entanglements between states and activists, the realm of the law with popular media representations, policies and opinion pieces with academic and scholarly work. In attending to these messy and complicated entanglements and imbrications, I explore how these discourses construct and disseminate notions of modernity and become tied to transnational debates around belonging and citizenship.

The transnational study of discourse, as Rebecca Dingo has argued, serves to "illustrate a matrix of connections between people, nations, economies, and the textual practices present in, for example, public policies and popular culture" (2012, 12). A transnational feminist approach to the study of discourse is, therefore, necessarily multisited, bringing into view both the visible and the less visible connections between different aspects of these discourses. Following the work of rhetorical studies scholars, this study is developed by "considering the transnational paths along which rhetorics travel" (Dingo, 21). The analysis in this work is thus guided by the circulations of the discourses of the honor crime in geographies I have intimately known and experienced either through living in them for extended periods or traveling through them as a result of the experiences of studying and conducting this research. While grounded in the specificities of these geographies, this work is not based on an ethnographic study conducted in these spaces. It is, in essence, a study of the political and material worlds that texts and discourses enact and disrupt in the specificities and intimacies of particular geopolitical contexts. What has led to this inquiry is an investment in contesting forms of gender violence that are intersectional and that require transnational feminist analytics and activisms in order to end gender violence in all its manifestations.

My analysis of honor crime discourses draws on multiple years of researching this topic and writing on violence in an effort to think about the ways in which feminism has theorized and actively confronted gender violence. Despite its grounding in feminist analytical frameworks, however, writing on violence that becomes known as honor-related violence raises many ethical and political conundrums. What does it mean to be able to write and produce research on incidences of gender violence that harm women and lead to or end in murder? How does one invoke the names of murdered women without playing into the sensationalized and exceptionalized rhetorics used to record, describe, or contest their murders? How can one speak against these crimes without reducing the lost lives of the people it targets to their final and macabre scenes? I have tried to address some of these concerns by focusing on the political and cultural workings of the discourse surrounding gender and sexual violence. I have done this while knowing that, at times, details of killing and murder are necessary and that recounting them, while risking sensationalism, is a crucial mode of remembrance and resistance of patriarchal erasure and denial of violence. In what follows, I trace what dominant and hegemonic honor crime discourses bring into view and what they obfuscate or disappear. In doing so, I focus less on the accounts of gender violence and more on the particular ways in which these stories are portrayed, represented, and, finally, contested. While doing this, I am aware of the dilemmas and pitfalls that Western-based academics and feminists, such as myself, encounter when writing about gender violence. As Nadje Al-Ali (2016) writes, "Representations of violence in scholarship, in the media, in popular culture, and, crucially, in policy discourses, reveal the complex and fraud [sic] ways our respective positionalities shape the registers we use to talk about and challenge violence" (8). Al-Ali rightly emphasizes the importance of challenging the limits of our own positionalities by developing our understanding of gender-based violence in "materially-grounded work" (11) that attends to both the discursive representations of violence and the realities of violence itself as it is experienced by people in local contexts. I have attempted to do this by not shying away from highlighting the multiple and intersecting experiences of gender violence that people encounter, speaking directly against them, and not reducing these experiences to the mere level of discourse.

In spite of this effort, writing on the honor crime in an academic work requires an acknowledgment of the violence of theorizing gender-based violence. It requires contending with how, as academics, the words we write, the books we produce, and the scholarly careers we build on them also enact certain omissions, lapses, and violences. There is no comfortable or easy way out of this reality—nor should there be. Writing on violence and the ethics of recounting violence in anthropological work, David Valentine states that this "analysis of violence therefore lies uncomfortably in the territory between representation and physical violence—*discourse as violence*—and how such facts are mounted to make a series of claims—*violence as discourse*" (2003, 33; emphasis in original). Valentine writes on the role of anthropology in confronting violence in all its messiness and complexities, stating "Violence, pain, suffering, like all other arenas of social life, are messy, cut through with ambiguity and contradiction. Violence is not only murder or beatings; it can be identified in a text or a political position" (45). In writing about the discourses surrounding the honor crime, my project also lies in the uncomfortable terrain of discursive violence and violent discourse that Valentine identifies. Like other scholars who write on violated or dead subjects, I am aware that a focus on discourses surrounding violence does not approximate confrontations of gender violence in the field, nor does it amount to a form of activism against its continued occurrence.

My goal in focusing on these discourses, tracing their genealogies, and the textual politics they deploy is to help develop an analytic framework that moves beyond the singularizing of this form of gender violence. To do so, I attend to the structural dimensions that give rise to the discourses of the honor crime and the multiple dynamics at play in their productions and circulations. I acknowledge that discourse analysis can offer a too-easy reliance on texts in order to make sense of the world and that it risks producing its own analytic foreclosures and certainties. In *Cultivating Development: An Ethnography of Aid Policy and Practice,* David Moss argues that while attention to text is important in understanding policies and practices that are enacted in its name, texts "cannot be read at face value without reference to the arguments, interests and divergent points of view that they encode and to which they allude" (2005, 15). In presenting honor crime discourses as they are named, discussed, and referenced in a broad array of texts, I seek to explore both their inner workings and their external associations. I explore the meanings they make when they are presented in tandem with or when they are set apart from other texts and contexts. Above all, I seek to present the different meanings that these discourses take on and the analytic openings and foreclosures they facilitate or prevent.

My critique of the workings of the dominant discourses surrounding the honor crime and their uses does not seek to gloss over the question of the politics and ethics of writing on domestic violence and the murder of women.

When we write on violated and dead subjects, to whom are we accountable? In her 2019 study on gender-based violence in Muslim communities, Juliane Hammer articulates a similar tension when she states:

> It is equally vexing for me to write about murder and violence in order to "reflect" on and develop an analysis of the ways in which domestic violence murders are discursively produced and approached. It seems macabre at times to theorize death in this way, and I have never achieved any level of comfort with participating in this endeavor. My only argument for the significance and ethical acceptability of this project is that awareness, public, communal, and academic, is an important tool for societal change and thus writing about these topics is important. (27)

Hammer's thoughtful questioning of the ethics and politics of writing on gender violence is significant, charting some of the problems of speaking and writing on this topic for academic audiences and academic purposes. In writing this book, I share many of her concerns and the concerns of other scholars who write on these topics and issues. Like Hammer, I am uncomfortable with the work of theorizing gender violence, and I struggle with the ethics of making meaning of the horrors inflicted on girls and women in the name of patriarchal systems that inhere and seek to regulate moral systems and social practices. Hammer finds some comfort in knowing that awareness can consequently create societal change. Like her, I too hope that this scholarly work on discourses surrounding gender violence known as honor-based violence can contribute in some way to the goal of ending violence that targets the lives of people in various ways and in creating safer environments for those struggling at the sites of multiple and intersecting forms of injustice and oppression.

A MAP OF THE BOOK

This book offers a genealogical approach to honor crime discourses, focusing on their dominant articulations and expressions. It does this by attending to past and contemporary historical formations of these discourses, tracing their emergence, circulations, and travels in multiple texts and contexts. Thus, *Gender Violence and the Transnational Politics of the Honor Crime* moves between histories, places, and spaces, seeking to unsettle what we know about the dominant honor crime discourses and their workings. By mapping these discourses and their appearances in specific historical, geographical, and political conjunctures, the following chapters "explore the geographies of public and private that shape power relations, that give meaning to difference, and that condition the political" (Staeheli and Kofman, 2004, 10). The chapters are organized around an examination of the ideological, institutional, and geopolitical underpinnings of the honor crime and its political uses. This organization moves between and through different contexts to present the distinct and (sometimes) overlapping ways in which honor crime discourses appear to work in each of the sites discussed here. In the chapters that follow, I trace the appearance of these discourses in public and popular works and explore the material, political, and economic conditions that allow for their continued acceptance and circulation. I do this by attending to the larger complex of violence in which gender violence is enacted and confronted.

In chapter 1, I explore how the story of a gender violence and femicide that occurred in Canada traveled to the US and then to Israel, to show how honor-related violence is depicted in media and the types of activism that it generates and helps mobilize. While much has been written about Aqsa Parvez and the story of her violent murder through its coverage in the Canadian press, considerably less attention has been paid to the ways in which this murder resonated far beyond the borders of the Canadian state. This chapter thus traces the travels of the narrative of Aqsa Parvez's murder from Canada to the US and then to Israel to show not only how stories of violence gain meaning but also how they make meaning by reproducing national boundaries and by reconfiguring relations of dominance, resistance, and power. By charting the transnational routes of gender violence as they are exemplified in the Aqsa Parvez murder and the narratives or stories it generated and the right-wing activism it mobilized, I make connections between the discursive and political configurations of this crime. In mapping these stories' movements and travels, as well as their tensions and contradictions, I show how the murder of (certain) Muslim women in crimes that become known as "honor crimes" is interpreted and deployed transnationally and in a number of interconnected geopolitical sites and registers. I argue that the production and commemoration of the honor crime as an exceptional violence authorizes posthumous solidarities that serve to buttress right-wing forms of political activism.

In chapter 2, I provide an analysis of the context of gender violence in Palestine, mapping the complicated contours of confrontations of gender violence in colonized contexts and their centrality to articulations of national sovereignty and sites of governmentality. In this chapter, I focus, in part, on the release in 2012 of the song "If I Could Go Back in Time" by the hip-hop group DAM. I analyze DAM's contestations of gender violence and the honor crime in the form of their popular and UN-funded song, placing this song and the controversies stirred by its release within their national and regional specificities and a wider discussion of the politics of speaking about gender violence in national and international contexts. That the ensuing debates between the artists, academics, and activists shifted to the question of authenticity prompts a careful consideration of positionality and accountability as central to feminist ethics and contestations of gender violence. This analysis charts the fault lines between activist and academic critiques of gender violence.

In chapter 3, I trace recent US government interest in honor-related violence as exemplified in President Donald J. Trump's Executive Order 13769. I argue that this interest is neither new nor coincidental, placing it in a longer historical context attuned to the imbrications between gender violence and terrorism in American discourses far before the issuance of this order. This chapter examines constructions of the honor crime in public discourses in the US and draws on the story of the murder of Tina Isa, an American teenager of Palestinian and Brazilian origins, who was killed in 1989 by her parents in St. Louis, Missouri. By reading this story and its public framings in relation to recent government interest in documenting honor-related violence and regulating US borders, I explore the messy racial politics underpinning national and public discourses on gender violence. This chapter analyzes the various political national and transnational registers that are often concealed, downplayed, or suppressed in public framings of gender violence in the US and their entanglement in debates around borders, migration, belonging, and citizenship.

In chapter 4, I turn to the Jordanian state and contemporary efforts to end gender violence by confronting the legal codes that are used to prosecute gender violence, including the honor crime and crime of rape. I explore how the law has become a prime site of analysis and critique in women's efforts to counter gender violence in Jordan. I argue that the state's investment in countering gender violence, and the legal codes long believed to sanction honor-related violence, enables the Jordanian state to simultaneously position itself as a modern state that upholds the rule of law while bolstering its criminal and carceral systems and frameworks. Here I show how developing nation-states employ efforts to end highly spectacularized forms of gender violence such as the honor crime to reconstitute themselves as modern nation-states committed to women's equality and empowerment. Rather than focus only on the state's capacity to utilize such discourse, I examine what is gained and lost when women's organizational efforts to end gender violence become aligned with the state in the service of justice that is wedded to the legal and juridical domains.

In the afterword, I connect the four geopolitical contexts that this book engages by investigating how honor crime discourses, operating differently across and between these sites, binds such distinct geographies and what the crime's contestations reveal about the current contours of the global fight against gender violence. In ending this book, I turn to the activist efforts of the Palestinian *Tal3at* movement and their contestations of rising incidences of gender violence in Palestine. I center their efforts as an example of transnational feminist praxis that attends to the complicated and messy intersections of violence in people's lives. Ultimately, *Gender Violence and the Transnational Politics of the Honor Crime* is a work about the power of rhetorics, discourse, and politics to shape antiviolence agendas and practices. It is a study of how this language came to be and of how and why it appears and is used in different spaces and places. It provides a critique of the mobilization of dominant honor crime discourses for state-building projects that work to cause harm and fortify the status quo. An analysis of this language and its working in multiple sites provides an alternative understanding of gender violence that may help us imagine different, more long-term, and sustainable strategies against its devastating and deadly effects on transnational communities across multiple borders and boundaries.

CHAPTER 1

Transnational Memorialization

The Politics of Remembering Murdered Muslim Women

ON THE MORNING of December 10, 2007, Aqsa Parvez was strangled to death by her father, Muhammad Parvez, and her brother Waqas Parvez. One of eight children, Aqsa was a first-generation immigrant to Canada and an eleventh-grade student at Applewood Heights Secondary School at the time of her death. Her family had moved to Ontario from Pakistan after her father was admitted to Canada as a refugee. Aqsa's father, Muhammad, was a taxi driver who, Canadian media reported, held a tight grip on his children and controlled their lives.[1] In dominant accounts of Aqsa's story, she is represented as an unruly daughter whose actions challenged her traditional, conservative, and patriarchal father (Mitchell and Javed 2010). Unable to make Aqsa adhere to his rules, Muhammad enlisted the help of her brother in carrying out her murder. Both pleaded guilty to second-degree murder charges on January 10, 2010, in what Crown Prosecutor Mara Basso described as a "chilling, gender-based crime" that was motivated "by patriarchal concepts of honour and shame" (qtd in Rosella 2017). In explaining the motivations for his violent actions, Muhammad is reported to have told Aqsa's mother, Anwar Jan Parvez, that he had killed his youngest daughter because she had insulted him and made him "naked" (*CBC News* 2010).

In the aftermath of the murder, the dominant story or stories of Aqsa's murder bore the familiar tropes of civilizational clash, culturalized violence, and multicultural collapse. In Canada the murder was quickly scripted as a case of honor-based violence, a cruel death that spoke to the unique danger posed by Muslim immigrants to Canadian national ideals of openness, racial harmony, and gender equality. Accounts of Aqsa's life displayed the telltale signs of youthful rebellion and an adolescent desire for freedom and social acceptance. And yet media interpretations continually narrated the teen's struggles in a way that emphasized the exceptional circumstances and unusual difficulties marking Aqsa's life. In so doing, Aqsa became recognizable to the Canadian public through her fatal encounters with rigid religious edicts and cultural codes that were antithetical to Canadian values. Unsurprisingly, public outcry about the murder was strong and served to amplify calls for a stricter interpretation and application of Canadian multiculturalism, a national policy codified by the Canadian Multiculturalism Act in 1988.[2] Thus, Aqsa's tragic death forewarned of a failing immigration system that ostensibly emphasized tolerance over assimilation, difference over sameness, and acceptance over coercion and thus promoted cultural practices that were violent to women. Her story reverberated far and wide because of audiences' ability to identify with Aqsa's struggles against her strict and, to many, foreign family structure and cultural norms.

The intensive mainstream media coverage of Aqsa Parvez's murder produced a discourse that resonated with the stories circulating in international press about the murders of Muslim women in multiracial and multicultural states.[3] Because of its Orientalist and racialized framings, coverage of Aqsa's murder renewed concerns about the status of religious and cultural minorities in Canada, the US, and various countries in Europe who do not assimilate into Western communities.[4] Functioning as a cautionary transnational tale, Aqsa's murder provided evidence of the dangers experienced by young girls and women living in cultural, racial, and religious isolation from within Western societies. As Beverly Weber argues in her work on honor crime discourses in Germany, narratives of violent Muslim men intent on victimizing innocent Muslim women have become part of a "systematically produced set of statements" that culturalize and exceptionalize familial forms of gender violence (2013, 42). Writing on the Canadian context, Yasmin Jiwani notes that "acts of violence are constructed as signs of the peculiarities of Other cultural traditions, peculiarities that reflect the traditional, barbaric, and inferior constructions of the cultures of the Others" (2006, 21).

Feeding into an anti-Muslim historical moment shaped by the global "War on Terror," the mass circulation of the story of this murder has served a number of competing agendas. News of Aqsa's death garnered mass condemnation for both her murderers and the Muslim community that some believed secretly condoned honor-related forms of violence. Conservative American columnists and openly anti-Muslim bloggers such as Pamela Geller of *Atlas Shrugs* and Robert Spencer of *Jihad Watch* have capitalized on Aqsa's murder to further anti-Muslim, anti-immigrant, and racist political agendas in the US and beyond. In 2011 supporters of these two blogs traveled to Israel from the US to commemorate the murder by dedicating the Aqsa Parvez Memorial Grove in Jerusalem's American Independence Park to victims of honor killings and honor-related violence across the world. Importantly, Aqsa's murder has also inspired feminist interventions from young, racialized, and Muslim Canadians who, in forming the Urban Alliance on Race Relations, commemorated Aqsa's life and death while also condemning gender violence and racism in Canadian society.[5] The range of responses to Aqsa Parvez's murder lays bare the complex and contradictory powers of narratives about honor-based violence and the persistence of naming and framing practices that appear to simultaneously "specify" *and* "single out" these crimes (Terman 2010).[6]

While much has been written about the murder of Aqsa Parvez and its coverage in the Canadian press and the politics of naming honor-related violence, considerably less attention has been paid to the ways in which this murder was memorialized. In this chapter, I trace the story of Aqsa Parvez's murder and its crossings from Canada to the US and then to Israel in order to show not only how narratives of death gain meaning but also how they make meaning by reproducing national boundaries and reconstituting relations of dominance, resistance, and power. In charting the transnational routes of honor-related violence as they are exemplified in the Aqsa Parvez murder and the narratives or stories it generated, this chapter aims to reveal connections between the discursive and political mobilizations of honor-related violence. In doing so, it does not aim to minimize the occurrence of gender violence and crimes that become known as honor crimes or to shield from critique or accountability Muslim perpetrators of honor-related violence and crime (Ziya 2019). Rather, it seeks to examine how certain acts of violence against women, and, in particular, acts of violence perpetrated by Muslim men against Muslim women specifically in Western contexts, are invoked, scripted, and utilized to further nationalist goals and right-wing political activism and memorialization efforts in this particular historical and political conjuncture.

Relying on transnational and critical race feminist theorizations of gender violence, this chapter charts three interrelated interpretive frames used to storify Aqsa's death in popular media and academic accounts. In the first part, I read Aqsa's murder in relation to its dominant framing as a form of "death by culture" by utilizing the theorizations of critical race scholars on representations of gender violence. I then turn to the national depiction of Aqsa's life as a young Muslim girl seeking to belong in a multicultural Canadian nation-state where agency, individuality, and personal choice are cherished, if not always realizable, goals. In the final section, I look at the discursive travels of Aqsa's story and narratives of honor-based violence from and between national and settler colonial contexts and its memorialization, paying particular attention to the deployment of women's causes for specific national, civilizational, and political gains.

Because honor killing narratives—both visual and discursive—gain traction with audiences from different backgrounds and with varying interests and stakes as these stories cross and are crossed between different sites, the effects of these narratives are always multiple and cannot be singularly understood (Narayan 1997; Whitlock 2007). By mapping these stories' movements and travels, as well as their tensions and contradictions, this chapter shows how the murder of Muslim women in honor-related forms of violence is interpreted, deployed, and memorialized in a number of interconnected geopolitical sites and registers between Canada, the US, and Israel. What this chapter aims to reveal are the ways in which stories of Muslim women's murders become mobilized by various nationalist and right-wing actors who turn the bodies of murdered Muslim women into subjects of rescue and memorialization.

CULTURE AS VIOLENCE

Shortly after Aqsa's murder, *Toronto Life,* a monthly publication covering daily news, current events, and social issues affecting Toronto, published a special issue dedicated to minority affairs in Canada. The issue features an article about Aqsa Parvez, whose picture appears on the cover of the magazine. This article alerts Canadians to the deadly consequences of a migration system that too readily accepts culture as sacrosanct. Titled "Girl, Interrupted," the article focuses on Aqsa's life and her desire to belong within Canadian society. In this work, Mary Rogan argues that Aqsa's family had put the teenager in a very difficult position that compelled her to make a choice between the stipulation that she wear a veil and her desire to be like other Canadian girls.[7] Aqsa is presented as a teenage victim of culture, whose innocent and youthful aspirations of belonging and desire for Western fashions are starkly juxtaposed with unbending cultural norms and fatal traditional expectations. Aqsa's murder leads Rogan to wonder whether this death was "the price of multiculturalism" (2008). Throughout her work, Rogan raises serious concerns about the threat that fundamentalist Islam and Islamic zealotry pose to Canadian society. Rogan's article thus claims Aqsa as a cultural victim, an innocent youth whose presumed social transgressions and the deadly price she paid for them foregrounded the problems of immigration, assimilation, and difference for a multicultural state and society like that of Canada.

Mary Rogan's article was criticized by a variety of groups who denounced the misrepresentations of Aqsa's life and its wholesale condemnation of multiculturalism. A press conference collectively organized by Muslim Young Women, the Metropolitan Action Committee on Violence against Women and Children, and the Urban Alliance on Race Relations took place shortly after its publication. The organizers advertised this event by situating Aqsa's murder within a larger framework of violence against women: "While this feature reveals a recognition that a young woman's life was tragically cut short, it reflects common stereotypes about Muslim and immigrant communities, diverting attention from the urgent issue of violence against women in Canada" (Urban Alliance 2008). The group's refusal to exceptionalize the violence that claimed Aqsa's life is important because it works against the cultural framework frequently invoked to explain her death. In their rejection of the limited and racialized explanatory frame offered in Rogan's article and in dominant media responses to Aqsa's death, the organizers also recast Muslim and immigrant communities as part and parcel of Canadian society. Rather than situate themselves at its margin, they assert their belonging within it by refusing to distance themselves from acts of gender-based violence that occur in their communities and in Canadian society as a whole. The importance of this act rests in its insistence on challenging constructions of gender violence that culturalize its meanings or manifestations.[8] Aqsa's body, through its depiction as a body violated by cultural norms and expectations that are at odds with mainstream society's conception of agency, subjectivity, and freedom, is situated at the nexus of the framework of culture as violence.[9]

Over a decade after Aqsa's murder, it remains true that the growing body of works appearing in Canada about this case did not place this crime within a broader continuum of violence against women in Canada. Instead, dominant representations of this crime repeatedly exceptionalized Aqsa's story, placing it in a framework that culturalized this murder and reproduced it as an imported phenomenon, brought over by immigrants who have refused to let go of the collectivist cultural practices in which they were raised. As Eve Haque demonstrates in an article on the limits of Canadian multiculturalism and Aqsa Parvez's murder, the discussion remained framed along a binaristic logic that pits those who believed the crime was an honor killing against those who argued that the case was an example of domestic violence and a manifestation of the universal practices of patriarchal violence. Haque shows how this latter argument hinges on the assertion of Islam's intolerance for such crimes. What remained missing from these discussions, as Haque rightly asserts, was a focus on the "socioeconomic material realities which if considered would throw into crises the linear integrative model which is the mythic promise of Canada's multiculturalism" (2010, 91). Absent from such analysis, the reigning stories told about Aqsa's murder help bolster myths of national innocence and reaffirm the image of Canada's superiority, its moral vigor, and its peacekeeping ways—national myths that are central to Canada's image on the national and global scales (Thobani 2007a). To understand the significance of this framing and its imaginative and figurative sway on dominant publics, we must attend to its liberal and secular underpinnings.

SEEKING FREEDOM: UNVEILED AGENCIES AND SUBJECTIVITIES

The killing of Aqsa Parvez was used to raise questions about the national belonging of Muslims, the status of Canadian society, and Canada's official commitment to the policy of multiculturalism. As one article that explores the meaning of Aqsa Parvez's murder puts it, the murder pointed to "a sign that that loathsome and barbaric practice of Muslim 'honour killings' is making its way from South Asia and the Middle East to Canada" (*National Post* 2007). This fear that Muslim immigrants would import gender violence to Canada masked the reality of its occurrence in Canadian society, helping further perpetuate the image of a harmonious, gender-equal, and antiracist Canadian nation-state (Olwan 2013). As an article published in the conservative Canadian newspaper the *National Post* put it in an editorial posted a few days after Aqsa's murder:

> Since 9/11, Western societies have begun to closely scrutinize the toxic cultural practices of unassimilated Muslims in Europe and elsewhere. These practices include not only honour killings, but also anti-Semitism, support for terrorism, misogyny, forced veilings and forced marriages. Several high-profile conservative columnists—some of whom appear on these pages—have been particularly vigorous about highlighting these pathologies. And so when a young Muslim girl gets killed by her father, there is a natural tendency to see it as an indicator that Canadian Muslims are about to follow the radicalized path of militant, unassimilated co-religionists in Paris, London, and Stockholm. (Kay 2007)

Painting a grim picture of Muslims as racists with terroristic desires, such articles reproduced the idea that Muslims constitute an internalized and perpetual threat for Western nation-states. This article served to retrench the idea that Muslim communities in Canada are following a prescribed path toward "radicalized" militancy and exclusion, a path that has already been paved by their fellow "co-religionists" who now live in and frequently terrorize major European cities.

Such editorials contributed to creating and sustaining a hostile environment in which Muslim immigrants were viewed as risky investments for the nation-state. It is this type of logic that, when taken to its full extent, casts the policy of multiculturalism as a failing or failed project. In this way, Aqsa's story serves an internal and regulatory function. Here Aqsa's death becomes a cautionary tale, a warning that the continued adoption of multiculturalism as a state policy ultimately harms racialized and immigrant women and, more significantly, damages an otherwise healthy and nonviolent Canadian society and state. Critiques of multiculturalism for its supposed tolerance toward bad cultural behavior is not new, and, as Sara R. Farris has shown in her important work on the rise of feminist nationalism in multicultural European states, "gender equality is presented as a pillar of the western European nation, and the declaration of respect for women's rights has been turned into a condition for settlement" (2017, 14).

In accounts of Aqsa's murder, the failure of multiculturalism as a state policy is exemplified in its tolerance of migrants who adhere too rigidly to cultural practices such as veiling, which is considered harmful to girls and women and inhibiting of their right to equality and freedom.[10] This is why various articles about Aqsa's murder reduced Aqsa's struggles with her family to veiling and her desire to dress in Western clothing. The hijab or head covering was referenced regularly to instill the point that Aqsa's struggles were both cultural and religious. In one article, Aqsa's murder was referred to as the "Canadian hijab case" (*Reuters* 2007). To further establish this murder as a case of culturalized violence, stories gathered from Aqsa's friends at school emphasized her pursuit of life interests that clashed with her family's religious identity and social norms. These personal testimonies played an instrumental role in constructing Aqsa's life in a way that rendered it legible to mainstream Canadian society. Two of Aqsa's friends, Dominiqua Holmes-Thompson (who was sixteen at the time of Aqsa's murder) and Natalie Rance (who was fourteen at the time), for example, discussed the fears that Aqsa experienced in her family life and attributed them to her desire to show off her beauty in ways that contradicted her family's values. Their accounts led Michelle Henry and Bob Mitchell (2007) of the *Star* to surmise that "vivacious and outgoing, Parvez wanted to dress like a Western woman in tight-fitting clothes and show off her long, dark hair by removing her hijab." Reflected in mainstream media, the friends' powerful words granted the Canadian public a privileged and arguably accurate view into Aqsa's life.

These personal and intimate—and thus truthful—depictions of Aqsa were quickly elevated to the level of testimony. Their frequent citations evidence the public's investment in a particular truth discourse that seizes on Muslim girls and women and their bodies as sites of contestation and resistance. As various scholars have argued, the power of testimony rests in its ability to find receptive audiences who can affirm the truths on which its claims are founded. For a testimony to be successful, it must be able to "find recognition from those others who will register and witness its truth" (Whitlock 2007, 79). By narrating Aqsa's life and her death in a way that corroborates prevailing assumptions about immigrant life in Canada in general, and Muslim girls in particular, the interviews with Aqsa's friends accrued value and played a significant—if not singular—role in the "framing of death of Aqsa Parvez as a question of culture versus domestic violence, and as the exercise of freedom through 'normal' Western dress codes and behavior versus the imposition of the hijab" (Haque 2010, 86).

Accounts such as those discussed above exemplify the media's preoccupation with stories that emphasize individual struggles against communal odds and cultural backlash. The implied audience of these narratives is empathetic to stories of young women who make provocative and nonconformist choices that place them at odds with religious or cultural collectivities. More importantly, these narratives appeal to audiences' notions of agency and subjectivity, concepts associated with the idea of unfettered or free choice. Through this lens, Aqsa's subjectivity is articulated through its refusal to adhere to her family's cultural expectations. Thus, Aqsa's unveiling efforts enact a form of what Saba Mahmood refers to as "positive freedom" (2011, 11). In her study of the Egyptian women's mosque movement, Mahmood argues that liberal theorists conceptualize freedom as the "absence of external obstacles to self-guided choice and action" (11). Through this paradigm, agency is actualized when a subject can challenge "cultural" dictates, when she makes choices that contradict practices considered traditional and thus abnormal. As Mahmood states, positive freedom "is understood as the capacity to realize an autonomous will, one generally fashioned in accord with the dictates of 'universal reason' or 'self-interest,' and hence unencumbered by the weight of custom, transcendental will, and tradition" (11). Aqsa enacts this free will by refusing to fashion her body through veiling. In the eyes of Canadian society, nonveiling becomes the main act through which Aqsa becomes recognized as an agential, independent, and nonconforming citizen/subject.[11]

At the heart of this configuration is the young migrant girl whose agency, while tentative, makes possible the reconstitution of migrant communities. In insisting on placing Aqsa's bodily and sartorial choices in a framework that highlights her individuality, prevailing depictions of her life gesture toward Aqsa's capacity to become like "us," to be Canadian. This desire to belong is emphasized by Canadian media in order to show the disjuncture between Aqsa's choice and her family's condemnation. While this framing lauds Aqsa's integration in Canadian society, it also signals the dangers entailed in this quest for young Muslim women whose bodies become the sites on which the battles between modernity and tradition are constantly articulated and fought. As Leti Volpp notes in her work on gender violence and cultural difference, such ideas about Muslim migrants and Western society "presumes a host society of the West that is progressive, democratic, civilized, and feminist, in contrast to immigrants—in Europe and in the United States after 9/11, most especially Muslim immigrants—as backward, barbaric, primitive, and misogynist" (2011, 92).

The frequency and pervasiveness of such ideas is not particularly new or unusual. In the 2005 case of the "honor killing" of Hatun Sürücü, an immigrant of Turkish origin, German media also underscored Hatun's successful integration into German society by lauding her life choices and her ostensibly open expressions of sexuality and her embrace of freedom. This was evidenced in her dating of a German man, her navel piercing, and her modern and Westernized clothing. Such acts signaled Hatun's assimilation into German society and her escape from her culture, narratives that parallel the depictions of Aqsa's integration and provide a rationale for her murder. In her detailed analysis of this coverage, Weber notes that "the figure of Sürücü exists in an uneasy space . . . where she has become 'German' but can only have done so by removing herself from Turkish culture and, by doing so, condemns herself to death" (2013, 65). Aqsa Parvez similarly occupies an uneasy space in multicultural Canada, a space where her body is simultaneously familiarized and estranged, remembered and forgotten, always caught in between a competing set of discourses that she can neither confront in life nor contest in death.

Drawing on the emotionally charged and politically vexed investments and meanings embedded in the bodies of young girls and women, stories such as the ones discussed above have the potential to both separate and bind audiences across moral and ideological divides (Galusca 2012). These stories gain particular meaning and appeal when they are centered on young girls whose bodies become sites for imaginative—but not actual—integration fantasies and desires. Though invested in the bodily and the physical, their power rests in their ability to conceal the material conditions of gender violence and the embrace of fantasies of freedom. In her analysis of the representation of girlhood and victimhood in Canadian media's coverage of another so-called honor crime that claimed the lives of three young racialized women, known as the Shafia murders, Jiwani shows how dominant representations often portray young women like Aqsa by downplaying "the structural reality of their location as marginalized and minoritized [girls] within a dominant host society that values whiteness" (2014, 30). In other words, such narratives gain their traction and appeal due to their ability to underplay or conceal the hierarchical values of worth and beauty embedded in a dominant society in which whiteness is prized.

Rather than an analysis of the systemic violence of migration and racism and the struggles that Aqsa may have encountered because of her cultural and racial differences, what is repeatedly emphasized is Aqsa's desire to become one with Canadian society. As Jiwani states, Aqsa and girls like her capture our imaginations because "these young women showed the promise, if not the actuality, of being/becoming like *us*" (2014, 30). This powerful promise relies on its ability to foreclose troubling discursive, material, and historical gaps that have the potential to unsettle rescue visions embedded in multicultural integrative myths. Thus, while it is important to dislodge the various dominant discourses that make Aqsa's life knowable to Canadian and international audiences, it is equally crucial that we attend to the type of work such knowledge performs when it crosses—or when it is made to cross—transnational borders and is converged with settler colonial logics.

TRANSNATIONAL MEMORIALIZATIONS

As various articles written on the subject of Parvez's death showed, acts of violence against women are abhorred but they are especially so when they are committed by Muslim men whose violence is understood to operate outside a continuum of patriarchal and heterosexual violence against women. And yet to assume that these narratives simply fuel a national and internal debate that remains contained within the borders of Canada is to miss how stories about honor crimes also travel and come to influence, stir, and advance nationalist and right-wing agendas in settler colonial states outside of Canada, including the US and Israel. In this section, I trace how the story of Aqsa Parvez's murder reverberated outside the borders of Canada to demonstrate what Lila Abu-Lughod has referred to as the "political work" that honor crime performs in national and international contexts (2011, 27).[12]

Without a doubt, 9/11, and the concomitant naturalization of the clash-of-civilization discourse that has followed these events, has contributed to the honor crime's current discursive and political entrenchment. As various critical race theorists have noted, the "War on Terror" marked Muslims as threatening to Western nation-states (Thobani 2007b; Razack 2009). But 9/11 alone did not catapult into being a new or unusual precarious form of belonging. Rather, it shored up *new-old* ways of constructing racial differences that authorize the violation of Muslim lives at home and abroad. As Inderpal Grewal, in her work on the gender and racialized constructions of otherness in the US, argues, "The creation of the Middle Eastern Muslim as a terrorist recuperated in new ways an old category of the Oriental" (2005, 209). The construction of Muslim otherness was solidified through the convergence between state-sponsored policies of emergency and representational practices that helped embed the figure of the violent Muslim other into American consciousness. This configuration of the violent Muslim, Arab, and brown other, as Grewal argues, was "gendered through representations of masculine violence, fanaticism, and barbarism" (2005, 210).

In this part of the chapter, I discuss the strategies in the representation, circulation, and deployment of honor crime narratives outside the national Canadian context by right-wing actors located in the US context. I explore these media accounts to better understand interest in Aqsa's story and right-wing mobilizations against honor-related violence. In so doing, I seek to address two interrelated questions: What happens when such stories of gender violence against Muslim women, which are often understood in the culturalized and racialized frames of the honor crime, become part and parcel of right-wing campaigns in the interests of settler states? What happens when they are—by virtue of their subject—"outsourced" (Grewal 2013, 2) and appended to global wars predicated on the promise of what Spivak long ago labeled "saving brown women from brown men" (1988, 296)?

To begin to tease out the transnational circuitries and travels of Aqsa's murder, one need look no further than an article published in the *Toronto Sun* in 2008 by Joe Warmington, which put into motion the transportation of Aqsa's story from Canada to the US and later to Israel. Titled "Aqsa Parvez Rests in Numbered Gravesite: Strangled Teen Dared to Be Different," the article inscribes this violent crime as an inherent feature of Muslim male violence against women. While denouncing both the violent act that took the young woman's life and the status of her burial site, Warmington paints a haunting picture of a teenager who is discarded in both life and death. He claims that, a year after her murder, Parvez lay in an unmarked grave that only bore the number "774." In his piece, the author laments the grave's lack of ornament, markers, and design, stating that it bore "no name, no date of birth, no date of death. No nothing."

Disturbed by his findings, Warmington asks why Aqsa's grave remains unmarked and, in his view, unremembered, save for the few flowers left at the graveside by her high school friends. Relying on the expert opinion of Tarek Fatah, a Muslim Canadian writer and journalist who offers regular commentary on issues related to Islam, multiculturalism, and integration, Warmington tells his readers that the victims of honor crimes are often left in unmarked graves as a punishment in death for the dishonor they brought upon their families in life.[13] After voicing his disgust at the "barbaric" practice of honor killings that "sadly occurs in some Muslim countries," the author concludes by reminding readers that Aqsa's forsaken grave can be reclaimed because "for $580, the cemetery can put a flat marker there—with her name, date of birth and death, and at least people can find her if they want to come to pay their respects."

Warmington's call to action incites the concerned Western reader who is impacted by cultural forms of gender violence and impelled to act on behalf of Muslim women to protect their rights. Shortly after the publication of the article, his appeal on behalf of Aqsa would garner the attention of the right-wing American political activist Pamela Geller. Geller is the editor and publisher of *AtlasShrugs.com* and the president of the American Freedom Defense Initiative and Stop Islamization of America, organizations that claim to protect the US from Islamist infiltration (Kumar 2012). In 2010 Geller was responsible for the successful elevation of anti-Muslim fervor in the US to the level of national hysteria over the proposed but never materialized Islamic center known as Park 51 or the Cordova House Project (Bever 2015).[14] Geller denounced the project as the "ground-zero mega mosque" (qtd in Barnard and Feuer 2010). In 2012, with the help of Robert Spencer of *Jihadwatch.org*, Geller held the "Jessica Mokdad Human Rights Conference: Islamic Law in America" in Detroit.[15] Organized by the two organizations, which Geller helped found, the conference bore the name of a murdered Muslim American woman despite pleas from her family that her name not be invoked for this anti-Muslim gathering. According to Geller (2012), the conference was "dedicated to increasing awareness of honor killings and gendercide under the Shariah."

In her writings, Geller often reproduces the clash of civilizations discourse that undergirds the "War on Terror." Geller's interest in Aqsa's murder can be read against this ideological backdrop where, as she often asserts, Western nation-states are at war with the growing religion of Islam, a religion whose followers are posed to overtake the Western world, undo Western freedoms, and defeat Christianity. Geller has issued frequent warnings to Americans about the threat that Islam in general, and Muslims in particular, poses to the integrity and sovereignty of the US and, by extension, to the health and vibrancy of Western states such as Canada and Israel and the world at large. Her interest in gender violence and the honor crime is motivated by a purported concern for Muslim women who, she argues, live under the threat of Muslim patriarchal violence. Writing on the central place that Muslim women's bodies occupy for neoconservative and right-wing American pundits and politicians, Juliane Hammer notes that "pointing out the abysmal situation of Muslim women, their oppression by Islamic law, their suffering at the hands of Muslim men, and even their own resistance to such oppression all serve to legitimate Islamophobic rhetoric in both domestic and international affairs," and it is this interest that provokes right-wing actors to script their political ideologies on the bodies of murdered Muslim women such as Aqsa Parvez (2013, 33).

Posing as a concerned activist, Geller used the story of Aqsa Parvez to further her agendas while claiming to seek justice for the murdered girl. She thus asked her readers to contribute to her project to purchase a headstone for the "unmarked" grave. With the support of her readers, Geller raised 5,000 US dollars. The proposed headstone was to include Aqsa's full name, her date of birth and death, and an epitaph that read "In Loving Memory of Aqsa Parvez . . . Beloved, Remembered, and Free." After contacting the Canadian cemetery where Parvez lay buried and acquiring their approval for the new plaque, Geller told her readers in January 2008 that all was "going according to plan" (Geller 2009). This was until Aqsa's family, having become aware of the plans made without their approval, refused Geller's efforts to revamp the gravesite. Outraged at the sudden interruption of her unsolicited efforts, Geller explored the possibility of purchasing a plot right next to Aqsa's grave. She discovered that this would not be possible, and, even more, that she could not make any purchase in the immediate vicinity of Aqsa's grave: "Not a tree. Not a rock. Not a bench. All the plots were owned by the Islamic Society of North America," she wrote to her readers on the *American Thinker* (2009), another right-wing American blog dedicated to American foreign policy issues and homeland security issues. Angered by her failure to transform Aqsa's actual burial site, Geller sought an alternative memorial site altogether.

Geller's desire to revamp Aqsa's grave was briefly realized when she joined forces with Scott McLeod, a fire chief of the town of Pelham, Ontario, who was also determined to remember the murdered teenager. Having read about and seen pictures of Aqsa's "unmarked" grave on *AtlasShrugs.com,* the chief collaborated with then town councilor Sharon Cook, and together they put

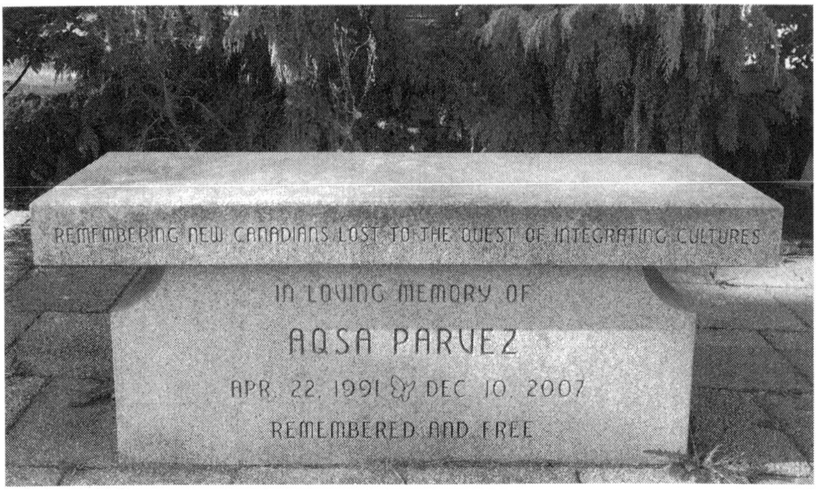

FIGURE 1. The Aqsa Parvez Bench in Pelham, Ontario. Photo taken by author.

forward a motion that would honor "Parvez and other immigrants who are caught between cultures" (Robinson 2009). On September 18, 2010, the town of Pelham, Ontario, dedicated a bench to Aqsa's memory that carried the following inscription: "Remembering new Canadians lost to the quest of integrating cultures: In Loving Memory of Aqsa Parvez—Remembered and Free" (see figure 1). When asked about the political implications of the inscription, Sharon Cook noted that "the memorial isn't against the Muslim faith. It's against the fact this young girl was murdered, allegedly for trying to integrate into Canadian culture" (qtd in Mitchell 2010).

While Geller wrote positively about the town of Pelham's courage on her blog, her public celebrations were cut short when McLeod denied any connection with the controversial blogger in an interview in the *Toronto Star* about the ideological aims of his project (Mitchell 2010). Even though he had personally thanked Geller for her efforts and generous financial donations to this project, McLeod refused to acknowledge any political motivations for his work. Unable to claim victory for her efforts to remember Aqsa in ways that bolster her brand of anti-Muslim politics, Geller put into motion plans for an alternative memorial site for the dead Muslim Canadian teenager. Her chosen spot was in Israel because, as she wrote in an article published in June 2009, "Considering the fact that Islamic honor killings were a global problem (over 90% of honor killings worldwide are Islamic), I approached the Jewish National Fund and worked to plant the *Aqsa Parvez Grove* in American Independence Park in Jerusalem, Israel, where the plaque before the grove

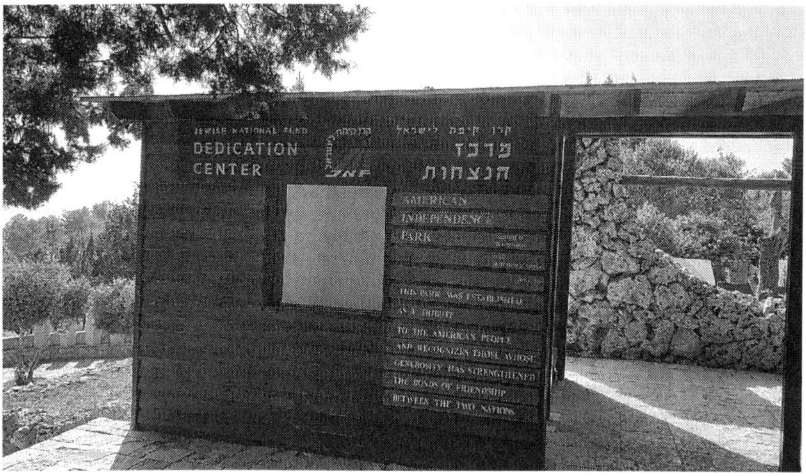

FIGURE 2. Entrance to the American Independence Park. Image courtesy of Majd Sidawi.

will read: *'In Loving Memory of Aqsa Parvez and All Victims of Honor Killings Worldwide.'* I loved the idea of a grove of trees that would continue to live and grow for decades in their name" (Geller 2011). A few weeks before the dedication ceremony, Geller encouraged her readers to "Stand with Atlas in Israel," where they could all remember the slain teen and support the State of Israel by attending the dedication ceremony and then joining radio commentator Glenn Beck's rally for Israel, which showcased right-wing Christian support for the Israeli state (Heller 2011). The plaque celebrating Aqsa's life is located in the American Independence Park in Jerusalem (see figure 2). Within the park there exists the "Wall of Eternal Life," established by the Jewish National Fund (JNF) to "provide a meaningful opportunity for the global Jewish community to tie themselves more closely to the State of Israel while memorializing the life of a loved one."[16] Aqsa's plaque exists on this wall alongside the names of many others.

Such strategies of selective memorialization register how the bodies of murdered Muslim women come to signify transnationally for political projects enacted in support of right-wing politics and settler colonial projects. Aqsa Parvez's inclusion in such public memorial projects specifically underscores the imbricated ways in which honor crime stories travel from one site to another and how their invocations are embedded in complex and highly charged political and historical processes of space claiming (see figure 3).

Geller's choice of Israel as the ideal location for the commemoration of Aqsa speaks to an alignment between the American Christian Right and sup-

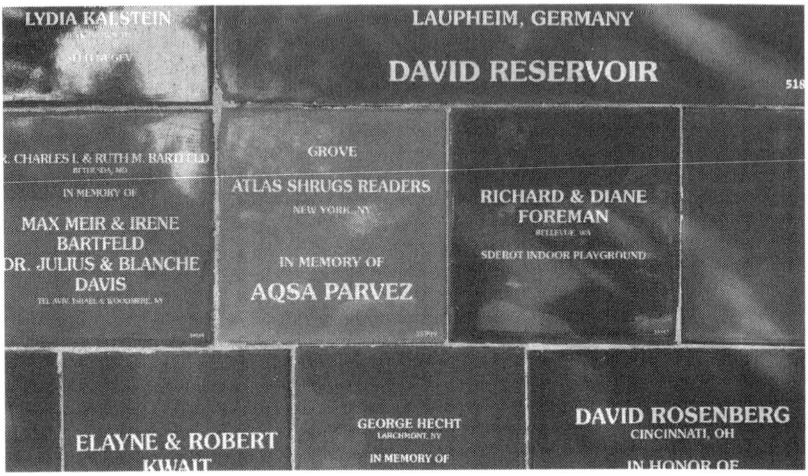

FIGURE 3. Aqsa Parvez's Memorial Plaque on the "Wall of Eternal Life" in American Independence Park. Picture courtesy of Majd Sidawi.

port for Israel. As Deepa Kumar has argued, the roots of such convergence lie in "a particular worldview that sees Israel as instrumental in advancing American power" (2012, 117). Geller's support for Israel emanates from the linking of Islam with terrorism and sexism—threats believed to be singularly faced by both the US and Israel under the dominant logic of the "War on Terror." This convergence often relies on the appropriation of women's rights discourses, rendering the political motivations behind Geller's selection of Israel as an ideal location for the commemoration of Aqsa's life and death unambiguous and tied to a historic conjuncture between right-wing American politics and the State of Israel. In this context, the violated and murdered Muslim woman's body is a central instrument for a politically motivated campaign premised on the false imperatives of empowerment, rescue, and emancipation that conjoin anti-Muslim discourses in both states. While efforts to memorialize Aqsa Parvez in Canada and Israel may operate at the symbolic level, an examination of the politics undergirding them reveals their material consequences and demonstrates that specific forms of gender violence continue to have an active transnational social and political life.

REMEMBERING MURDERED MUSLIM WOMEN

What makes *some* Muslim women's deaths *count*? What politics underpin the ideologically motivated interest in these murdered bodies? How can we make sense of the inordinate attention given to Muslim women's bodies murdered (or honor-killed) by Muslim men in the context of the settler colonial states of Canada, the US, and Israel? Beyond the obvious anti-Muslim racism driving the increased attention given to the bodies of some murdered Muslim women, what are the ramifications of such interest and concern, and how might we ethically oppose gender forms of violence against Muslim women specifically and women more broadly? How, in other words, can we confront what Jennifer Hyndman has called the "utilitarian calculus of death and loss" shaping the geopolitics of right-wing transnational remembrance practices that are exemplified in the story of Aqsa Parvez (2007, 39)?

In this chapter, I have drawn on the rich body of literature and the theoretical framings of critical race feminism to demonstrate how honor crime narratives are mobilized to buttress the dominant logic of multicultural and settler colonial states. I aimed here to show how, in death, Muslim women's bodies gain particular meaning and use value by right-wing actors who are, openly and publicly, strong opponents of Islam and Muslims. For these anti-Muslim actors, the bodies of murdered Muslim women are convenient subjects of remembrance that are routinely and conveniently deployed to perform a number of regulatory and political functions. In death Muslim women's bodies can be used to redraw civilizational borders, corroborating narratives of Western superiority and Muslim difference and inferiority. These narratives buttress stereotypical beliefs about Muslim migrants and their experiences of settlement and integration. In this narrative, attention to the political and economic constraints of migration disappears, while the individual and cultural failures of migrants and their inability to assimilate are overemphasized. As a highly gendered script, this narrative necessitates the construction of Muslim women as victims of patriarchal violence at the hands of Muslim men. Functioning in tandem with one another, these narratives are neither new nor unfamiliar, drawing on racialized representations of Muslim alterity and difference.

In tracing the narratives of Aqsa's death and their memorialized deployments, this chapter examines the recalibration of stories of gender violence in the service of the ideologies and interests of right-wing actors and settler states. It does so neither by diminishing the seriousness of the crime and forms of gender violence to which Aqsa was subjected by members of her own family, nor by ignoring the vexed political, scholarly, and theoretical terrains in which honor-related violence is enacted, enmeshed, and inserted (Terman 2016). It argues that the confluence of neoconservative, anti-immigrant, and anti-Muslim right-wing agendas over the murder of Aqsa Parvez showcase how, as victims of gender violence, the bodies of some murdered women, and the narratives generated through and on them, are particularly useful and ripe for co-optation. As the story of Aqsa Parvez amply demonstrates, Muslim women's bodies not only mark the ideological, political, and racial limits of the Western nation-state but also enable its regulatory functions precisely through the assumption of their susceptibility to certain forms of cultural and gender violence. Claimed in death, they are also used to cloak right-wing, anti-immigrant, anti-Muslim political forms of activism. Attached to agendas they cannot contest, the bodies of Muslim women become useful tools, deployed to corroborate assumptions of cultural violence, racialized difference, and inherent victimhood. By experiencing gender violence, Muslim women's bodies acquire special status and relevance because they can be used to construct myths of gender equality and to erase and rewrite past and ongoing histories of violence, occupation, and war committed in settler colonial states. In other words, these dead bodies and the constructed narratives produced about them *count* precisely because they cannot refute the ideological work to which they are put in death. As such, they are convenient subjects for political and ideological remembrance acts that masquerade as solidarity and care.

CHAPTER 2

Between the Artist and the Critic

Palestinian Confrontations of Violence

IN 2012 DAM, a Palestinian hip-hop group, received funding from the United Nations Entity for Gender Equality and the Empowerment of Women to produce a music video, titled "If I Could Go Back in Time," as part of its album *Dabke on the Moon*. Featuring Palestinian artists Amal Murkus and directed by Jackie Salloum (of the documentary *Slingshot Hip Hop*), the song was widely circulated and garnered the already popular Palestinian band transnational acclaim from a number of musical groups, activists and workers for justice in Palestine, and women's and human rights organizations, whose multiple locations and heterogeneous social origins and political investments traverse neat divides between the foreign and the authentic, the real and the virtual, and the local and the global. As an officially acknowledged sponsor of DAM's work, UN Women (2013) commended the song for its commitment to "combatting all forms of violence against women," celebrating the band's work in supporting "women's advocates and human rights organizations in changing the laws that support the [practice of honor killings] in Palestinian society."

Shortly after the song's release, however, the band found itself at the center of a debate about the politics of speaking about gender violence in colonial contexts that instigated a broader conversation about contesting forms of violence directly shaped by the intersecting systems of patriarchy and settler colonialism. On one side of the debate, DAM and its supporters argued for the importance of adding their voices to growing local activist efforts to end gender and sexual violence within Palestinian society and in historic and occupied Palestine. Despite acknowledging some of the song's limitations, its supporters urged audiences and critics to acknowledge the occurrence of gender violence within Palestinian society. The song's detractors, while emphasizing the importance of activisms against gender and sexual violence, shed light on the dangers of advocacy work that does not attend to the intersections of these forms of violence with multiple systems of power, including settler colonialism and that, in the process, becomes part and parcel of dominant and transnational scripting of the honor crime as a "cultural-legal category" (Abu-Lughod and Mikdashi 2012a).

Discussed on the pages of *Jadaliyya*, an e-zine that has played an instrumental role in reshaping popular and academic understandings of the Middle East during the Arab uprisings and since, the debates brought to light anxieties over what feminist rhetorical studies scholar Wendy Hesford has described as the "ungovernability" of transnational visual, discursive, and rhetorical representations of gendered and sexual violence (2011, 98).[1] While the two sides of the debate surrounding DAM's song have been understood as diametrically opposed, I want to argue that they share a commitment to interrogating and confronting sexual, social, and political forms of violence that structure the politics of life and death in Palestine today. Despite their diverging methods and tactics, arguments for and against DAM's song become recognizable and legible through a focus on issues of authenticity, positionality, and accountability—issues central to feminist research methodologies and feminist praxis. Both sides thus urge us to ask: *Who* has the right to speak about gender violence, and from what locations? What brings together or sets apart academic discussions from artistic and activist efforts to end forms of violence known as honor-based violence in Palestine and elsewhere? Put differently, what is the relationship between theory and praxis, and how can they work (together or separately) to end all forms of gender violence, including the violence of the honor crime?

To address these questions, I focus on the specificities of settler colonialism and occupation that structure the phenomenon of gender violence in Palestine. I thus map how the category of the honor crime became intimately tied to state-making projects in Palestine and what its confrontations reveal about the problem of gender violence in occupied contexts. After analyzing this context, I offer a close reading of DAM's video and its transnational receptions. I explore how the song is placed and was later circulated within a laden political context that works to spectacularize, exceptionalize, and culturalize honor-related violence. Rather than simply rehash the terms of the debate in which this song became deeply imbricated or oversimplify the complex arguments and positions over the song, I explore what its narrow (and narrowing) contours can reveal about the ways in which gender violence is narrated, consumed, and confronted in and across settler colonial geographies where aid works to govern people's realities and shape their subjectivities. Primarily I am interested in mapping the tensions that this debate indexes in order to reflect on the possibilities and limits of feminist interventions in efforts to address forms of violence that are themselves intersecting, cross-cutting, and relational.

A central question that animates the discussion I offer in this chapter is the issue of authenticity and the question of who gets to speak on Palestine, and under what conditions local players can contest gender violence that is produced and sustained by both the context of settler coloniality and local articulations of patriarchy. I show how the local scenes of Palestinian activism blur the line between state and nonstate actors, local organizations and global funders, producing complicated sites of intervention in and prevention of the phenomenon of gender-based violence in Palestine.

In what follows, I contextualize mobilization efforts against gender violence, showing how activism against honor-related violence communicates ideas about Palestinian society and its relationship to state-making projects and human rights campaigns aimed at ending violence against women. I explore how the varying geographies of occupation and settler colonialism in historic Palestine shape and delimit efforts to contest gender-based violence in protracted, dissimilar, and complicated ways. This chapter brings into view what popular representations of the honor crime often disappear and obfuscate: namely, the shrinking political space for transnational feminist contestations of ubiquitous and overlapping forms of gender violence that demand complex, multiple, and divergent strategies, resistances, and solutions. I use the debate surrounding this song to speak to the politics of contesting gender violence in spaces of occupation and settler coloniality such as that of Palestine.

CONTEXTUALIZING VIOLENCE AGAINST WOMEN AND STATE-MAKING PROJECTS IN PALESTINE

In 2011, a year before the release of DAM's song, the Palestinian cabinet endorsed a nine-year national strategic plan to combat violence against women, which was developed by the Palestinian National Authority (PNA) or the Palestinian Authority (PA).[2] The plan put into place a series of strategies to identify and address violence against women occurring in the Occupied Palestinian Territories.[3] Developed by members of the National Committee to Combat Violence Against Women, a committee formed under the auspices of the Ministry of the Women's Affairs of the Palestinian National Authority, the strategy report provides a contextual approach to its understanding of the phenomenon of gender violence.[4] *Violence* is seen as a broad term that encompasses a range of harms and violations, including discrimination against women that adversely impacts their right to live and work. The strategy's authors seek to end the occurrence of violence against women because they see it as a public and national problem impacting all Palestinians, viewing its continuation as an impediment to the overall health of all segments of their society, including men, women, and children. The strategy identifies three areas of primary concern for its efforts to end violence against women: violence that occurs as a result of Israeli occupation, domestic violence that occurs within the family, and violence against women taking place in the workplace. Taking a dual "developmental" approach to the phenomenon of violence within Occupied Palestinian Territories, the *National Strategy to Combat Violence Against Women 2011–2019* recognizes the interaction between "the culture, norms and traditions which reinforce roles division between males and females" and the impact of Israeli occupation on "increasing the marginalization of Palestinian women both directly and indirectly" (National Committee to Combat Violence Against Women 9). The report states:

> Palestinian women experience various forms of violence at two levels: at the international and national levels, on the one hand, and at the local level, on the other hand. At the international level, the Israeli occupation increases the level of violence in Palestinian society in general and affects all social groups, not women exclusively. Thus, the occupation puts all members of Palestinian society, men, women, boys and girls, at risk of getting involved in cycles of violence. Yet, for women, the oppressive policies of the occupation are a double source of violence, reinforcing the violence they experience as a result of their already compromised social role and status at the internal, domestic level, where they often find themselves beyond official systems of protection in the Palestinian society, especially legal protection. (9)

I cite this part of the report at length to demonstrate the complexities of the terrain of gender violence in Palestinian society. Palestinian women face compounded and multiple forms of oppression. As members of communities that emphasize traditional specific domestic obligations for women, women have social roles that are often truncated and confined to the private sphere. Israeli occupation policies compound these difficult realities, leaving Palestinian women prone to abuse and violence, at the hands of both local patriarchs and the administrators of Israeli occupation, including the army, whom women interact with at checkpoints and other military and administrative posts. The multiyear strategy report grounds all its past and future efforts to confront violence against women in Palestinian society within the inseparable political realms of occupation and the social domain of local Palestinian patriarchy.

Noting the absence of current statistics on gender violence in the Occupied Palestinian Territories, the report relies on a number of previous studies to represent the scale of the problem of violence in an accurate way. It records statistics acquired from the Domestic Violence Survey conducted by the Palestinian Central Bureau of Statistics (PCBS) between December 2005 and January 2006 on over 4,212 households in the West Bank and Gaza, where 61.7 percent of "ever married" women were exposed to psychological violence, 23.3 percent were exposed to physical violence, and 10.9 percent reported being exposed to sexual violence by their husbands at least once during the period in which the survey was conducted (2006, 11). The strategy pays considerable attention to the killing of women and labels these crimes examples of femicides (or the killing of women) carried out under the pretext of family honor. In developing a strategy to combat the rising rates of violence in Palestinian society and to protect women from all forms of violence, including murder, the report puts forth a plan that relies on cooperation and interaction between formal and informal sectors of Palestinian society. The strategy identifies the Palestinian Basic Law as an important formal avenue for justice, especially when buttressed by international law agreements and framed within the discourse of human rights.[5]

In addressing the necessity of making legislative changes to end the phenomenon of gender violence, the report's authors note that "the political circumstances in the oPt, circumstances which affect its legislative process, have turned the legal situation in the oPt into a major dilemma rarely faced by other societies" (19). Recognizing the multiplicity of actors needed to put an end to violence against women, the strategy also attends to "informal protection mechanisms" that include the tribal and family systems, women's organizations, and political parties (24). In the document, there is a clear recognition of the interplay between the law and the tribal system in enforcing patriarchal codes; the strategy goes so far as to identify the extended family system that often resolves cases of femicide in ways that benefit the male offender as an impediment to efforts to end gender violence in Palestinian society.

The strategy is an important national document not because it registers the stated will of a pseudo-government to address the problem of violence against women in occupied Palestine but because it indexes the magnitude and the complexity of potential confrontations which are caught between the specificities of the Palestinian legal context itself, the realities of settler colonial occupation in the West Bank and Gaza, and the backdrop of patriarchal traditions and customs that shape and regulate life for Palestinian men, women, and children. Steeped in the rhetoric of development and equality, the report is structured by a vision to "promote the principle of the rule of law based on respect for women's rights and improving institutional mechanisms in Palestinian society in order to protect and support abused women and allow them to live in a society free from all forms of discrimination, and based on equality, dignity, and respect for human rights" (39).

In its identification of gender-based violence as an issue of national concern requiring a multiyear strategy commitment, this report stakes for the emerging Palestinian state a definable position through a human rights framework. It shows how local national actors such as the Palestinian Authority have engaged gender violence as a site of governmentality, a social problem that can be mitigated or stopped through the intervention of state and nonstate actors in issues that challenge the sovereignty and power of an emerging and yet-to-be-realized Palestinian state. Gender violence is understood as an impediment to the development and progress of Palestinian society and as a problem deeply rooted in the nexus of patriarchal and colonial rule that subjects Palestinian people's lives but one that, ultimately, must be confronted in the interests of the state.

As Rema Hammami (2019) has shown, the Palestinian strategy on fighting violence against women emerged from a longer genealogy of combating violence against women as a social problem with global and local ramifications. In Palestine, violence against women was first statistically measured through the Palestinian Central Bureau's statistical report *Domestic Violence in the West Bank and Gaza* (479).[6] This measure lead to the establishment of a task force for fighting violence against women and later to the authoring and release of a government-approved strategy. Hammami's work brings into focus the "complex set of geopolitical relations and processes through which Palestinian domestic violence came to be articulated in specific ways, made visible, and then constantly circulated through and across a range of intersecting local and global domains, where it became privileged as Palestinian society's most prominent social problems as well as its particular violence problem" (482). As we will see, confronting violence against women in general and the honor crime in particular had become a nationally identified priority and concern before the UN-funded release of DAM's song. This is due, in part, to the rising rates of femicide within Palestinian society at the time of the report's publication and the national recognition that the problem's continuation was an impediment to Palestinian statehood and the Authority's recognition of what Hammami aptly terms "the productive life of domestic violence in Palestine" (495). It is precisely within this context that DAM's musical intervention and its particular representation of gender violence must be placed and analyzed.

Immediately prior to the release of DAM's song, the killing of women for what honor-related reasons was on the rise in the West Bank and Gaza. While the number of reported murders had dropped in 2011 to five cases, the figure rose in 2012 to thirteen women and doubled in 2013 to twenty-six.[7] The staggering rise in murder cases led to increased negative local and international media attention to this phenomenon, prompting various women's agencies to pressure the Palestinian Authority to take a public and explicit stance against this violence. This pressure reached a zenith in 2011, with news of the discovery of the gruesome murder of Aya Baradiyah, a twenty-one-year-old university student, a year after she had gone missing from her family's home in the village of Surif.[8] Aya's family had reported Aya missing the day after her disappearance on April 20, 2010. Shortly after news of her disappearance became known in the village, rumors impugning her respectability and honor began to circulate in her community, and members of her own family stopped visiting her parents' home for fear of having their reputation tarnished by association. Prior to her disappearance, Aya was engaged to a man seventeen years her senior after she had managed to convince her father of his suitability as a suitor. Her father reluctantly agreed to her request but stipulated that the marriage not take place until after Aya completed her university studies. On the day of her disappearance, Aya had visited the home of her uncle, who would later confess to murdering her, with the help of two of his friends, by covering her head with a bag and leaving her in a well to die. Aya's remains were discovered there by accident a year after her disappearance from her family's home.[9]

Aya's murder gave rise to broad mobilization efforts against the murder of women within Palestinian society. In addition to the international and local coverage that the crime received, a local campaign called "Mapping Her" was developed by a nongovernment organization called *Taghyeer* for Social Media. The organization launched *Hamlit Bint Al Balad,* releasing a powerful infographic with details of Aya's murder.[10] The campaign's name translates roughly to "Daughter of the Nation" or "Daughter of the Homeland." It indicates the belonging of murdered women in Palestine and the identification of the campaign's members with them through the insistence on claiming them as part of the Palestinian nation. Titled "Discarding Aya Baradiyah in a Well While Alive," the poster includes a picture of Aya that names her as a victim of physical violence and provides details of her age and her marital status as a single woman. The poster also details Aya's murder:

> The virginal girl Aya Baradiyah, who was 21 years old and a university student, was kidnapped and murdered in a cold-blooded and premeditated crime at the hands of her uncle and his two friends because of a claim that she had established a relationship with a man who had asked for her hand in marriage. While she was still alive, the offenders threw her into a well located in the remote area of Khalet Abu Sulaiman, which lies to the west of her village, Surif, located in the Governorate of Hebron in the south of the West Bank. Aya was found there thirteen months after she had disappeared. (My translation)

This account of the murder of Aya Baradiyah insists on her sexual innocence by introducing her as a "virginal girl" killed by a member of her family based on a false claim of social or sexual impropriety. In doing so, the campaign reverts to traditional coverage of honor-related crimes that denounces the murder of women and invokes sympathy for them by asserting their sexual purity and morality. This "hymen status line," as Ebtihal Mahadeen names it in her work on Jordanian media portrayals of honor-related violence, is a common part of such accounts (2013, 83). It is a rhetorical strategy that establishes the distinction between worthy and unworthy victims of gender violence in Arab media discourses.

While its presence helps confirm the innocence of some murdered women, its absence marks women who have been murdered by members of their family or by their spouses as guilty subjects, deserving of the violence they have encountered.[11] Its appearance in representations of Aya is intentional, verifying her innocence and squelching any gossip that questions her reputation or marks her as deserving of her death. The description of Aya's murder in this poster goes further by casting doubt on the veracity of the rumors that she had engaged in improper behavior—rumors that may have cost her life. As is well known in the literature on honor-related violence, rumors and gossip are central drivers of violence against women. They function to first propel or initiate the planning of the act of violence and later to sanction its occurrence or to diminish its significance.[12]

In Palestinian accounts of Aya's murder, Aya is represented as an honorable young woman whose reputation was above reproach. Accounts of the murder allude to Aya having a relationship that her uncle did not approve of; these stories have been refuted with assertions that her father, as the male head of household, had approved her engagement. This appeal to the official nature of Aya's relationship with her fiancé is significant, emphasizing that Aya was a respectable young woman who adhered to cultural expectations and who therefore did not deserve to be killed by her uncle.[13] While the description of Aya's murder reproduces the morality and honor logics used to sanction violence against women, the poster also insists on rooting Aya and her murder within the specificities of space, place, and time in Palestine. This can be discerned through the specific cartographic details given about the murder. Attached to the description of Aya's murder is a map of historic Palestine that shows where the crime occurred, rooting both Aya and her murder in the intimate geographies of Palestine. Rather than denying the occurrence of this crime or disappearing it from national purview, the poster makes Aya's murder a Palestinian problem, a serious social issue that Palestinian society as a whole must confront.

In claiming Aya as a daughter of the nation, or *bint al balad,* a girl who belongs in Palestine, the campaign purposely challenged dominant representations of murdered Palestinian women as sinful members of society who are to be discarded by the nation or cast out by members of their own families and communities. By using such strategies, the campaign challenged some of the social and discursive frames used to sanction gender violence, employing what can be understood as a feminist geopolitical praxis that emplaces such violence within the geographies of occupied Palestine. The organization thus makes the act of mapping political, claiming it as a feminist form of activism that can shed light on social issues that have been ignored or previously denied. As their website states, "Mapping Her is a digital tool, made to map the marginalized, harassed, unprivileged, invisible and hurt women. By doing so we'll map their pain for people to find, explore, discover and make a change."[14]

In addition to placing Aya's murder within the geographies of Palestine, the organization showed that the crime was denounced by Aya's family members (including both her father and her brother) and her Palestinian community at large, thus refuting the assumption that honor crimes are tolerated within Palestinian society. In all accounts, Aya is recognized as a valuable member of the community and someone whose murder was nationally deplored, contested, and mourned. *Bint Al Balad*'s campaign to end violence against women in Palestinian society was funded by the German nongovernment organization Heinrich Böll Stiftung: The Green Political Foundation and other local nongovernment organizations, such as *Taghyeer* for Social Media, the Palestinian Counseling Center, the Palestinian Non-Governmental Organization Against Domestic Violence Against Women (Al Muntada), and Women's Media and Development.[15] This collaboration between a Western-based, nongovernment organization and local NGOs is not unusual in the Palestinian context, where interactions between local activists and the NGO discourse on development, human rights, and equality shape activist confrontations of gender violence in Palestine in highly important ways. The strength of this particular campaign, however, lies in its ability to use social media platforms to publicize its message among Palestinian youth, recognizing in them a powerful constituency that can bring about positive social change. In addition to using posters written in Arabic, the campaign developed an interactive application that allows community members to add information about violence against women occurring in Palestinian society. Following the publication of the poster of Aya's murder, the campaign launched an electronic letter in support of missing and murdered Palestinian women that called on Palestinian society to advocate for sweeping legal reforms that would protect women from violence and guarantee their right to a dignified and safe living.

A review of media responses to Aya's murder shows that the crime produced collective Palestinian outrage that was directed both at the Palestinian Authority for its failure to protect Palestinian women and at the murderers themselves for taking the life of an innocent woman.[16] Calls for the imposition of harsh sentences on the murderers were echoed in various media accounts, including television programs where young women called for the imposition of the death penalty on the perpetrators.[17] At her funeral, thousands of people joined Aya's family to mourn the murdered woman. In a letter to Aya's family from Palestinian prisoners incarcerated in Israeli jails, the murder was denounced as alien to Palestinian culture and Aya was claimed as a Palestinian martyr, a sign of the high esteem in which Palestinian society held Aya and their unequivocal condemnation of the murder.[18] This particular rhetorical and political strategies used by the campaign demonstrates how the murder of women deemed honorable can elicit national outrage that allowed Palestinians to claim Aya to be a martyr, someone who occupies, through her murder, the highest echelons of Palestinian society.

This collective and national outrage surrounding Aya's murder led President Mahmoud Abbas, in a televised meeting with family members of Aya and with her grieving mother and father that was broadcast on Palestinian national television, to claim that existing laws would be changed to prevent such murders, which are unacceptable "by mind, logic, or religion."[19] Abbas would further state, in a paternalistic tone, that no one could be silent in the face of such crimes that target "our daughters," asking God to protect the Baradiyah family and their offspring and offering to fund the family's pilgrimage to Mecca that year. Despite the public and performative aspects of Abbas's meeting with the Baradiyah family, there is little doubt that Aya's murder was a catalyst for national response against gender violence in Palestine. Following his meeting, Abbas issued a presidential decree that froze article 340 of Penal Code 6 of 1960 in the West Bank and stipulated an amendment to Penal Code 16 of 1960 enforced in the West Bank, and Penal Code 74 of 1936 enforced in Gaza (Melhem 2014).[20] The president gestured his opposition to honor-based violence by stating his commitment to place restrictions on laws that allow for mitigated or commuted sentences for men who murder women. However, as many would later note, these changes operated at the cosmetic level only, since article 340 functions as part of a trifecta of legal codes that provide extenuating circumstance as cover for perpetrators of violence against women and because the president had shown no serious political will to alter or eradicate such laws in the aftermath of the murder beyond public spectacle.[21]

Aya's murder and honor-related violence in general remained in the spotlight as a result, in large part, of local activist efforts to pressure the Palestinian Authority to adopt a stronger position on violence against women (Odgaard 2014). One such campaign, launched by a coalition of Palestinian women's groups, called "In Palestine killing is permitted," issued 120 letters to the office of the president to urge him to adopt more stringent laws against men who murder women under the pretense of honor.[22] After ignoring their various calls for legal reform, successful pressure by various women's organizations, including demonstrations in Palestinian cities that sought draw attention to this crime, led the president to sign a number of international human rights agreements focused on women's rights, including the ratification of the Convention for the Elimination of All Forms of Discrimination Against Women (CEDAW) on April 2, 2014. In ratifying this agreement and others like it, the Palestinian Authority sought to establish itself as an independent entity, one that had the power and sovereignty to enter and enforce international agreements. While ostensibly informed by a commitment to women's rights and the protection of their safety, such acts also reflect the desire of the Palestinian Authority to be recognized by the international community and its willingness to opportunistically seize on the women's rights discourses to improve its image and legitimate its authority.

The rush to ratify national agreements that ensued in this period coincides with the Palestinian Authority's statehood bid that was submitted to the United Nations Security Council and was preceded by the granting of Palestine observer and nonmember status at the United Nations in 2012.[23] Such acts are important for their political as well as their symbolic meanings, showcasing how the uptake and deployment of human rights discourses can mark entry to or exclusion from the project of modernity for nation-states and their citizen subjects. To be admitted into the international community, civilized nation-states and governments must revoke gender violence at the national, legal, and cultural levels. They do this by publicly stating their opposition to violence and declaring their commitment to instituting laws, policies, and practices that guard against violence against women and guarantee women's right to security and safety. Progress on challenging these crimes not only provides states platforms to assert their concern for women's rights on a global stage but also opens opportunities for membership and recognition within the international community of nation-states, where stated commitments to women's rights, progress, and development are essential rhetorics of statehood.

As Sally Engle Merry has argued, ratifications of international agreements such as CEDAW occur within "the spaces of transnational modernity" where state representatives "produce a social reformist, fundamentally neoliberal vision of modernity governed by concepts of human rights" (2006, 100). By representing itself as a state that is not only conversant in but also compliant with human rights instruments for measuring and ending violence against women accepted and adopted worldwide, the Palestinian Authority sought to acquire a place for itself among international state players.[24] In essence, it hoped that the ratification of such agreements would register its readiness to become a recognized nation-state in fulfillment of the promises of the Oslo Agreement signed between the Palestinian Authority and Israel in 1993.[25] Such efforts reflect the opportunistic nature of state discourses surrounding gender-based violence, discourses that often use and usurp local activism in the name of protecting women from violence.

For various developing states, commitments to contesting gender violence are often intimately tied to funding opportunities in the form of international aid and nongovernment donations.[26] This includes funding from nongovernment organizations and entities such as the UN, funding that also supported the project of monitoring the progress of the PA on its national strategy for confronting violence against women discussed earlier.[27] In the case of Palestine, the promise of nationhood has become intimately connected to the Palestinian Authority's ability and willingness to repudiate legal codes that exonerate male perpetrators of honor-related violence or that provide them lenient or reduced sentences. President Abbas's decree and his stated commitment to end gender violence in Palestine cannot be separated from the broader national and international contexts that use the stated position of a government on issues of gender and sexual violence and women's rights as a measure of its worthiness and ability to belong to the international community. While DAM's musical work on gender violence in Palestinian society does not directly emerge from the context of the occupied Palestinian territories of the West Bank and Gaza, placing the group's intervention within this landscape serves to simultaneously historicize and de-exceptionalize their efforts to combat violence in Palestine. It shows how such efforts are always already shaped by local and transnational politics of modern subject-making that demand that gender violence be understood within the recognizable framework of human rights infractions. It also situates activism against gender violence and the murder of women in Palestine against the backdrop of state-making practices that seize contestations of violence against women as sites of governmentality.

FEMICIDE IN PALESTINE

In an important article on the politics of gender violence, Nadera Shalhoub-Kevorkian (2002) named the violence that occurs in Palestinian society a form of "femicide," referring to the forms of abuse that women experience as "'living death'" (2003, 591). Through her scholarship and advocacy, Shalhoub-Kevorkian attends to the personal and political dimensions of gender and sexual violence. Her work uses an intersectional form of analysis that pays attention to the details of the killing of women and does not begin at the site of the murdered body but with attention to the social and political contexts in which women experience violence, including verbal, psychological, physical, and emotional abuse and the threat of murder. Refuting the singular focus on honor-based violence that dominates accounts of violence against women in Palestine, Shalhoub-Kevorkian invited researchers to "learn more about women's realities by mapping the political landscape of these contexts and analyzing their relationships and intersections with women's lives in general, and with women's lives within the family in particular" (2003, 593).

I begin with this theoretical framework in order to explore the complex political, social, and legal context of femicide in historic Palestine, showing how activists and local actors confront increasing rates of gender and sexual violence against the backdrop of Israeli settler colonialism where Palestinians live in conditions of poverty, compounded by limited educational and work opportunities (Sultany 2012). If the previous section provided some insights into the terrain of confrontations of gender violence in the shadow of the Palestinian yet-to-be-realized state, this section showcases the difficulties and complexities of this work within the settler colonial state of Israel for Palestinian subjects/citizens who experience a form of double marginalization as a minoritized population in the Jewish state that is relegated to what Nimer Sultany describes as "separate and unequal status" within Israel (194).

Palestinian citizens of the state of Israel constitute 20 percent of the population, or roughly 2.2 million of Israel's nine-million-plus population.[28] They exist in what is known as 1948 Palestine, or within the "green line."[29] They are the descendants of Palestinians who, at the founding of the Israeli state in 1948, either remained or were able to stay in their own towns and villages or became internally displaced persons within the green line. As a minority population existing within a Jewish majority state, some Palestinians were granted citizenship within Israel, but their citizenship was immediately restricted through emergency regulations that curtailed their movement, their ability to purchase land, and their ability to pass citizenship on to members of their own families.[30] Such regulations were implemented to guarantee the growth of a Jewish majority state. As Nadim N. Rouhana and Areej Sabbagh-Khoury (2015) explain, the form of citizenship granted to Palestinians in 1948 evolved over four distinct historical periods that worked to consolidate what they describe as a "settler-colonial citizenship" practice employed to manage and regulate the life of Palestinians in the Israeli state.[31]

As second-class citizens, Palestinians with Israeli citizenship often live in cities and towns that are socioeconomically impoverished and geographically marginalized. In these geographies of engineered difference and inequality, poverty rates within the Palestinian population are double that of the Jewish Israeli population. A recent report found that 47.1 percent of Palestinians live below the poverty line as opposed to a national average of 28.4 percent (*Middle East Monitor* 2018). In 2018 a report published by the Knesset Research Center covering the period 2014 to 2017 found that there were, on average, 100 murders per year in Israel, and that 64 percent of the victims of such murders were non-Jews (Khoury 2018). The report points to the lack of security experienced by Palestinians, a situation shaped by a combination of government neglect and worsening economic conditions that impact Israeli society as a whole but that target the Palestinian population as a minoritized population systematically locked out of economic opportunities and racially targeted for management, surveillance, and incarceration. Such facts are exacerbated by urban planning policies and practices favoring the Jewish population and confining Palestinians to geographies of poverty, criminality, and exclusion.[32] Tamer and Suhell Nafar, lead singers in DAM, for example, hail from a town known for high rates of poverty, drug trafficking, and violent crime.[33] It has been dubbed a "murder city," and accounts of drug- and gun-related violence in the city and other "mixed cities" proliferate in local Israeli media and in the international press, often blaming this type of violence on Arab and Palestinian residents (Patrick 2013).

At the time of DAM's release of the song, there was a noticeable increase in recorded instances of violence against women in the context of 1948 Palestinian towns and villages. In Lyd, a city twenty minutes from Tel Aviv, at least thirty-five women had been murdered between 2004 and 2014. In explaining the staggering rates of violence, activist Samah Salaime explained that the issues facing Palestinians living in Lyd are not the concern of the Israeli authorities (Salaime 2014). As Salaime makes clear, poverty and easy access to weapons have created unsafe living environments for women and children, making violence ten times more likely to occur in this town than in other Palestinian towns and villages. This assessment resonates with those of Aida Touma-Sliman, who served as the chairwoman of the Knesset Committee for the Advancement of the Status of Women in 2016. During that time, Touma-Sliman took a strong stance on the rising rates of violence against Palestinian women, calling out Israeli police for their refusal to fully investigate the murders of Palestinian women and for their failure to provide adequate protection to Palestinian women facing violence (Harkov 2016). This position has also been shared by the political party *Balad,* which advocates for the rights of Palestinians with Israeli citizenship. In 2016, after a staggering rise in the number of murders of women, the party released a statement condemning such attacks, reminding Palestinians that femicide was a crime against the entire society and that confronting these crimes was a collective responsibility of Palestinian society. In its statement, the party also decried Israeli state reluctance to curb this violence, arguing that many of the Palestinian women victims had, in fact, requested the state's protection prior to the occurrence of violence that lead to their death, but that this protection was not granted even though the state regularly monitors and surveils Palestinian people. Balad's statement reflects a general sentiment shared in Palestinian society that the death of Palestinian women within the state of Israel is not the subject of the state's concern.

Based on this condition of state neglect, Palestinian feminist scholars have shown that the disappearance and murder of Palestinian women cannot be understood outside the particulars of Israeli colonization of Palestinian life. Writing on honor-related violence in Palestinian society, Manar Hassan states that such violence is a "product of a conscious policy of social and political control whose price tag is minimal: no more than a few [Palestinian] female corpses per year" (2002, 23). In Israel the murder of Palestinian women in the name of honor is an institutionally sanctioned crime, upheld through the actions and inactions of both the Israeli police and welfare and social departments responsible for protecting citizens of Israel. These crimes are thus often simultaneously culturalized and tacitly condoned, revealing a blatant disregard for the life and death of Palestinian citizens of the Israeli state. As Nadera Shalhoub-Kevorkian and Suhad Daher-Nashif state in their study on gender violence and the politics of colonization in Palestine, the police "do not treat the murder of Arab women as homicide cases, but as expressions of a cultural norm, or of 'traditional' attitudes toward woman" (2013, 306).

By labeling violence against women in Palestinian society "crimes of honor," police are released from the duty to fully investigate them and readily relegate them to an internal Palestinian affair demonstrating this society's regressive social, moral and sexual codes. This fact is widely known in the Palestinian context, and Palestinian women activists have long lobbied the state to alter the language it uses to describe gender violence against Palestinian women. Samah Salaime, founder of the NGO *Na'am*- Arab Women in the Center, states her opposition to the use of the term *honor* because of the role it plays in licensing police neglect. As she argues, "What made us really angry is how police deal with gender crimes [in the Arab sector] and how the Israeli media are talking about it . . . They say it's 'honor crimes,' that 'this is Arab men doing what they're taught to do.' It's not about the honor of anyone, it's about men who want to control a women's [*sic*] life" (qtd in Lidman 2016). In opposing such discourse, Palestinian women activists recognize how the language of honor can be used to cover up and sanction crimes committed by Palestinian men under the guise of protecting and upholding Arab cultural codes and thus rationalize state nonintervention. Activists oppose this labeling because it provides license to Israeli society and Israeli state apparatuses (such as the police and the criminal justice system) to ignore these crimes, and to dismiss them as endemic to Palestinian society and as signs of Palestinian social and cultural inferiority. It also allows Israeli policy to affect displays of cultural sensitivity and respect toward Palestinian society and its internal system for the management of gender violence.

In 2010 Palestinian Knesset member Ahmad Tibi proposed a law that would ban the use of the term *honor killings* (Lis 2010). The proposed law aimed to prohibit Israeli police, courts, and media from using the term to describe the murder of Palestinian women (Lidman 2016). Although the law did not pass, the police stopped using the language of honor killings and its variant of explaining a murder as being killed for "romantic reasons" in 2012 (Weinglass 2015). The state thus shifted the language it used to describe these crimes to another troubling discourse that places blame on the victim's "independent conduct," implicitly attributing this crime to the behavior of the victim. This discourse was used when the Israeli police finally made arrests in the case of the 2014 murder of Bisan Abu Ghanem, who was the tenth victim in her family to be murdered, in the town of Ramleh.[34] The Israeli police used the language of "independent conduct" to avoid accusations of culturalizing this form of violence (Salaime 2015). The result, as Samah Salaime rightly points out, is the further subjugation of Palestinian women and the questioning of their right to act as independent human beings. Salaime (2015) writes, "If until now the grounds of honor killing pointed the finger toward a woman's sexual conduct, and hinted at control over her body and her sexual life, now comes 'independent conduct' and expands the domains of control in almost every conceivable direction."

At stake in this formulation is the assumption that a Palestinian woman is not a fully independent subject, a person having the right to act independently and freely. Instead, the Palestinian woman is configured as a dependent subject, a person who must be punished for her actions and behaviors if and when they constitute a break with common and collective cultural norms and understandings by members of her own community. In other words, in an effort to stop culturalizing this violence, the Israeli police have adopted victim-blaming rhetoric that robs Palestinian women of their agency. Significantly, Palestinian feminist discursive contestations against the culturalization of violence against women by Israeli state apparatuses and the press are not simply about language or its problematic usage but over the right (and the likelihood) that cases of gender violence against Palestinian women will be adequately investigated by the police and that the perpetrators of these crimes will be prosecuted for their criminal acts to the fullest extent of the law and not provided reduced sentences by the colonialist state apparatuses.[35]

If the Israeli police response to this type of violence frames it within a logic of culturalization, the response from state welfare departments extends this logic by confronting what they view as regressive and traditional social codes in Palestinian communities. In attempting to protect Palestinian women fleeing violence or experiencing the threat of it, welfare departments often enforce upon Palestinian women solutions that render them vulnerable and make them outcasts in the eyes of Palestinian society. One such example is the insistence on placing Palestinian women in shelters outside their communities in predominantly Jewish cities (Shalhoub-Kevorkian and Daher-Nashif 2013). Stuck between colonial and patriarchal logics of informal and formal, state and nonstate institutions, Palestinian women are compelled to resort to the protection of a local network of Palestinian men who are positioned as mediators between the Israeli state and Palestinian society (Shalhoub-Kevorkian 2014). This network is empowered to intervene in such cases through a strong alliance with the formal sectors of the Israeli state. Extended the title of "honorables," this group of men (often including men from the clergy, the courts, or those who have prominent roles in their families due to age, profession, wealth, or reputation) are sometimes able to prevent violence against women by appealing to traditional family values and the need to preserve Palestinian social connectedness and cohesiveness in the face of Israeli colonization (Lang 2005; Shalhoub-Kevorkian and Daher-Nashif 2012). Poised as mediators between the family and the girl or woman who experiences violence, these men often enact their power in ways that confirm, rather than challenge, patriarchal control structures. To secure and protect women who live under the threat of violence, bargains with local patriarchies are struck that help further strengthen their grip over Palestinian women's lives. Palestinian women experiencing or facing the threat of gender violence are thus caught between two powerful systems that consolidate control over women's lives in ways that extend, rather than challenge, the settler colonial logics of the Israeli state (Shalhoub-Kevorkian and Daher-Nashif 2012).

Due to its complex manifestations, Palestinian women's resistance to the phenomenon of femicide in 1948 Palestine is multifaceted and ongoing. Women's groups have called into question state neglect of the murders of Palestinian women while also challenging patriarchal codes and structures within Palestinian society that seek to control and delimit women's lives. They have also shown how conditions of settler colonialism create unsafe and unhealthy environments in which women's lives become both disposable and dispensable. Palestinian women activists have thus sought to ground their analysis and praxis in a critique of gender violence that does not abnegate or disappear from view the settler colonial context of Israeli occupation and its role in producing conditions that render gender violence against Palestinian women possible. This type of analysis holds a multiplicity of actors and a complicated set of structural factors accountable for femicides against Palestinian women, furthering a politics of contestation that simultaneously refuses to pathologize Palestinian society in the interests of the Israeli state or to absolve it of the responsibility to protect the lives of Palestinians from everyday forms of violence, including the violence of family members and the settler colonial state, an analysis that will be put into praxis in the work of the feminist group *Tal3at* that I discuss in the afterword.

Against this intricate and complicated backdrop, DAM's intervention into gender violence in Palestine is informed by a commitment to altering the conditions of social and political life for Palestinians. DAM, like other members of Palestinian society, understands the interconnected and multilayered ways in which violence against women in Palestine is enacted. As Tamer Nafar states in an interview after the release of the group's album *Dabke in the Moon*, featuring DAM's musical intervention on gender violence in Palestine:

> There is a huge connection, directly and indirectly, between violence and the occupation, especially as regards Arab-on-Arab violence. Lyd, where I live, is considered one of the biggest crime and drug markets in the Middle East. When Arabs [in Israel] get killed, cases are not even opened, no one investigates, and no one is arrested. It's easier to pull a trigger on another Arab knowing nothing will happen to me. This is general, and it similarly impacts Arab women. Of course when there is occupation, there is poverty, when there is poverty, there is less education. Honor killings happened before the occupation, but the occupation is responsible for increasing the percentages. (qtd in Nesheiwat 2012).

DAM's work in confronting gender violence does not part from an intersectional comprehension of the operations of colonial structures of power and their impact on the social problem of gender violence. In their recognition of the interconnections between gender violence and colonial contexts, DAM engages an analytic and political framework furthered by Palestinian feminists that readily places instances of gender violence within its historical, political, and socio-economic contexts. Whether this framework was incorporated and reflected in the song "If I Could Go Back in Time" or not would become a central point of contention in the debate that ensued after the song's release.

BETWEEN AGENCY AND AUTHENTICITY

DAM's first appearance on the international musical scene coincided with the group's recording and distribution of the hit song *meen irhabi* (or "Who's the Terrorist?"), in the aftermath of September 11, 2001, and the American-led "War on Terror," and in the midst of the second Palestinian *intifada,* or uprising.[36] Composed originally of the two brothers Tamer and Suhell Nafar and their friend Mahmood Jrery, DAM is a Palestinian hip-hop group whose work engages a diversity of issues, including occupation, settler coloniality, Zionism, racism, freedom, gender equality, and Arab nationalism.[37] An abbreviation for Da Arabian MCs, the band's name also spells out the Arabic word *dam,* which translates to the noun *blood* and the verb *remain* or *stay.* This naming works to tie the group to the land of Palestine and to discourses of resistance and revolution that the blood analogy is meant to invoke. The group members' ability to write and perform songs in Arabic, Hebrew, and English, as well as their particular experiences as marginalized Palestinian citizens of the Israeli state and as residents of 1948 Palestine who deftly negotiate an online presence and multiple local and global audiences, have allowed them to reach audiences across vast geographical, racial, and linguistic boundaries.

Since its beginnings in the 1990s and its rise to fame, DAM has become known for their subversive musical lyrics that speak to the realities of dispossession, marginalization, and oppression punctuating life for Palestinians within historic Palestine and in the diaspora. As grandchildren of the generation of Palestinians who experienced the *Nakba,* or the ethnic cleansing of Palestine in 1948, and who continue to live on lands that have been appropriated and that now exist within the borders of the Israeli state, this group navigates the difficult position of being a minoritized indigenous population in a predominantly Jewish state that is also the occupier of at least four million Palestinians in the West Bank and Gaza. Writing on this particular point, Sunaina Maira, in an important book on Palestinian hip hop, notes that "one of the central paradoxes created by the settler colonial state for [1948] Palestinians is that their citizenship in Israel makes them suspect for other Palestinians and Arabs, yet their identity as Palestinians is erased and suppressed by Israel" (2013, 97).[38] In response to this dual position, DAM members have created music that addresses their minoritized status and that speaks frankly about issues of policing and surveillance characterizing their experiences within the Israeli state. In their music, they repeatedly emphasize their belonging in spite of Israeli violence and their indigeneity and emplacement within Palestine.[39] Although navigating this terrain of identity is at the heart of DAM's work, the group has also not shied away from making discussions of gender and sexuality, as well as Arab patriarchy, central to their musical legacy.

In fashioning its musical style, DAM has emphasized its ability to write songs that simultaneously look inward toward Palestinian society and outward toward its colonial oppressor.[40] As band member Mahmood Jrery states in an interview, "It's a matter of growing up . . . We realized that if we want to take on the state that is conquering the Palestinian people, we must be brave enough to look in the mirror and criticize our own society. There are a lot of things in our society that we hate, and the time has come to talk about them, not to keep silent" (qtd in Shalev 2012). This idea of breaking the silence surrounding violence and other issues taking place in Palestinian society is significant, as the band members continually position themselves as a groundbreaking force, unafraid of speaking about topics that are considered social taboos. This is why, in other songs, they have discussed issues like violence against women and the relationship between liberation and feminism (in "Freedom for My Sisters"). In response to the criticisms they have received regarding their focus on gender violence in Palestinian society, DAM released a new song, "*min inta*" ("*Who You Are*"), which takes aim at Arab patriarchy and challenges hegemonic and toxic forms of masculinity.[41] With the addition of Maysa Daw, a female lead singer, to the group in 2014, the band's music has explicitly addressed sociopolitical issues pertaining to Palestinian society, including the control of women's bodies ("*jasadik-hom,*" or "your body of theirs") and, most recently, the pressure placed on Palestinian men and women to marry (in "*emta njawzak yamma*").[42]

"If I Could Go Back in Time" centers on a story of a woman who is killed by her family. The video suggests that she is murdered because she refused to marry her cousin and had prepared to run away from her home. In the video and in the lyrics, the song documents the woman's life but narrates it in a shifted time frame: It begins with her murder and segues back to her birth while offering snapshots and glimpses of her adult life and her experiences with her family. The first part of the song thus states:

> Before she was murdered, she wasn't alive
> We'll tell her story backwards from her murder to her birth
> Her body rises from the grave to the ground
> The bullet flies out of her forehead and swallowed into the gun
> The sound of her echo screams, she screams back
> Tears rise up from her cheeks to her eyes
> Behind the clouds of smoke, faces of her family appear
> Without shame, her brother puts the gun in his pocket
> Her father throws down the shovel and wipes the sweat off his forehead
> He shakes his head, satisfied from the size of the grave
> They drag her back to the car, her legs kicking
> Like a sand storm, she's erasing her own tracks
> They throw her in the trunk, she doesn't know where she is
> But she knows that three left the house and only two will return
> They reach the house; throw her to the bed in violence
> "So you want run away huh?" they wake her with violence ("If I Could Go Back in Time Lyrics")[43]

The first scene opens with a bloodied woman rising from her bed to face the barrel of a gun directed at her face. The violent scene depicts the woman's brother shooting his sister and her father digging the grave in which she is buried. Through its rewinding techniques, the song constructs an imaginary modern-day honor crime, showing the role that family members (both men and women) play in planning, negotiating, and ultimately carrying out this form of gender violence. As the woman is dragged back into the trunk of a car, she becomes aware of the fate that awaits her: "But she knows that three left the house and only two will return. They reach the house; throw her to the bed in violence 'So you want run away huh?' they wake her with violence" ("Lyrics"). This rhetorical question shifts the blame from a brother who shoots his sister and violates her right to life to a woman who has broken unspecified social mores in pursuit of individual goals and desires, and thus invites death upon herself.

Alternating between "real" depictions of family life and a fantasy of life after death, the song situates the gender violence that the woman experiences in a broader social context where women are subjects of patriarchal control, discipline, and punishment. This tension between communal demands and individual desires undergirds the entire song, catapulting outrage and moral condemnation from both listeners and viewers. The violent opening scene is followed by the chorus, which is performed by Amal Murkus:

> If I could go back in time
> I would smile
> Fall in love
> Sing
> If I could go back in time
> I would draw
> Write
> Sing

Joined by a number of women who appear happy and jovial, Murkus is in a fantasylike space. Within a few seconds of seeing Murkus singing, the woman who was shot by her brother in the song's opening scene finds herself on a bed surrounded by trees, shimmering light, and glowing colors. She awakes, after her murder, happy and smiling, while Murkus sings about what it would mean to go back in time and how she would, if given the chance, draw, write, and sing. The jarring juxtaposition between this fantastical scene of life and the gloomy opening scenes of death makes gender violence and the honor crime appear to be a common and festering problem in Palestinian society.

By blurring the boundaries between truth and fiction, "If I Could Go Back in Time" depicts the struggles faced by the woman in simplistic ways: her choices and sexual freedoms are placed at odds with social demands and cultural expectations. In DAM's condemnation of gender and sexual violence, agency is depicted as the powerful and independent rejection of familial pressures and patriarchal interventions; it is the enactment of a desire to live a willful life, uncomplicated by the choices, demands, or expectations of those with whom we may share a sense of space and place (Abu Lughod and Mikdashi 2015). The woman's tasting of "forbidden fruits"—a reference in the song, indicating that she may have broken some unnamed but known code or expectation—her unwillingness to marry her cousin, and her departure plans all evidence her commitment to an independent reality, an alternative future freed from the demands of her family and collective life. It is this active resistance to a predetermined life path that renders the story of her death so tragically familiar to its audiences. The struggles that the main protagonist appears to embody resonate with audiences because the figure of the oppressed woman whose independent will is undercut by the collective will of those around her is situated in the familiar enclosures of freedom and unfreedom.

In her refusal to adhere to social norms, the protagonist's agency becomes known to listeners and viewers, and she becomes recognizable as an independent and worthy subject who desires freedom as an articulation of her right to be fully human. Through this paradigm, agency is actualized when a subject challenges cultural norms, when she seeks freedoms that affirm her individual identity and her desires, and when she confronts practices considered traditional and thus harmful—even at the risk of experiencing further violence, a theme earlier witnessed in narratives about Aqsa Parvez's murder. Noting the complex ways in which individuals negotiate and develop their sense of agency in relation to rather than in opposition of cultural demands, Diane Baxter contends that "agency, in this sense, is not about the efforts to achieve one's efforts *against* the weight of hegemonic forces, but rather as part of a specific set of hierarchical relations" (2007, 745). DAM's song resonates because the struggles of its doomed protagonist to assert herself by escaping her fate are effectively rendered cultural and exceptional; she is posited as an individual fighting against a collective family structure that wishes to rob her of the ability to make decisions that are her own.

A critical look at this construction calls into question what Inderpal Grewal and Caren Kaplan have named the "tradition-modernity" binary. In 2001 the authors called upon theorists of gender and sexuality studies to rethink models of inquiry that inhere sexuality as a site of knowledge formation and excavation separate from broader studies of race, class, nation, and religion (666). They emphasize the importance of placing the study of sexuality in a framework that recognizes varying "conceptions of the body" and that attends to "the political economies of the family" (667). Without such analysis, theorists risk creating "sexual subjects as traditional in order to create feminist modern subjects" (669). By recentering normative understandings of sexuality and freedom, the song alludes to the possibilities and promises of normed subjectivities and subject positions that are vacated from complex iterations of individual and collective identities, histories, and experiences. In DAM's song, the Palestinian woman is cast as the individual victim of tradition, while transnational audiences are placed as the idealized subjects of modernity who have the agency to experience freedom and who can, in turn, seek and secure it for others. DAM's song reproduces the powerful binary of static and unchanging tradition versus progressive and malleable (and thus sexual) modernity. In DAM's video the Palestinian woman is stuck between her desire for freedom and her family's restrictive expectations. Against these odds, she chooses to flee, to escape her family's grip and to seek an alternative life outside of Palestine, a depiction that invariable leads to the disappearance of the "very thickness of Palestinian lives" (Abu Lughod and Mikdashi 2012a).

In their response to DAM's song, Lila Abu-Lughod and Maya Mikdashi (2012a) argue that the song disappoints its fans because "it succumbs to an international anti-politics machine that blames only tradition for the intractability of (some) people's problems." Highlighting the vanishing context of Israeli occupation in which gender violence in Palestine occurs, a context that this chapter has sought to bring to the fore, Abu-Lughod and Mikdashi focus on the ways in which such depictions help reify Orientalist assumptions about and stereotypes of Palestinian men and women and thus consciously and unconsciously misrepresent their realities. But this critique, as the response of DAM to its critics suggests, does not comfortably fit when it is transfixed on Palestinian society. To dismantle the claims of the authors, DAM takes aim at their location in the US academy, ignoring their transnational and long-standing connections and embeddedness in the region. Undergirding DAM's defense of its work is a troubling claim to authenticity that enshrines the right of practitioners to produce interventions (artistic or otherwise) placed beyond the pale of critique (academic or otherwise). In defense of their work, DAM maintains that their musical interventions are not only warranted but are also direct products of the "greatest historical moment" of 2012, when uprisings across the Arab world signaled hopeful social and political transformations for many disenfranchised Arab youth (Tamer Nafar, Suhell Nafar, and Mahmood Jrery [DAM] 2012). This is why DAM argues that "we should dispense with concerns over how we may be read (particularly by the West)" and focus, instead, on issues that have been identified as "society's taboos" (Tamer Nafar, Suhell Nafar, and Mahmood Jrery [DAM] 2012). As DAM members boldly proclaim, they are part of a "new artistic movement in Palestine that is secure enough to take on occupation and domestic violence, [as well as] racism and sexism" (Tamer Nafar, Suhell Nafar, and Mahmood Jrery [DAM] 2012).

Orientalism, DAM seems to suggest, does not function in a uniform or singular fashion; its contestations thus need to be attentive to differential geographies of power and resistance: *where* we are located inflects *how* we encounter and resist gender violence. While challenging Orientalism can hold some intellectual promise and political appeal for academics in Western contexts, it may not be the end goal of activisms and pursuits situated outside these spaces. As DAM says, "When we write songs, we do not sit and think, 'what would America or Israel think of this?' We open the window and document what we see" (Tamer Nafar, Suhell Nafar, and Mahmood Jrery [DAM] 2012). Although I am sympathetic to the arguments made by DAM regarding the importance of activisms informed by the immediacy of place and the situated realities of experience, two core imperatives of embodied forms of feminist activism, I am wary of arguments that stake for activists a position of innocence or moral high ground and that cleave academic debates from artist and activist endeavors, enshrining the latter beyond the pale of critique.

In this context, academics are seen as detached from the social problems they study and analyze by virtue of the politics of where they are located and the spaces from which they lodge their critique and their mode of analysis. This specific point is conveyed by Tamer Nafar in response to criticisms DAM received regarding the song. As he states, "We were attacked in an article, saying that we are giving fuel to Western propaganda. The funny thing is we wrote the song in Arabic, in Palestine, and the ones criticizing us are sitting in America, writing in English, on an American website, in an American university" (qtd in Nesheiwat 2012). Not only do Nafar's words claim for himself and DAM a position of proximity and authenticity vis-à-vis Palestine and Arab culture and the Arabic language in which they often sing in; they do so by simultaneously dismissing DAM's song's detractors precisely because of their assumed lack of proximity to or their actual distance from these markers of authenticity due to their location in the US, their use of the English language for the production of knowledge, and their employment within the American academy.

Here we see how the claim of authenticity can be wielded to defray the charge of complicity. While I am aware of the privileges that academic spaces such as those of the US academy can afford some academics, privileges that Nafar alludes to and that I, too, benefit from as a Palestinian academic located in a US university who writes in English to English-speaking audiences and who has not lived in occupied Palestine, I am interested in thinking about the ways in which Orientalism as a structuring logic and a disciplinary power haunts confrontations of gender violence and the honor crime in DAM's musical intervention. I am invested in thinking about how Orientalist tropes work to suture DAM's analysis to a discourse that works to exceptionalize honor-related violence by activating, intentionally or unintentionally, entrenched ideas about Arab violence and patriarchy often used to cast Arab societies as backwards, oppressive, and antiwoman.

In DAM's song, Orientalist representations of Arab life proliferate, serving to culturalize familial forms of gender violence. The list of angry, irrational, and violent Arab characters who populate the three-and-half-minute video is long: we have the violent Arab brother who beats and later kills his sister by pointing a gun at her face; there is also the father who, together with other men in his family, plans and authorizes his daughter's murder. There is a mother who collaborates with family patriarchs by revealing her daughter's escape plans and thus willfully endangering her life. In their interactions with one another, family members are emotional and aggravated. These scenes rest on assumptions about Arab men and their propensity for violence against Palestinian women, who are depicted as victimized subjects whose power to make choices that are their own is repeatedly foreclosed by patriarchal family structures upheld by dominant and controlling Arab and Muslim men.

Although DAM can claim that its message is not geared toward Israeli or Western audiences, its depictions of honor-related violence and the honor crime are nevertheless shaped by and steeped in the colonial context of Israeli occupation, where Palestinians are routinely depicted as violent, patriarchal, and culturally backwards and thus deserving of the violence enacted upon them by the state. The discursive categories reproduced throughout the song rest on and borrow from transnationally deployed depictions of Muslims, Arabs, and Palestinians that traffic in assumptions of their inherent violence, irrationality, and excessive sexual control over women. DAM's depictions of sexual violence in Palestinian society, of course, are not singular. Rather, they are the product of a particular historical and political conjuncture where Muslim and/or Arab cultures are routinely stigmatized, targeted, surveilled, and violated at both the symbolic and the material levels. In the aftermath of September 11, 2001, and the "War on Terror," and drawing on a longer history of Orientalism, anti-Blackness, colonization, and racism, the Arab/Muslim man has come to represent an essentially dangerous body whose masculinity signifies as both patriarchal and terroristic threat. His body thus serves a double function: internally, he is responsible for terrorizing women and for enforcing his patriarchal order on them. Externally, he also terrorizes (or threatens to terrorize) civilians and endangers the safety and lives of innocents at home and abroad, a trope that will be seen again in chapter 3 in representations of Zein Isa and the murder of his daughter Tina.

In light of such configurations, it is significant that in DAM's rendition of the honor crime, it is the woman's brother who kills her, but only *after* local family patriarchs authorize the violence. Although this representation serves to show the collective decision-making process that takes place before an honor crime is planned and authorized, the perpetrator of the crime is the young Palestinian man who is positioned as a violent authority figure, capable of physically hurting and later executing his own sister.[44] In the video it is the protagonist's brother who punches his sister, shoves, yells, shackles, and forcefully pushes her into the car, and who, ultimately, points the gun at her face and executes her. This casting of Palestinian men as an undifferentiated, collective, and murderous mass that controls and violates the bodies of Palestinian women refracts a normative lens produced through assumptions of racial, national, and cultural differences. This lens showcases Palestinian masculinity as inherently threatening and violent, capable of maiming, endangering, and even ending the life of women.

Drawing on a broad corpus of affective and material registers of fear and terror, this type of representation not only rehashes an all too familiar and dominant Orientalist and anti-Muslim script but also, in effect, *indigenizes* it—thus providing local sanction and license for its transnational circulation and uptake. While debate around the song has focused on how it may be heard outside of Palestine, it is perhaps equally important to consider how it might be heard within Palestine and what ideas it constructs and disseminates to Palestinian society about itself. It is also important to ask how its circulation upholds an exceptionalized understanding of gender violence that separates it from the structural conditions and contexts that both create and sustain it.

In making this argument, I do not minimize the immensity of gender violence or absolve Palestinian men who commit violence against women and who utilize honor as an excuse and sanction for their violent behaviors. Certainly, there are fathers, brothers, uncles, husbands, and sometimes mothers who kill. I am not suggesting that, in the interest of saving face, we must exonerate such murderous acts or shroud them in secrecy and silence. Rather, I am invested in showing how representations of the honor crime are always mired in global and political struggles over meaning that extend rather than resolve, interrupt, or end interconnected and multiple forms of gender violence. As DAM's musical intervention and its reception makes clear, the honor crime is situated within a field of ungovernable signifiers that reinscribe binaries, reproduce polarizations, and enact reductionisms. When DAM circulates messages about Palestinian society that have the effect of rendering gender violence a culturally endemic problem, they lend credibility and legitimacy to dominant and normative representations of the honor crime. They do this by separating violence against women from the historical context in which it occurs, a context that the song's makers deeply understand and viscerally experience and one which the song, by design or by accident, repeatedly occludes.

It is this vanished context that Palestinian feminists Nadera Shalhoub-Kevorkian, Sarah Ihmoud, and Suhad Daher-Nashif brought to view after the fallout over DAM's song. In a 2014 article on the relationship between gender violence and Israeli settler colonialism published on *Jadaliyya,* the authors carefully demonstrate the historical links between the formation of the state of Israel and targeted attacks against Palestinian women's bodies. Weaving historical events with personal accounts from survivors of gender violence, the authors show the necessity of a feminist analysis that reads the "targeting of Palestinian women's bodies and sexuality" as "structural to the Israeli settler colonial project's racialized logic of elimination." Using a comparative settler colonial studies framework, the authors make clear that "our struggle for indigenous sovereignty within anti-colonial activism as feminists is necessarily situated in the protection of Palestinian women's bodily safety and sexuality, family, and communal right to life."

The ideas presented in this article expand upon Shalhoub-Kevorkian and Daher-Nashif's (2012) intervention in the immediate aftermath of the debate surrounding DAM's song. Writing from their position as "therapists, activists, and scholars who have worked with abused women, and conducted social anthropological studies on the killing of women in Palestinian society," both authors shift the terms of the debate to focus on the relationship between killing of women, or "*qatl al-nisa,*" and "the realm of the political." Their work emphasizes the need to think about the act of naming and representing violence against Palestinian women and its intersections with the intertwined domains of politics, morality, and ethics. Inspired by a desire to provide a view from within Palestine regarding the debate, the authors state their respect for DAM's and for Abu-Lughod and Mikdashi's important "clear interventions in addressing the criminalization and politicization of Palestinian women by their family members." The intervention by the Palestinian feminists, while also privileging the politics of location, shifted the terms of the debate to the question of responsibility. While acknowledging the occurrence of femicide in Palestinian society in historically specific ways, the authors invite readers to ask the following questions: Who benefits from violence against women? Who benefits from femicide? These questions shine a spotlight on the role of the Israeli colonial and criminal systems in bolstering the killing of women in Palestinian society, thus recalibrating the terms of the debate beyond its discursive fault lines and back to the issue of gender violence in Palestinian society.

As a sign of the strength of the honor killing discourse in which the song is invariably mired, it is important to remember that the song never directly uses the term *honor crime* to describe the act of violence that the woman experiences, nor does it actually invoke Palestinian society by name in its lyrics or in the video itself.[45] Instead, it is listeners and viewers and the concomitant activist/scholarly debates surrounding this song that come to define it as a work about honor crimes and their occurrence within Palestinian society. This reading makes apparent the power of the very discourses and imagery that DAM refutes or claims not to engage or centralize in their response to Abu-Lughod and Mikdashi. Even when DAM does not use the exceptionalized language of honor-based violence within the work itself, the song nevertheless remains connected in the minds of its listeners to this crime because of the various "paratexts" or messages that exist outside the song itself that help shape how it is received, consumed, and understood as a work against honor-related violence (Genette 1997). Among these are the song's association with a UN-funded project to mobilize Arab youth to combat violence against women in general and the honor crime in particular. This association is celebrated through UN Women's launch of the song on their website before its worldwide release. As the UN Women (2012) news release announcing the song states:

> Across the world, the United Nations estimates that 5,000 women and girls are murdered and abused every year by male relatives as punishment for a range of behaviors judged to have damaged the family reputation. Between 2007 and 2010, 29 women in the West Bank were reported murdered in the name of honour and at least nine cases have already been reported since the beginning of 2012.

Repeating the claim that 5,000 are murdered in honor crimes each year, this collaboration between DAM and UN Women structures the type of discursive and political intervention and analysis that DAM makes about gender violence in the video itself and elsewhere in the band's interviews about the work. What is at stake is not the collaboration itself but rather the ways in which such collaborations ultimately become fitted within the confines of UN discourse and strategies for ending violence against women.[46] This type of focus neatly aligns with what Jutta M. Joachim labels the UN's "criminal justice framework" that seeks to achieve the two interconnected goals of making family violence signify as a crime and prosecuting perpetrators of violence against women so "society communicated that violence was unacceptable and made the offender personally responsible for his actions" (2007, 119). Both goals are central to the song's message, which, while highlighting the collective nature of this gender violence, also emphasizes the need for broad societal disapproval.

As a band composed of young Palestinian men, DAM is positioned as a potential leader of a campaign to mobilize Arab youth against gender forms of violence that the UN links to family reputation and honor. The connection between the song and the UN-led campaign against honor-related violence is further documented in the final scene in DAM's video, which lists the names of the songs' funders and in which the song's creators remind their Arabic-speaking audiences that "there is no relationship between the killing of women and honor—Murder is a crime. Say no. Unite to end violence against women" (my translation). The English version of the text, which appears under the Arabic version, states: "Say NO—UNite to end violence against women." The capitalization of *UN* in the word *unite* draws attention to the role of the organization in funding this work. The slight differences between the Arabic and English version of the texts are significant. While the Arabic version calls on Arabic-speaking audiences to oppose honor-related violence and to confront such murders as crimes that violate the lives of women, the English version calls on audiences to confront violence against women in a general and broader sense. Without a doubt, these liminal messages, which exist in the very margins of the text of the song but which nevertheless structure how it is heard, received, and understood, help cement the link between the work and the laden discourse of the honor crime in which DAM's song is enmeshed.

"If I Could Go Back in Time" is not a documentary or a scholarly study about gender violence. It is an artistic and activist engagement with social issues, a work that contests gender violence against women and that seeks to produce outrage and to solicit action on behalf of victims and survivors of gender violence in and across colonial and contexts. The song's creators see themselves as active participants and members of the Palestinian community who are engaged in local and important conversations and domestic forms of activism against the phenomenon of gender violence within Palestinian society. Situated within the settler colonial context of Palestine, they position themselves as authentic agents, activists, and artists who have the right to define and speak on issues they deem significant to their own communities on their own terms, but their contributions cannot be dissociated from the broader political and discursive texts and contexts that are used to portray and enact gender violence within Palestinian communities.

THE ACTIVIST, THE CRITIC, AND THE DISAPPEARING TEXT

The debate over DAM's song has emblematized a widening gulf between the work of academics and activists, one that continues to demarcate the theoretical and political fault lines around a range of issues such as the honor crime, female genital cutting, queer subjectivities, and queer rights.[47] In dominant narratives about these issues, activists and academics are positioned as polar opposites: one has the privilege to write and study and reflect upon social realities and problems; the other lives them, often at a heavy and personal cost. While academics accrue value and accolades and secure their livelihoods in Western academic institutions through their production of studies about such issues, activists continuously face physical, political, and socioeconomic risks for doing and embodying the work that academics produce and disseminate knowledge about. Transnational academics located in US contexts travel between spaces of academia and activism, often usurping knowledge from activist interlocutors and taking up space in conversations about difficult and challenging social issues and political realities. The relationship between the two is thus uneven, structured by global socioeconomic realities that position Western-based academics as privileged in relation to activists located in third-world contexts where their basic rights to freedom, security, and dignity are frequently abrogated. If academics produce theories and texts, activists engage in praxis and do work, and the two are constantly cleaved from one another. Where one is performative, disengaged, and produced in the ivory towers of academe, the other is immediate, authentic, and informed by material hardship and struggle.

Feminists have long inquired into the possibility of overturning these unequal power structures. As Melissa W. Wright explains, "Reckoning with the power dynamics inherent to the production of knowledge continues to represent a challenge for feminist theorists and activists as they negotiate over whose knowledge counts as 'official' knowledge, in whose language is this knowledge formed, and who is able to represent this knowledge, have access to it, and reap the rewards of its circulation" (2008, 380). More than anything, the debate over DAM's song reveals that such reckonings remain ongoing and unresolved. Lurking in them is an implicit but never quite stated question about who has the right to speak on gender violence in Palestine, under what terms, and from what locations. Rather than contest the power structures that impose and reproduce these divisions and distinctions, debates over DAM's song, and the larger conversations around gender violence they animate and map, have tended to reify the line between subjects and objects of knowledge. They have worked to widen or foreclose, instead of bridge or open up, the possibility of engagements that bring together activist and academic contributions to ending the phenomenon of gender violence. In constraining the terms of the debate to individual actors and questions of positionality and authenticity, the shrinking political space for confronting gender violence is even further limited.

In an article on the broader feminist politics animating the debate over DAM's song, Rochelle Terman inquires into how "particular characterizations, modes of argumentation, omissions, and framings work to discursively normalize a paradigm of legitimate or illegitimate positions on the issue of gendered violence in Muslim contexts" (2010, 3). Terman lays bare a feminist analytic field of inquiry structured by a "double bind" between anti-imperialist and postsecular modes of critique. Where one camp (the "anti-imperialists") curtails analyses of gender violence because of fear of how it might be used to service Islamophobic and imperial goals, the other (the "postsecularists") focuses on confronting such issues despite the risks associated with these contestations. Terman seeks a "multidimensional analysis of the main lines of domination facing women in Muslim contexts, including anti-imperialist critique of those political formations that can escape scrutiny precisely because they present themselves as anti-imperial movements" (23). While I am drawn to Terman's invitation to analysis that weaves together anti-imperialist and antiviolence positions, it ends up inadvertently reasserting the binary of activists versus academics by assigning activists a more privileged position of critique due to the politics of location rather than the substance of their interventions.

What is emphasized in here and in defenses of DAM's right to produce work that intervenes in the social problem of gender violence is that members of DAM, like other activists and artists who confront gender violence from within their communities, actually do live in Palestine. Certainly, this fact provides DAM and local Palestinian activists immediate experiences and crucial insights into the dual context of colonial and patriarchal violence and the strategies for confronting this violence from within Palestine in indigenous and localized ways. Missing from Terman's analysis, however, is the content of these strategies or the vanished text of DAM's musical intervention, which is the very subject of the debate between the anti-imperialist and postsecular, activist, and academic camps she identifies. To rethink the terms of the debate, then, we would need to consider not only *where* DAM is located but also *what* strategies and interventions they reproduce and make possible in their work about the honor crime and how these strategies fit within broader strategies of confronting gender violence.

The controversy over DAM's video invites us to carefully reflect on and challenge the boundaries of knowledge production between activists and academics on issues like gender violence. It calls on us to think with, through, and beyond the politics of location in ways that bring into view a multiplicity of actors, strategies, and analytics for contestations of gender violence. Accusations of complicity, like claims to authenticity, work to foreclose possibilities of collaboration and engagement across real and imagined borders of location, subjectivity, and positionality. By pitting the academic against the activist other, they eclipse the substance of both the activist interventions and their academic critics. More importantly, they disappear from view the complexities in which protracted social problems such as gender violence in settler colonial contexts are undoubtedly mired and in which discussion of honor-related violence must be placed. These discursive and political fault lines render impossible future collaborations that have the potential to open up spaces "where academic agendas and frameworks can be interrogated and recast, and where we can generate new transformative possibilities in the fissures, gaps, absences, and fallibilities of our critical frameworks whose cutting-edge status we may have taken for granted" (Nagar 2014, 110). While Nagar's invitation is offered to feminist academics located primarily in Western contexts, what would such collaborations look like if taken up by *both* activists and academics working together to wrestle with the complexities of the phenomenon of gender violence which are disappeared in the liminal, binary, and noxious spaces of the debate? And how might they help us get through the impasses that such debates ultimately leave in their wake?

CHAPTER 3

Against Exceptionalism

Historicizing US Discourse on Gender Violence and Racial Terror

ON JANUARY 27, 2017, a few days into his presidency, Donald J. Trump issued Executive Order 13769, "Protecting the Nation from Foreign Terrorist Entry into the United States." Known by its critics as the "Muslim ban," the order ushered into law a number of rulings that effectively overhauled the US immigration system. The ban stopped refugee admissions for 120 days while subjecting the US immigration system to review and indefinitely suspending the Syrian refugee admission program and preventing from entry to the US citizens of five Muslim-majority states.[1] In addition to its subjection of visa applicants to "extreme vetting," the first version of the executive order specifically stopped from entry to the US anyone who would "engage in acts of bigotry or hatred (including 'honor' killings, other forms of violence against women, or the persecution of those who practice religions different from their own) or those who would oppress Americans of any race, gender, or sexual orientation."[2] In putting this language into the words of the order, President Trump drew power from the text of the Immigration and Nationality Act of 1952, which gives the president the power to "suspend the entry of all aliens or any class of aliens as immigrants or nonimmigrants, or impose on the entry of aliens any restrictions he may deem to be appropriate" if their entry is deemed detrimental to US interests.[3] Claiming to protect both the interests of the US state and those of American citizens in danger of potential forms of sexual, racial, and gender violence from foreign-born terrorists, section 10(ii) of the order mandated that government agencies such as the Department of Homeland Security collect, track, and publicize information about "foreign nationals in the United States who have been radicalized after entry into the United States and engaged in terrorism-related acts." In the name of "transparency and data collection," section 10(ii) also required state agencies to report on major crimes and to collect "information regarding the number and types of acts of gender-based violence against women, including honor killings," committed by foreign nationals.

In its sweeping language of border control, the ban sought to implement policies that would strengthen US immigration law and further regulate entry of foreign nationals into the country. Its supporters argued that such a step was necessary because of the existence of legal loopholes in the immigration system that allowed false refugee claimants to abuse US law and endanger the country and its citizens. This position was echoed by former Homeland Security Secretary John Kelly, who argued, "The fact remains that we are not immune to terrorist threats and that our enemies often use our own freedoms and generosity against us . . . We cannot risk the prospect of malevolent actors using our immigration system to take American lives" (qtd in de Vogue et al. 2017). At the time of its issuance, American public opinion on the ban was split along party lines. A poll conducted by CNN in 2017 found that 53 percent of Americans opposed the order, that 47 percent were in favor, and that at least three of ten people interviewed wanted to see it expanded (Sparks 2018).

The differing opinions on the ban reveal the convergence of US immigration and notions of safety and securitization that were further reinforced in a post-9/11 and "War-on-Terror" world order.[4] Reactions against the ban ranged from legal battles in courtrooms across the country to airport protests in US cities against the detention of migrants to marches on the US Capitol.[5] This activism helped open up spaces for the questioning of the US immigration system and its transnational practices and reach; they called into focus the logics of racial discrimination and difference that undergird the operations of the US national security and settler colonial state.[6] Critics of Executive Order 13769 (EO1) and its revised version 13780 (EO2 and EO3) have highlighted the devastating impact of Trump's policy on migration and refugee and asylum policies and practices in the US. They have shown the order's materially adverse effects on refugee communities, both those inside US borders and those with hopes of resettlement and reunification with families fleeing persecution or war. Many have demonstrated the problematic and differential notions of citizenship and belonging that the ban enshrines while also lamenting the atmosphere of racial and religious tension, suspicion, and animosity that the ban provokes and licenses at the national and transnational levels.

In legal contestations of the ban's validity, critics have argued that the ban is unconstitutional because it "reveals an invidious anti-Muslim intent" and thus breaches the Establishment clause of the First Amendment that prohibits the making of laws targeting specific religious groups (Anderson et al. 2017). Although discussions of the Muslim ban have focused on the issue of its inherent—if not stated—bias against Muslims, others have also noted its invocation of honor crimes as cause for feminist alarm and concern. As feminist and Middle East studies scholars have convincingly argued, the invocation of honor violence is a "dog whistle," intended to malign and further target Muslim communities and to further link Muslim cultures and peoples to specific forms of gender and sexual violence in order to fuel anti-Muslim and antimigrant sentiments and ideologies (Gökariksel 2017). In her response to the ban, legal feminist scholar Leti Volpp (2017) highlights the irony of a Muslim ban from a party that attacks same-sex marriage, opposes adoption by gay parents, and invokes states' rights to deny bathroom facilities to transgender people while claiming to protect the nation from Muslim migrants and refugees who are banned "both as putative terrorists and as a purported threat to gender equality and sexual liberty."

Beyond the anti-Muslim fervor driving this ban, what is at work in its reference to honor crimes? And how did the honor crime become part of Trump's migration agenda? To answer these questions, I trace iterations of the honor crime in US political discourses. While various feminist scholars have written convincingly on the problems associated with the executive order and its relationship to anti-Muslim sentiments expressed directly and indirectly by the Trump administration, there has been less focus on the longer genealogies of this discourse in US politics and its racial underpinnings. As we will see, analytic frameworks that read Trump's policy initiatives as the most recent and recurrent expression of colonial feminism that usurp contestations of gender violence for antimigrant agendas and policies do not fully capture the historical imaginaries that inform the rise of such discourses and the historical specificities of their development, circulation, and uptake. In this chapter, I read Trump's ban, and its invocation of the honor crime, against the logic of exception in which it has often been mired. Following Puar's lead in shifting analysis from the temporalities of emergency to the "temporality of regularity" (2007, 81), this chapter places the crime within a historical context attuned to the imbrications between gender violence and terrorism in American legal, political, and social discourses long before the issuance of the order. As I show, representations of honor-related crime as a racialized and culturalized form of violence do not emerge suddenly at the time of Trump's ban. Their nascent appearance marks the intertwined and interwoven contours of gender violence, racial terror, and terrorism through which the honor crime has long been understood. By unraveling the links between constructions of the racialized crimes of terrorism and the honor crime, this chapter explores how certain forms of violence work to define not only who is allowed to belong in the US but also what forms of gender violence are socially contested and under what legal and juridical conditions they come to be so. My aim is to show how the appearance of honor killings in Trump's executive order is an extension of, rather than an aberration from, a US global agenda on gender violence that is tied to domestic governance and foreign policy. An exclusive focus on the Muslim ban that does not attend to such genealogies ignores how the more recent appearance of the honor crime in Trump's executive order is tied to longer histories of criminalizing Arabs and Muslims through the lens of culturalized gender violence.

GENDER VIOLENCE AND "INTIMATE TERRORISM"

On November 6, 1989, in St. Louis, Missouri, Tina (short for Palestina) Isa was confronted by her father and mother for alleged illicit social and sexual behaviors. Upon her arrival, Tina was told by her father that that night would be her last and that she was going to be killed. Tina physically struggled against her mother and father who stabbed her to death. In a seven-minute audio recording captured by an FBI intelligence device placed in the Isa home, the incident is documented and later reproduced in various American media outlets (*State v. Isa 1993*).[7] The recording, which was used in court in the trial against both Zein and Maria Isa, helped convict Tina's parents of the charge of first-degree murder, for which the jury requested capital punishment for both parties.[8] Tina Isa was the daughter of a Palestinian American father and a Brazilian American mother. Her father had immigrated to the US after he and his family had lived, briefly, in Puerto Rico, Brazil, and the West Bank. I begin with the story of Tina Isa's murder because I am interested in tracking narrations of honor crimes in American media and because this particular crime shows how certain forms of domestic violence, patriarchal power, and racial difference are scripted as terroristic acts. Reading the story of Tina Isa's murder and its subsequent uptake in two US courts shows how the seeds for the interlacing of terrorism and domestic violence and honor killings were planted in the US almost three decades before the issuance of Trump's executive order. In rereading Tina Isa's murder case and linking it to the executive order, I rely on Leti Volpp's (2010, 2011) groundbreaking work and careful collection and representation of details of the case that helped challenge dominant representations of the murder. I reread Tina Isa's case alongside Volpp's analysis because it carries with it signposts of the contemporary inscription and co-option of the fight against gender violence for the revival of racial and cultural fears, the stoking of immigration debates, and the ongoing US fight against terrorism.

In media coverage of her life and death, Tina is described by her friends as a fun-loving, happy American teenager who wanted normal things, such as a part-time job, a boyfriend, and a late curfew. Her parents are portrayed as struggling with her desire for freedom and autonomy, and Zein Isa is represented as having a violent temper toward his youngest daughter. An article in *People* magazine explains Tina's murder as a crime that "defies understanding, reflecting as it does cultural and generational conflicts that are alien to most Americans" (Treen 2002). To explain this crime, the author argues that neither Tina's father nor Tina's mother assimilated into American culture, and that their failure to do so had made them suspicious of their American daughter, who was, as her friends would later testify, also very free-spirited. Tina's parents disapproved of her extracurricular activities at school, including her joining of the soccer team, the tennis team, and the cheerleading squad, and of her having a Black boyfriend.[9] This behavior, as media reports demonstrate, threatened Zein Isa's sense of honor and his desire to have his daughter remain a virgin who would, soon after graduating from high school, be married to a Palestinian man in Beiteen, where she would ultimately live and settle (Krajicek 2013).

At the parents' trial, expert defense witness Nicolas Gavrielides, a State University of New York anthropology professor who was born and raised in Jerusalem, testified that Tina's way of life had offended her traditional father's sense of honor. In court, he claimed that "everyone growing up in the Middle East knows being killed is a possible consequence of dishonouring the family" (qtd in Treen 2002). This trope of honor and its possible infractions dominated the story of Tina's murder in American newspapers at that time and was later emphasized in court when the parents tried to utilize culture as rationale for their murder of their daughter (Volpp 2011).[10] Predictably, the story was understood as a clash of civilization, a narrative that reveals the struggles of first-generation immigrants whose children wish to live an American life and hope to integrate into the social fabric of the US but whose choices are repeatedly undercut by parents who cling to traditional conceptions of culture and honor. Such discourse is echoed in representations of the murder of Aqsa Parvez discussed in chapter 1.

In 2013, writing for *New York Daily News,* David K. Krajicek captured the murder thus:

> Like many teenagers, Tina Isa didn't listen to her parents.
>
> They lived in different worlds, in effect.
>
> Her father, Zein Isa, was a Palestinian Muslim with Old World ideas about how his child should and should not behave. His wife, Maria, a Brazilian Catholic, was more a martinet than a mother.
>
> But Tina was a headstrong modern girl growing up in big-city St. Louis, not some medieval village.

By and large, public framings of Tina Isa's murder clung closely to readily recognizable political and discursive frames: they positioned Tina Isa and the fatal violence that she experienced within spaces of "alterity" that reproduce the charge of otherness attached to both the crime and its perpetrators (Ticktin 2008, 865). While the narrations of Tina Isa's murder generally adhered to this familiar script, they also exceeded them in an important way through their linking of Tina Isa's murder to another crime of difference and alterity; the crime of terrorism.

As court records reveal, the murder of Tina Isa by her parents was captured on tape by the FBI (*State vs. Isa 1993*). The FBI's monitoring of the Isa home had spanned more than two years, during which the state agency sought to collect evidence of terrorism against her Palestinian father, Zein Isa, for his alleged involvement with a US-based branch of the Abu Nidal Organization (ANO).[11] In 1997 ANO was designated by the US State Department a foreign terrorist organization in accordance with the Antiterrorism and Effective Death Penalty Act of 1996.[12] The organization was accused of carrying out terrorist attacks in twenty countries and killing or injuring at least 900 people.[13] Its members were thought to operate mostly internationally, but some were believed to be located within the US. Based on the State Department's suspicion that Zein Isa was a local and US-based operative of ANO who was actively plotting against US interests, his home was subject to FBI surveillance, including wiretapping.[14] During the trial for the murder of their daughter, the FBI evidence would play a key role against Tina's parents, who were described in a report from the *Associated Press* (1991) as "fundamentalist Muslims," helping to convict Isa and his wife of murder, a crime for which they both received a death penalty sentence. While on death row, however, Zein Isa and three fellow Palestinian co-conspirators who were naturalized citizens of the US were also indicted by a federal grand jury in St. Louis for planning to bomb the Israeli embassy in Washington, DC, and for their involvement with ANO (Ostrow 1993).[15]

At that time of Tina's murder images of terror from the Middle East had dominated US news media since the Iran hostage crisis of 1979–81. In the

1990s the US became involved in the Gulf War amid rising fears of terrorist threats against US national and international interests, including worries about home-grown terrorist attacks which were realized in the first World Trade Center bombing in 1993 and the Oklahoma City bombing in 1995 (Semati 2010). These events, as various scholars have shown, helped reify a link between Islam and terrorism and served to construct the figure of the Muslim suspect turned terrorist essential to the operations of the "War on Terror" (Puar 2007; Stampnitzky 2013). As Lisa Stampnitzky argues in her work on the invention of terrorism, the linking of Muslims and terrorism began to take place in US public discourse as early as the 1970s, but it was in the 1990s and with the bombing of the World Trade Center that "advocates of the 'Islamist terror' threat mobilized current events as proof of this new form of terrorism that was irrational, that broke from predictable routines, and that held the potential for mass violence" (143). Terrorism thus became a problem associated with irrationality and public violence, a phenomenon that needed government intervention in order to be managed and curbed.

Under the federal Racketeer Influenced and Corrupt Organizations (RICO) statutes, the four men were indicted for "obtaining illegal weapons, such as a rocket-propelled grenade launcher; procuring and using bogus passports; illegally transferring money overseas; and conspiring to murder Tina Isa" (Worthington 1993). In addition to these charges, the four men were accused of conspiring to murder Tina because she posed "a threat to the secret existence and continuity of the enterprise" (Jehl 1993). During the terrorism trial, Tina's murder was believed to be the result of her discovery of her father's involvement with ANO and his fears that she might cooperate with US authorities against him and his co-conspirators, further demonstrating the link between the two interrelated crimes (Volpp 2011).

The suspicion that Tina had knowledge of her father's terroristic activities was later repeated by special agent James C. Van Rhein in an affidavit submitted to the Missouri court:[16]

> The tape evidence demonstrated that before the killing, Tina had over the years (at least between 1986 and 1989) become aware of all the defendants' membership in the ANO. Tina also had general knowledge of the ANO activities of all the defendants. The tape evidence also demonstrates that, before the killing, Tina Isa had rebelled against and rejected her father's criminal association with the ANO. Tina Isa had also rejected her Palestinian heritage. Tina Isa simply wanted to be an American teenager. (United States District Court, Eastern District of Missouri, 5)

The three men whom Zein Isa was associated with pleaded guilty and served two years in prison, but charges against Tina's father were dropped because he was already serving a life sentence and was on death row for his daughter's murder.[17] Importantly, the intelligence information collected from the Isa home and used in the federal trial against Zein and Maria Isa thus inadvertently reframed the murder from a cultural crime about safeguarding a father's honor to one about eliminating a potential and familial threat to the suspected terroristic and political activities in which he engaged. Tina Isa is transformed from a daughter murdered by her father over cultural differences to someone murdered in an altercation over politics. Rather than being a victim of domestic violence, Tina Isa becomes an American patriot willing to risk her life to expose her father's engagement in illegal activities against the US state. The state's reliance on the information collected from spying on the Isa home for the father's suspected terrorist activities, in effect, collapsed the distinction between gender violence and terrorism. Not only was information about terroristic activities and gender violence shared between the two separate courts, the crimes of domestic violence and terrorism became inseparably intertwined. In Zein Isa's case, evidence from one court shored up the legal charges brought against him in another. The disappearance of the distinction between these two crimes was thus legally secured through the suturing together of gender violence and terrorism, an act that is similarly reproduced in the text of the executive order.

In her work on Tina Isa's murder and gender violence and their representation in US courts and media, Leti Volpp (2011) has effectively shown how certain violence has been framed in popular and academic discourse as culturalized violence. Volpp demonstrates how such representations reproduce notions about otherness rooted in Orientalist and anti-Muslim associations between Arab and Palestinian culture, on the one hand, and violence toward women, on the other.[18] In discussing representations of Tina's murder, Volpp critiques academic work that reproduces these narratives, showing how this scholarship forecloses the potential for uncertainty about "the web of factors that shape incidents of gendered violence" (95). Volpp goes further to show how Zein Isa's identity as a Palestinian American involved with a designated terrorist organization evacuated him from the category of citizenship itself and the associated privileges that it bestows on (some of) those who carry it.[19] In other words, it is by coupling Zein Isa's murder of his daughter with acts that are threatening to the US state that Zein Isa comes to occupy the new identity of "noncitizen other," someone whose involvement in terroristic activities helps provide an explanatory framework for his violence toward women and vice versa (96). By analyzing the multiple dimensions of the crime against Tina Isa, Volpp explores the possibility that her murder was about not only the tensions between modernity and tradition, as popular framings repeatedly suggest, but also "the relationships between cultural difference and the U.S. state, terrorism, surveillance, and immigrant communities—relationships only made more complicated after 9/11" (96).

With the trying of Tina Isa's murder in two separate courts, and the linking of a case of gender violence to the crime of terrorism, Tina Isa's case does what feminist geographer Cynthia S. Gorman describes as "jump[ing] scales," wherein a case of domestic violence becomes situated in a broader legal terrain where contestations over citizenship rights and practices of belonging loom large (2018). Gorman's analysis offers an important entry for reading Tina Isa's case and its discursive and political significance decades after the crime's occurrence. By re-examining this crime, we can begin to see how the legal, political, and rhetorical differences between perpetrators of culturalized violence against women (namely, honor crimes) and the racialized crime of terrorism are effectively disappeared (3).[20] As a foreign-born US citizen, Zein Isa is found guilty of two crimes attached to registers of racial and sexual difference in US political and social imaginaries. Both crimes are tied to bodies configured as outsiders to the US dominant publics or as internally threatening to its power.

Similarly, the honor crime is a racialized crime insofar as its occurrence is associated with certain groups and peoples who are configured as culturally and racially inferior to dominant white publics and whose violent acts exist outside a framework of domestic violence, a framing that is again operationalized in the executive order. When these crimes occur within Western nation-states, they are viewed as importations, problems that are linked to othered bodies that now exist within the borders of the US and thus constitute a threat to its social order, a connection that was similarly made in relation to the murder of Aqsa Parvez in the Canadian context. A Palestinian man who migrated to the US as an adult, Zein Isa is an outsider citizen, an other to US society long before he murders his daughter. Because of his racial identity and the Arabic language he speaks at home, Zein Isa is a body that draws suspicion from the US security state and that therefore invites its surveillance and tracking.[21] Zein Isa's connections to the Middle East, his engagement in a form of organizing and politics linked to transnational circuits and networks of terror, and his religious and cultural identity as a patriarchal and violent Arab man coalesce to shape how the crime becomes popularly known and remembered and how it plays out in the domain of the legal. His actions aid in the figurative and, later, the legal conjoining of gender violence and terrorism in an explicit way and thus set the stage for what seems to be a more recent political order associated with the Trump era that uses these co-linked crimes to shore up border control policies and procedures.

This link between gender violence and terrorism has been established in a number of popular and scholarly works in order to draw attention to the idea that domestic violence and terrorism share similar lineages and characteristics and that investigating or establishing a correlation between the two can curb their occurrence. In one of the first works to address these links, Isabel Marcus argues that "there are strong and striking parallels and similarities between terrorism as a strategy used to destabilize a community or society consisting of men and women, and the abuse and violence perpetrated against women in intimate or partnering situations" (1994, 32). Marcus likens experiences of political terrorism to those of domestic violence, as both are "designed to maintain domination and control, to enhance or reinforce advantages, and to defend privileges" (32). Enacting gender violence on others is here uncritically accepted and normalized as a precursor of terrorist activities, an act that signals the propensity of an individual to harm and showcases a desire to control and impose particular rules and orders on them.

In noting similarities between the acts of terrorism and intimate violence, Rachel Pain (2014) provides the explanatory framework of "intimate terrorism" to explain the links between social and political forms of terror. As the evidence shows, domestic terrorism is often initiated by men who have histories of violence and who need to assert traditional notions of masculinity and power through the exertion of force against women and other vulnerable subjects with whom they have close contact. The home is also the space where heterosexual norms and practices are defined and imposed and where claims to dominant and hegemonic forms of masculinity are often expressed. In this research, the distinctions between the spaces of the domestic or the private and the spaces of the public are disappeared. In other words, the domestic space becomes a realm where terrorists enact their violence on intimate partners (including women and children) as practice for the enactments of future violence outside the home on civilian targets. As a private space that is often shielded from public scrutiny, the home is seen as a site of danger, where the right to personal and physical safety is constantly challenged for victims and survivors of domestic abuse and intimate violence by perpetrators of gender violence who are predominantly, but not exclusively, men.[22]

Proponents of these theories suggest that recognizing the links between gender violence and terrorism helps draw attention to the significance of the phenomenon of violence against women, here reframed from a private and individual threat to an issue of mass and public concern. Arguing for the importance of recognizing the continuities and disjunctions between domestic violence and terrorism, Rachel Pain notes that the reframing of domestic violence "muddies the boundaries between forms of violence that are usually framed as public, political and spectacular, and forms that are usually framed as private, apolitical and mundane" (2014, 534). Pain's work calls on feminist geographers and the field of geography at large to question the singular focus on terrorism that leads researchers to ignore the ubiquitous phenomenon of gender violence, which is not only connected to political and global terror but also informed by it. Pain acknowledges how race, class, and gender shape understandings and confrontations of these forms of violence, insisting on the development of policies and provisions that incorporate structural analyses, and that demonstrate how "terroristic intimate violence is a specific and common pattern of abusive behavior which cuts across class, ethnicity and sexual orientation" (534). With the rise of international and domestic terrorism in the US and elsewhere, including the UK and Europe, such theories have gained traction because of their ability to link public and geopolitical forms of violence with "their presence in the intimate" sphere (Pain and Staeheli 2014, 345).

While Pain's work offers a grounded analysis of intimate violence and its relationship to global scales of violence, the linking of domestic violence and terrorism poses a number of challenges to transnational and critical race feminist investigations of these crimes. Prime among these is their tendency to universalize patriarchy, to flatten out differences between intimate violence that is directed toward nonqueer and queer subjects, and to reaffirm the connections between terrorism and racialized (primarily brown and Muslim) people. The tying of domestic violence to terrorism in a uniform way disappears from view more complex frames of political and social analyses. In such discursive usage, the term *terrorism* is emptied of historical significance, bound as is it to individual actors who align themselves with ideologies deemed terroristic in accordance with state definitions of terror and terrorism. As Lisa Stampnitzky shows, this type of work relies on an "anti-knowledge" about terrorism that operationalizes the two tropes of evil and irrationality (2013, 189). The connection of gender violence with terror serves to mire this crime in discourses of evil and irrationality that can be used to obfuscate either or both of these acts of violence in ways that facilitate their rescripting.

The linking of terrorism and domestic violence is a powerful theoretical and political move because it is able to elude historical specificity, to appear to maneuver out of discursive constraints. As the Tina Isa case demonstrates, this coupling occurred in US courts long before the release of Trump's order. By centering Tina's case in readings of Trump's executive order, it becomes apparent that the collapsing of the distinction between domestic violence and terrorism is a politically useful and expedient act. Its operationalization works to amplify racial difference and associate with it culturalized acts of domestic violence. Theories that enable such uncritical linkages without attending to their potential misuse and or deployment can help lay the ground work for dangerous and racist policies and procedures enacted in the name of protecting the national safety and security of all.

GENDER-BASED VIOLENCE AND THE US NATIONAL SECURITY AGENDA

In order to understand the operations of the honor crime and violence against women in Trump's executive order and refuse to exceptionalize their appearance in state records, we must first ask where and how violence against women became a problem that warrants state attention. How did particular forms of violence against women come into the purview of the state, and under what conditions? To answer these questions, we can trace the contemporary folding of gender violence back into the US global agenda during the Obama regime. In 2017 President Obama issued *The United States Strategy to Prevent and Respond to Gender-Based Violence Globally.*[23] The strategy outlined the fight against gender-based violence as a cornerstone of Obama's administrative commitments to the "three pillars of U.S. foreign policy—diplomacy, development, and defense" (5). The US policy strategy was informed by President Obama's Executive Order 13623, "Preventing and Responding to Violence Against Women and Girls Globally," in which the president charged the government with implementing the US strategy and creating an interagency working group that would address gender-based violence and report on strategies and information pertaining to its prevention.[24] The working group was to be co-chaired by the Secretary of State and the Administrator of the United States Agency for Development (USAID).[25] In his executive order, President Obama made a link between violence against girls and women and economic, political, and social prosperity and growth. Obama's order also described violence against women as a "public health challenge," one further exacerbated in areas and times of conflict, unrest, and emergency. In response to this order, the government developed a multipronged, multiyear strategy for preventing gender-based violence, building on the legislation promoted in the International Violence Against Women Act (I-VAWA), which was adopted in 2007 and which helped assert for the US a global leadership role in the fight against gender-based violence and reassert the value of the US State Department in fulfilling this work (Treuthart 2016).[26]

The battle against gender violence became central to the operations of the US state as early as the 1990s. As Sara L. McKinnon shows, US interest in promoting an antiviolence agenda was woven into the fabric of the security state through the marking of some forms of gender-based violence as an exceptional "construct that is deployed ideologically and rhetorically in the service of the U.S. state" (2016a, 415). McKinnon focuses in her work on how female genital cutting and female genital mutilation were made central to the US agenda against gender-based violence, arguing that US rhetoric worked at times to offshore their occurrence to the African continent and African nation-states. This narrative is employed in the US strategy document that articulates the US Congress's commitment to fighting gender-based violence in this way:

> The U.S. Congress has long championed efforts to prevent and respond to gender-based violence, including in the context of child, early, and forced marriage, female genital mutilation/cutting, sexual violence, human trafficking, and region-specific gender-based violence, from Latin America and the Caribbean to the Middle East and Sub-Saharan Africa. (6)

In this discursive formulation, the US Congress is lauded for its efforts to confront and end gender-based violence occurring outside US borders. In addition to fighting "female genital mutilation/cutting," the strategy identifies forced marriages, sexual violence, and human trafficking as specific and interconnected forms of gender violence that the US battled. While naming is an important step toward identifying different forms of violence that people experience, the strategy also ties their occurrence to broad and externalized geographies of otherness such as those of Latin America, the Caribbean, the Middle East, and Sub-Saharan Africa. The strategy, then, imagines gender-based violence as a problem that happens over there, one that the writers of the strategy would have us believe, as McKinnon rightly suggests, "that the end of gender violence in the United States is *fait accompli*" (2016b, 128).

Although the opening pages of the strategy focus on the occurrence of gender violence elsewhere, the strategy document adopts a broad definition of gender-based violence that emphasizes the global magnitude of the problem of violence against women:

> GBV is a global problem: it occurs in every country and society. It happens in public and private settings, including but not limited to digital and online spaces, educational settings and schools, the home, workplaces and in transit. Types of GBV include, but are not limited to: child, early, and forced marriage; female genital mutilation/cutting; so-called "honor"-based

> violence and killings, and other harmful practices; acid violence; dating violence; domestic violence; female infanticide; femicide or gender-related killing of women and girls; all forms of human trafficking; intimate partner violence; sexual harassment; stalking; all forms of sexual violence, including reproductive and sexual coercion, and rape, including marital rape, so-called "corrective" rape, and rape as a tactic of conflict. Other types of violence that are sometimes gender-based include, but are not limited to: abandonment; neglect; bullying; child abuse; corporal punishment; and elder abuse. (6)

The definition of gender-based violence used in this document insists on its occurrence in every country but never specifically names the US as a site where this violence may be present or from which such violence may emanate. Instead, the strategy upends the binary between private and public forms of violence, refusing to privatize gender-based violence or to place it beyond public purview and intervention. Adopting a notion of gender-based violence that acknowledges its occurrence in virtual space as well as work and educational spaces, the strategy explicitly focuses on the sexual aspect of this form of violence. As such, its names *sexual harassment, sexual violence,* and *reproductive and sexual coercion* as forms of gender-based violence. Unlike Trump's executive order, which focuses on the broad term *violence against women* and selectively chooses to single out the honor crime, the strategy uses the broader term *gender-based violence.*

This usage signals its authors' understanding that gender violence can impact people of all genders even though girls and women are disproportionately more likely to be targeted by this violence than men. In addition, the definition names early and forced marriage, female genital mutilation (FGM), acid violence, and honor-based violence and killings among a variety of forms of gender-based violence potentially experienced in all countries, disappearing the distance between violence occurring outside the US and violence occurring within it. This definition acknowledges the magnitude of gender violence as a global phenomenon, an acknowledgment that is absent in Trump's executive order. While the document includes honor killings as an example of gender-based violence, its authors appear aware of the politics of language surrounding this term, placing the word *honor* in quotation marks and adding the word *so-called* in reference to the fact that perpetrators often use the language of honor to exonerate their own actions. The wide-ranging and inclusive approach reflected in the definition of gender-based violence section offered in the strategy pays tribute to the complexities associated with efforts to define the term. Rather than foreclose the parameters of the definition of gender-based violence that it offers and thus narrow the types of violence that the state regulates and opposes, the strategy widens it, referencing "other" forms of violence which include but are not limited to "abandonment; neglect; bullying; child abuse; corporal punishment; and elder abuse." This encompassing rhetoric helps stake for the US state a very broad and far-reaching mandate through which to confront gender-based violence on the local and global stage in the service of state interests, a discursive setup that is later employed—if indirectly referenced—in Trump's executive order.

Known for its championing of women's rights, the Obama administration's strategy for confronting gender-based violence linked violence against women with the instability of nation-states and the urgent and growing threat of terrorism. During his tenure, President Obama spearheaded an agenda that made violence against women central to US government policies.[27] Among the recorded achievements of his administration in the fight against gender-based violence are the appointing of the first White House Advisor on Violence Against Women, the signing of the third reauthorization of the Violence Against Women Act in 2013, and the prioritizing of federal funding and programming in support of efforts to end gender-based violence.[28] On the global front, the Obama administration addressed violence against girls and women as a "foreign policy priority," one that was backed by the dedication of at least $150 million in support of projects responding to or preventing gender-based violence around the globe.

Noting the elevation of gender-based violence to national security agendas, Corinne L. Mason (2013) argues that gender-based violence and women's rights in general were "genderwashed" and "used to communicate the changes in US foreign relations and to bolster national security at home" (63). This historical shift, Mason suggests, helped enact the emerging US policy on violence against women, one spearheaded by then secretary of state Hillary Clinton (2009–13). Described as the "Hillary Doctrine," the doctrine viewed ending gender-based violence as both a political and an economic issue for the US. In a much-cited TEDWomen talk in 2010 that the subjugation of women constitutes a threat to national security for the US and the world.[29] This speech built on previous remarks that Clinton had made at the Beijing Conference in 1995, when she argued that "women's rights were human rights." Although the Hillary Doctrine and the IVAWA agendas unfolded separately, they are politically and rhetorically connected, as "both define violence against women as a national security issue and generate a sense of urgency around the issue by using already circulating discourse of safety and security in a post-9/11 world" (Mason 2017, 34).

The Hillary Doctrine placed the protection and empowerment of women at the heart of US national security concerns, suggesting that the promulgation of the former can further US interests in curbing the rising tide of terrorism globally. The connection between women's disempowerment and the antiterror agenda of the state and the government's stated political commitment to successfully fighting both rests on a biologically essentialist belief that terrorism is reduced in societies where women have equal rights and where they have opportunities to act as deterrents to men's radicalization by making their opposition to violence known within their families, communities, and states. The validity of this hypothesis, which is premised on the idea that women tend to be more inclined toward peace, has been empirically tested by Nilay Saiya, Tasneem Zaihra, and Joshua Fidler (2017), who argue that the denial of women's political, economic, and social rights forecloses women's ability to disrupt terrorism. The authors thus understand the Hillary Doctrine with its emphasis on women's empowerment to be a vital moral and political issue and one that represents "an important but underused counterterrorism tool" (429). In addition to weaponizing the fight against gender-based violence in the service of the "War on Terrorism," the Hillary Doctrine tied its prevention to commonsense fiscal and economic concerns for women's development and prosperity.

In an op-ed published in the *Guardian* in 2011 on the devastating impacts of violence against women on communities throughout the world, Clinton argued that "gender-based violence is an intolerable violation of human dignity" that has both unquantifiable physical and emotional costs for its survivors and quantifiable economic costs for the communities in which they belong. As her op-ed states:

> No one can quantify the personal pain and anguish of any form of abuse. But medical bills and legal costs, lost wages and lower productivity, health costs including an increased risk of HIV—these are things on which we can put a price. And when we do, we see—in dollars and cents—how much violence against women and girls truly costs everyone in a society.

Clinton's speech adopts a neoliberal approach to ending violence against women that centers the costly economics of lost wages and declining productivities in a capitalist setting. Her agenda, as stated in this work, delineates the end of violence as a development issue separate from the structural conditions that lead to women's economic and political disempowerment globally. Instead of an approach that would offer a recognition of the ways in which capitalism and the ideas of wages and productivity mourned as losses in Clinton's speech have exacerbated gender-based violence nationally and globally, Clinton promotes an ideology of ending violence against women that urges their recuperation and salvaging.[30] Uniting her analysis of the violence against women with an emphasis on economic progress and development, Clinton declares the fight against gender-based violence "an issue of international human rights and national security." This converging of the fight against gender-based violence with the neoliberal discourses of development and the US national security agenda heralds a US state that tactically deploys interest in both to amass US power on the global stage.

Toward the end of his second term, in 2015, President Obama traveled to Kenya, where he delivered a powerful and popular speech in which he emphasized the connection between development, stability, and women's progress. In this speech, Obama delineated the three pillars necessary for the progress of Kenyan society as "strong democratic governance; development that provides opportunity for all people and not just some; a sense of national identity that rejects conflict for a future of peace and reconciliation." Obama drew on his own personal story and struggles and success to remind Kenyan youth in the audience of the importance of hard work and resilience in the face of difficult life conditions. He also spoke about the unique challenges facing Kenyan society by comparing the different struggles faced by countries across the world. In his speech, Obama addressed how the continuation of gender-based violence in Kenyan society prevents development, growth, and success. In a speech that embraced teleological narratives of progress, Obama called on Kenyans to let go of harmful practices that are upheld in the name of maintaining "tradition." Likening the continuation of violence against women in Kenya to the tradition of raising Confederate flags in the US, Obama stated:

> Well, so around the world, there is a tradition of repressing women and treating them differently, and not giving them the same opportunities, and husbands beating their wives, and children not being sent to school. Those are traditions. Treating women and girls as second-class citizens, those are bad traditions. They need to change. (Applause.) They're holding you back.
>
> Treating women as second-class citizens is a bad tradition. It holds you back. (Applause.) There's no excuse for sexual assault or domestic violence. There's no reason that young girls should suffer genital mutilation. There's no place in civilized society for the early or forced marriage of children. These traditions may date back centuries; they have no place in the 21st century. (Applause.)
>
> These are issues of right and wrong—in any culture. But they're also issues of success and failure. Any nation that fails to educate its girls or

> employ its women and allowing them to maximize their potential is doomed to fall behind in a global economy. (Applause.) (The White House 2015)

President Obama's speech offers insights into the US strategy for fighting gender-based violence and its attaching of an antiviolence agenda to civilizational discourses. Posing as a sympathetic and resolute father who wishes to see his Kenyan compatriots embrace national success and development, Obama urged Kenyans to let go of "bad" cultural practices such as sexual assault, domestic violence, and female genital mutilation. He then tied gender-based violence to the failure to educate girls and women and the inhibiting of their potentials to contribute to society. The success of any nation, Obama suggested, is dependent on the contributions of all members of its community. Obama's investment in ending gender-based violence and female genital mutilation in Kenya echoed remarks he had made in the US at the US–Africa Leaders Summit held in Washington, DC in 2014 when his opposition to this tradition was clearly stated: "Female genital mutilation—I'm sorry, I don't consider that a tradition worth hanging on to. I think that's a tradition that is barbaric and should be eliminated" (qtd in Dukureh 2015). In both remarks, the former president placed acts of violence such as female genital mutilation and cutting within the frame of "harmful traditional practices, such as early and forced marriage, female genital mutilation/cutting, and "'honor' killings" (The White House 2012).

In 2016 President Obama issued a statement to mark "The International Day of Zero Tolerance for Female Genital Mutilation/Cutting" in which he asserted his administration's commitment to combatting this phenomenon both in the US and globally:

> Thirteen years ago tomorrow, four first ladies in Africa came together and declared an International Day of Zero Tolerance for Female Genital Mutilation/Cutting (FGM/C). They knew that by targeting and holding back girls, this practice harms and holds back entire communities. Since then, countless others—from the Middle East to South Asia to here in the United States—have joined these women to say that FGM/C has no place in any community and undermines our efforts to celebrate and empower women and girls. (The White House 2016)

In this statement, President Obama joined world efforts to combat female genital mutilation and cutting, an effort that received global support when the UN General Assembly adopted a 2014 resolution that called on states to implement laws that target and eliminate FGM.[31] Obama also restated his opposition to traditional practices that are harmful to girls and women, a position that was also echoed by then secretary of state Hillary Clinton, who stated, "We cannot excuse this as a cultural tradition. There are many cultural traditions that used to exist in many parts of the world that are no longer acceptable. We cannot excuse it as a private matter because it has very broad public implications. It has no medical benefits. It is, plain and simply, a human rights violation" (qtd in UNFPA 2012).

Recognizing that the problem continues to exist within US borders, the statement articulated the president's commitment to fighting this phenomenon by outlawing the transport of American girls outside of the US for such surgeries:

> In the United States, we have criminalized the transport of girls to undergo FGM/C, worked with religious leaders and community-based organizations to raise awareness—especially in some immigrant communities, where the pressures to engage in this practice remain—and provided grant opportunities for domestic NGOs implementing innovative prevention strategies. (The White House 2016)

Obama's reference to the criminalization of the transportation of girls or the banning of "vacation cutting" recalls an amendment to the Federal Prohibition of Female Genital Mutilation Act of 1995. In its original form, the policy stated that anyone circumcising "the whole or any part of the labia majora or labia minora or clitoris of another person who has not attained the age of 18 years shall be fined under this title or imprisoned not more than 5 years, or both."[32] The policy also directed the Secretary of Health and Human Services to compile information about the procedure, identify communities that practice it, and develop educational recommendations for students in medicine and osteopathic medicine about "female genital mutilation and complications."

During Obama's presidency, the policy was amended twice, first by the introduction in 2011 of the "Girls Protection Act," and later through a 2013 amendment to the National Defense Authorization Act which altered the existing policy to include a directive against anyone who takes part in the transportation of a minor for the undergoing of this procedure.[33] As the new directive in the "Transport for Female Genital Mutilation" act states:

> (d) Whoever knowingly transports from the United States and its territories a person in foreign commerce for the purpose of conduct with regard to that person that would be a violation of subsection (a) if the conduct occurred within the United States, or attempts to do so, shall

> be fined under this title or imprisoned not more than 5 years, or both. (US Code, Title 18, § 116, 2013)

The tightening of state regulations around female genital mutilation and cutting in the US coincides with the increase in the number of migrants to the US from countries where female genital mutilation and cutting is practiced (Mather and Feldman-Jacobs 2016). In 2016 the Centers for Disease Control and Prevention (CDC) published a study which estimated that "approximately 513,000 women and girls in the United States were at risk for FGM/C or its consequences in 2012, which was more than three times higher than the earlier estimate, based on 1990 data" (Goldberg et al. 2016, 340). The study also noted that the increased risk of FGM in the US has continued "despite the fact that FGM/C prevalence has not increased in practicing countries (and has seemingly fallen in many countries). Rather, the increase resulted from the fact that the U.S. population originating from FGM/C countries has risen sharply in recent decades" (343).

In response to reports about the increased rates and risks associated with this phenomenon, the US government has issued a "Fact Sheet on Female Genital Mutilation/Cutting" which is distributed on the US visa section of the US Department of State's website and also featured in targeted US consulates globally.[34] In it, the government recounts its commitment to ending female genital mutilating and cutting and states its prohibition of this act. The fact sheet provides a definition of the procedure that emphasizes its nonmedical nature, specifying the criminalization of this act under both US criminal and immigration law. Under a section on the immigration consequences of violating laws against female genital mutilation, the fact sheet states the following:

> Violating the laws against FGM/C—even without a criminal conviction—may have significant immigration consequences, including making one inadmissible to or removable from the United States, as well as ineligible for some immigration benefits. (U.S. Department of State—Bureau of Consular Affairs)

As this statement makes clear, engaging in FGM/C constitutes a violation of both US federal and immigration law. As such, it would render someone inadmissible or removable from the US. The fact sheet asserts that, in the case of migrants to the US, a violation of the laws against FGM/C can be established "even without a criminal trial." In other words, a migrant can be removed from or considered inadmissible to the US for being suspected of violating laws around FGM/C. The fact sheet also distinguishes between those who violate US laws surrounding FGM/C and the girls and women who have experienced FGM/C, who are not considered to have violated any US laws. For anyone who has undergone the procedure or believes to be at risk of it, the US State Department provides a free 1-800 tip line and an email address that is associated with both the Department of Homeland Security and the Immigration and Customs Enforcement agency, showing how the gender violence agenda is central to the nexus of immigration, security, and law enforcement that structures social and political life in the US.

In summer 2017 US Immigration and Customs Enforcement (ICE) launched Operation Limelight at major US airports such as Dulles International and JFK. Operation Limelight is designed to raise awareness of the practice of female genital cutting and to prevent its occurrence. The operation brings together trained investigators from the Department of Homeland Security and the FBI to discuss with families who are about to board international flights and who are "bound for connecting hubs or destinations with high prevalence rates of FGM" the dangers of female genital cutting and its criminalization under US law (US Immigration and Customs Enforcement 2018). As a press release about the program issued by ICE (US Immigration and Customs Enforcement 2017) states, the Department of Homeland Security

> is in a unique position to engage with the traveling public at U.S. borders and ports of entry, where the local enforcement operations focus on the prevention of "vacation cutting," or sending children out of the United States for the purpose of FGM. As part of Operation Limelight USA, special agents who complete FGM-related training speak to passengers flying to or from high-risk countries, offering informational brochures and identifying potential victims and violators of FGM. These discussions both educate passengers on the consequences of involvement in FGM and provide passengers with a means by which to refer cases or receive victim assistance.

As an organization well known for its role in implementing the most egregious aspects of US immigration policies, including immigration raids, forced removal and deportation of migrants, and the incarceration of migrant children, ICE's seemingly benign and benevolent expansion into this area of governance is stunning. In this press release, ICE claims that its role in monitoring migrants departing from US airports is confined to speaking to passengers who are here reconfigured as "traveling publics" and offering them information on the dangers of the practice. Drawing on the work of

Michel Foucault, Patricia Clough and Craig Willse note that the word *publics* engenders a politics of government and management, one that pulls together populations based on "groupings of characteristics, features, or parts" (2010, 51). Publics, the authors argue, "are engaged at the level of affect and sensation, being drawn into images and commentary that are full of passions and prejudices in order that affective states might take on a facticity without employing a logic of evidence" (51). The traveling publics invoked in ICE's release are thus a racialized entity, a population that is both imagined and constructed as simultaneously responsible for FGM and in need of education and protection from its dangers. It is therefore constituted as a population that ought to be brought under the authority of US legal regulations. As educators on FGM, special agents from ICE utilize borders and ports of entry by targeting specific populations either deemed to be responsible for violating FGM/C policies or constituted as victims (or would-be victims) of the practice. The role of ICE is here confined to that of being a seemingly neutral informant, working in the interests of potential victims in need of ICE assistance and care.

Modeled after a British program that carries the same name, the US version of Operation Limelight targets airports where communities associated with female genital mutilation are believed to currently reside. Describing how the program works at US airports, Brett B. Dryer, assistant special agent in charge of Homeland Security Investigations in Newark, states:

> We are here to look at travelers, screen travelers, and identify potential victims and girls at risk, and possibly the violators that would be encouraging or performing these procedures in girls . . . We will be interviewing them, educating people about the law, and notifying them it's against the law and it's something the federal government is looking at. (qtd in Alvarado 2018)

Dryer's words appear to develop the role played by ICE officials beyond official rhetoric surrounding the practice. Here Dryer renders apparent that ICE officials engage in acts of screening and labeling that help them identify both potential victims and possible violators. Invoking the threat of federal law, Dryer makes clear that ICE officials not only educate people on the practice but also conduct interviews with them and utilize US law to instill fear around the dangers of its potential violations. As emissaries of an organization founded on an immigration system that "has institutionalized a set of values that dehumanize, demonize, and criminalize immigrants of color," ICE's foray into this domain of gender-based violence advances an investment in antimigrant carceral politics and practices (Hing 2009, 3).

The increased attention to female genital mutilation has led at least twenty-seven states to issue strict policies against these crimes (Wamsley 2017). In 2017 Michigan passed an anti-FGM law that made those who engage in performing the procedure or transporting any girl for it a felony punishable for up to fifteen years in prison.[35] In 2018 federal legislation surrounding FGM took center stage when a Michigan court judge ruled the 1996 federal ban against the procedure unconstitutional (Forliti 2018). The judge's ruling was issued in relation to the case against Jumaina Nagarwala, a doctor accused of performing procedures on at least nine girls from Michigan, Illinois, and Minnesota (McVeigh 2018). In his historic decision, the judge dismissed the case against the defendant and argued that the federal government did not have purview to legislate against what is essentially a criminal activity (Thoet 2018). The decision has been criticized by anti-FGM organizations, with some arguing that the judge's decision provided "legislative blessing" for this procedure (qtd in McVeigh). While the debate surrounding legislation against FGM continues, US government reports emphasize the importance of increased federal legislation, and bipartisan state efforts to target and raise awareness about this crime are on the rise.[36] The various legislations issued around the practice of FGM, and the increased and continuing visibility of this crime in public and state-sponsored discourses, signals the importance of gender-based violence to the agendas of the state.

In her study of US political discourses surrounding FGM, Sara McKinnon notes the elevation of this issue within the realm of "U.S. international defense, security, and development policy" (2016a, 422). McKinnon's incisive analysis demonstrates how US efforts against FGM range from overseas interventions through USAID to local interventions that are played out in US courts. Drawing on this work, we can view US state investment in curtailing FGM, an aspect that forms an essential part of the US global agenda to end gender-based violence, as emerging from the same discursive and legislative body that targets particular acts of violence for management. In both cases, exceptionalized forms of gender violence act as a constitutive link, fusing together the disparate parts of the antiviolence agenda of the US state and its immigration control mechanisms with its national and foreign policy goals. The recognition of these crimes as particularly egregious forms of gender violence that must be managed, regulated, and ended not only animates iterations of colonial state feminism but also emboldens the constitutive practices of the anti-immigrant state and its targeting of brown, Black, Arab, and Muslim people. Despite the distinctions in the approaches between Obama's policies and Trump's executive order highlighted here, both mobilize gender-based violence in the service of nationalist configurations, tying gender-based violence to iterations of terror. A focus on the US global agenda on fighting gender-based violence, and in particular its more recent campaigns against female genital mutilation and cutting, reminds us that "securitized approaches to gender justice have been able to ascend to the highest platforms of US and global politics" (Bernstein 2018, 162). A relational examination of this agenda as a crucial precedent that lays the legal and political groundwork for Trump's Executive Order 13679 helps shed light on the convergences, overlaps, and imbrications between and among them.

READING EXECUTIVE ORDER 13769

Less than one hundred days into his presidency, Donald. J. Trump had signed thirty-two executive orders, a number that exceeded not only that of his predecessor, President Barack Obama, but also all US presidents since World War II (Reene 2017). Trump was a vocal critic of what he perceived as Obama's reliance on executive orders during his presidency, constantly calling out his inability to negotiate with Congress on important issues such as immigration and health care, a point Trump repeatedly made on the campaign trail and on his Twitter account (Hayes 2019). While many of President Trump's orders have been issued to media fanfare geared toward public ceremony and pomp, some have had a broad impact on large numbers of US and non-US citizens. This includes his determination to oppose the Affordable Care Act, to restructure the immigration system, and to declare a national emergency at the border which primarily targets Mexican migrants and asylum seekers (Bierman 2019). Trump's most controversial decisions have been challenged in US courts and in Congress, and the latest battle has been around the Trump administration's quest to add a citizenship question to the 2020 US census, a request that has been overruled by the US Supreme Court (Thomsen 2019). Trump's use of executive orders has not gone unchallenged, as was amply demonstrated after President Trump's issuance of Executive Order 13769 (EO1).

Shortly after its release, EO1 was mired in a number of legal battles and contestations that challenged its validity.[37] On February 3, 2017, two weeks after its issuance, Judge James Robart issued a nationwide Temporary Relief Order (TRO) that, in effect, blocked the application of the order (Stern 2017). Arguing against the executive order, Washington State Attorney General Robert W. Ferguson stated in the original complaint that the order was "motivated by discriminatory animus and bears no relationship to its purported ends" (*Washington v. Donald Trump*).[38] Ferguson's complaint also noted that, while homeland security and protecting the country from terrorist attacks was an important goal, the order did not further that purpose. In his historic decision siding with the State of Washington, Judge Robart argued that providing a TRO was appropriate since "the Executive Order adversely effects the States' residents in areas of employment, education, business, family relations, and freedom to travel" (qtd in Barrett and Frosch 2017).[39] In court, Judge Robart side-stepped the issue of the constitutionality of the order and focused instead on the topic of national security, whose proponents have argued is the primary motivation behind the ban's issuance (Ford 2017). In this section, I provide a close reading of Trump's executive order that demonstrates how the appearance of the honor crime became a political prop or tool that, as Nadine Naber and Junaid Rana (2019) demonstrate, "institutionalizes the racializing of Muslims as a religious group and continues the legal history of racialized exclusion in the United States."

Although they are named only once throughout the document to condemn attacks on Americans of all genders, races, and sexualities, race and religion played a significant role in shaping Executive Order 13769. In its first iteration, the order asserted the authority and power of the US presidential office to "protect the American people from terrorist attacks by foreign nationals admitted to the United States" (Exec. Order No. 13,769 [2017]). The invocation of terror in the first paragraph of the order is intentional, bringing into focus real and imagined national security threats to the US founded on racialized discourses of otherness and immediately linked to Muslims. In an effort to distance itself from the charge of racial bias and racism, the order does not attach the terroristic activities it seeks to ban to any particular bodies but makes a political and discursive correlation between terror and the "foreign" Muslim-majority states it targets for inclusion in its directive. The order goes further and states in the purpose section that proper screening for visa issuance in US consular offices is central to the protection of US citizens (Volpp 2019). In rationalizing the need for the order, its authors remind readers that the terrorists responsible for 9/11 had been foreign nationals who received visas in US consular offices, insinuating that the visa screening process that facilitated their entry into the US was somehow lackluster or improper. Contrary to popular assumptions about the extreme nature of this request, visa vetting is a mechanism that has been used since the founding of the country and can be traced back to 1645, when the Massachusetts Bay Company prevented from entry into the US "poor or indigent persons" (Borjas 2016). Borjas argues that "immigrant vetting, and even extreme immigrant vetting, has a very long tradition in American history. Since before the founding even, US policies about whom the country chooses to welcome and reject have changed in response to changing conditions."

The call for more extreme visa vetting was a core campaign issue for Trump but one that has a historical precedent in a number of US policies, including President Obama's 2016 "Visa Waiver Program Improvement and Terrorist Travel Protection."[40] In a major speech that foreshadows the issuance of the executive order given shortly before his ascension to power, Trump focused on terrorist attacks committed in the US and elsewhere to call for policies that would inhibit past or would-be members of terrorist groups (and their sympathizers) from entering the US:

> In addition to screening out all members or sympathizers of terrorist groups, we must also screen out any who have hostile attitudes towards our country or its principles—or who believe that Sharia law should supplant American law.
>
> Those who do not believe in our Constitution, or who support bigotry and hatred, will not be admitted for immigration into the country.
>
> Only those who we expect to flourish in our country—and to embrace a tolerant American society—should be issued visas.
>
> To put these new procedures in place, we will have to temporarily suspend immigration from some of the most dangerous and volatile regions of the world that have a history of exporting terrorism. (qtd in Politico Staff 2016)

Juxtapositions of migrants who oppose the Constitution and engage in terrorist attacks with those who wish to prosper in and become part of a "tolerant American society" ripple throughout Trump's speech, reflecting a common belief that imposing a stricter immigration screening process would safeguard US interests and protect its citizens from hostile migrants who, among other things, wish to "supplant" US law with *Sharia* law.

Trump's investment in stricter visa screening processes was developed further in Executive Order 13679 and elevated to the level of national policy. In the first version of the order, Trump called for vigilance and proper visa screening procedures that would guard the US against similar or future attacks:

> In order to protect Americans, the United States must ensure that those admitted to this country do not bear hostile attitudes toward it and its founding principles. The United States cannot, and should not, admit those who

> do not support the Constitution, or those who would place violent ideologies over American law. In addition, the United States should not admit those who engage in acts of bigotry or hatred (including "honor" killings, other forms of violence against women, or the persecution of those who practice religions different from their own) or those who would oppress Americans of any race, gender, or sexual orientation. (Exec. Order No. 13,769 [2017])

Echoing the language of his speech, this section asserts that entry into the US necessitates ideological pledges of allegiance to the Constitution and to the founding principles of the state. In the name of safeguarding US citizens, the order makes admittance for foreign-born nationals contingent on implicit agreement with both, reasserting the power of the US nation-state to determine which foreign-born nationals are worthy of entrance to the country and which ones must be kept out. Although the "Purpose" section does not state how personal disagreement with or allegiance to the Constitution from foreign-born nationals can be determined, it nevertheless makes a link between those who oppose the Constitution and those who "would place violent ideologies" above US law. Here it is important to note that the executive order, in the interest of guarding its writers from the charge of anti-Muslim bias, removed mention of *Sharia* law or references to religious affiliation. The order bars foreign-born nationals who may have ideological or political disagreements with the US Constitution and its founding ideologies, linking opposition to both with the likelihood of engagement "in acts of bigotry or hatred" targeting Americans of all races, genders, and sexual orientations. In a clarifying subtext placed in parentheses, the order specifies certain acts of hatred, singling out "'honor' killings," violence against women, and religious persecution as exemplars of bigoted acts that the US state opposes. Although they are placed in quotation marks and confined to parenthetical subtext, the naming of these crimes in the purpose section of the order is central, bringing into view a rationale about who the document seeks to forbid from entry into the US and why.

On first glance, the inclusion of "'honor' killings" in an order that seeks to protect the US state from foreign-born terrorists and domestic terrorism appears curious. What links the seemingly distinct crimes of terror and gender violence that this act opposes? The order's specific naming of honor killings as a form of violence is significant for a number of reasons. First, the placing of the word *honor* in quotation marks appears to trouble the inclusion and singling out of the crime or at least point to some disagreement or uncertainty regarding its rhetorical meanings and deployments, a tension that will be played out in the revised versions of the text and the subtle changes used in the naming of the crime which the revised order undergoes (Volpp 2019).[41]

Second, the order of appearance of the honor killing in the parenthetical text is also noteworthy. In the earliest version of the executive order, honor killings are placed before and apart from "other forms of violence against women." This position is not accidental but serves to simultaneously separate the honor crime from a broader spectrum of violence against women and to specify it as a more extreme variation of it. It is also significant that the order rhetorically ties gender violence to racial terror through a reliance on an implicit, rather than an explicit, coded script about the nature of the violence itself and the assumed racial background of its perpetrators. Although the order neither defines what constitutes an honor killing nor gives examples of the varieties of violence against women it seeks to guard Americans against, both are figuratively and discursively connected to the bodies of foreign-born terrorists who oppose the founding principles of the US and who are thus likely to enact violence against its citizens due to religious, racial, gender, or sexual differences.

In her detailed legal analysis of this order, Leti Volpp states that "while the surface of the text of EO-1's 'Purpose' section suggests that the administration is concerned about gender violence, discrimination, and inequality, we can understand the rationale of these passages as reinforcing the presumption that Muslims must be kept out of the United States, as particularly engaged in these forms of abhorrent behavior" (2019, 143). In addition to attaching abhorrent crimes to the foreign-born migrants from primarily Muslim countries, perhaps the most significant aspect of the purpose section of the order is the absence of specific temporal and geographic referents to the violent acts committed by those seeking entry to the US which the order seeks to regulate. In the text, it is not clear whether the state should not admit to the US people who have committed past violent and bigoted acts in their home countries or whether it should withhold entry from those who are likely to do so in the US in the future. On its surface, the order appears to protect from criminal acts such as violence against women both US-born citizens and noncitizens. Through its capacious language, the order expands the state's authority to both morally condemn and legislate on past, present, and future forms of violence against women in general and the honor killing in particular, whether committed in the US or transnationally. In other words, the US state is able to usurp for itself a "pastoral" and protective role on both the domestic and the global fronts, a role that has been annexed in the service of military projects that are premised on the welfare and rescue of women (McKinnon 2016b, 33).

The honor crime makes a second appearance in section 10, "Transparency and Data Collection," of the first version of the order, which directs the Secretary of Homeland Security and the Attorney General to provide the American public with information about crimes committed by foreign-born nationals, including

(i) information regarding the number of foreign nationals in the United States who have been charged with terrorism-related offenses while in the United States; convicted of terrorism-related offenses while in the United States; or removed from the United States based on terrorism-related activity, affiliation, or material support to a terrorism-related organization, or any other national security reasons since the date of this order or the last reporting period, whichever is later;

(ii) information regarding the number of foreign nationals in the United States who have been radicalized after entry into the United States and engaged in terrorism-related acts, or who have provided material support to terrorism-related organizations in countries that pose a threat to the United States, since the date of this order or the last reporting period, whichever is later; and

(iii) information regarding the number and types of acts of gender-based violence against women, including honor killings, in the United States by foreign nationals, since the date of this order or the last reporting period, whichever is later; and

(iv) any other information relevant to public safety and security as determined by the Secretary of Homeland Security and the Attorney General, including information on the immigration status of foreign nationals charged with major offenses. (Exec. Order No. 13,769 [2017])

In this section of the order, President Trump charges two government agencies central to the operations of the "War on Terror" with the role of informing US publics of the dangers that foreign nationals seeking entry to the US may pose to their safety and security. The Department of Homeland Security, founded under the auspices of President George W. Bush in the aftermath of 9/11, has the official mandate of "protecting the American people from terrorist threats" and promoting "a secure and resilient nation that effectively prevents terrorism in ways that preserve our freedom and prosperity."[42] The US Attorney General represents the US government in all legal matters and has, in certain instances, executive power to enforce US laws. The order requires both bodies to collect and report information on terrorism-related offenses and the number of people who have been radicalized since entry into the country. These two tasks operationalize a claim made by a government-issued fact sheet about the executive order which states that "the United States has the world's most generous immigration system, yet it has been repeatedly exploited by terrorists and other malicious actors who seek to do us harm."[43]

Deploying moral panic about would-be terrorists who have taken advantage of an overly generous immigration system, the order enlists the power of these two government agencies to produce and disseminate information about a problem that does not exist on the scale that the order's writers would have audiences believe (Volpp 2019). As Michael Welch convincingly shows in his review of human rights violations in the "War on Terror," "moral panic and pseudo-disasters commonly precipitate new laws placing additional restrictions on existing freedoms, liberties, and due process" (2004, 4). But the order also goes further than spreading and trafficking in by-now common associations of migrants with terror and terrorism, bringing into its purview information on both "the number and types of acts of gender-based violence against women, including honor killings" committed by foreign-born nationals in the US. In this version of the order, the honor killing is a concern secondary to gender-based violence against women, but it is, nevertheless, a bona fide crime that no longer exists in tentative quotation marks as the previous textual appearance suggests. If the purpose section was unclear about the limits of the geographies of violence that the order sought to govern, this section makes obvious its investment in collecting information on crimes that occur within the US (Volpp 2019).[44]

The requirement that the government track and report on gender-based violence committed by migrants, a directive now in place due to the Supreme Court's upholding of the revised executive order, serves to exceptionalize this form of violence and to separate it from a large order of crimes that target women and violate their bodies in the US. In her critique of the order, Leila Milani (2017) makes the same point, stating that "there are multitudes of crimes that would fall under the category of violence against women—such as domestic violence, rape, human trafficking, and female genital mutilation/cutting—which far outnumber the cases of 'honor killings' in the U.S." The order's singling out of honor killings also perpetuates the notion that migrants commit gender-based violence in disproportionately higher numbers than US citizens, a point that again betrays an interest in the opportunistic use of violence against women to manage targeted populations rather than address or curb the phenomenon itself.

In their brief on honor killings and the executive order, the group Muslim Advocates provides a clear and succinct genealogy of the appearance of honor crimes in the US popular discourse, arguing the following:

> Given the absence of any information suggesting that "honor killings" are a distinctive problem in the U.S.—or one that is in any way related to national

> security or to the populations of the countries identified in the Orders—President Trump's decision to track and publish figures of these crimes in the U.S. reveals an interest in stigmatizing Muslims and the nationals of the Muslim Ban's targeted countries, rather than in actually combating violence against women. (September 2017, 4)

In this account, the authors challenge the "common sense" (Volpp 2019, 169) idea that ties Islam and Muslims to violence against women, revealing the politically based and insidious motivations beyond the government's focus on such crimes. The authors effectively trouble the association between gender violence and terrorism that appears in the text of the order as a naturalized extension of the government's stated concern with protecting US publics from instances of terror in which both crimes remain largely and conveniently undefined.

Legal contestations of the executive order have sought to expose the political motives behind the president's declared interest in fighting violence against women, revealing the anti-Muslim animus undergirding the order's exclusive focus on honor-related violence. As Nadine Naber writes in her analysis of the Muslim ban, "The orientalist privileging of societal and cultural forms of gendered and sexualized violence obscures gendered and sexualized US state violence enacted on bodies perceived to be Muslim" (2019). In two amicus briefs, opponents of the executive order relied on testimony provided by experts on the honor crime to help establish how it configures in today's political landscape as a form of violence that is both exceptionalized and routinely linked to Islam and to Muslim male perpetrators. In her declaration in support of the brief submitted in the case *Universal Muslim Association of America INC., et al., vs. Donald J. Trump et al.*, Lila Abu-Lughod explained the appearance of "honor killings" and its corollary the "honor crime" in the text of the order:

> My research has demonstrated that the term "honor killing," or "honor crime," has become a means of signaling a class of violence purportedly linked to Islam and committed by Muslim men. I have also demonstrated that invocation of "honor crimes" has become a way of stigmatizing and demeaning Islam as a faith and Muslim men as a group as uncivilized and dangerous. In this way, rhetoric about "honor killing" or "honor crime" is a means of implicitly but powerfully conjuring negative and misleading stereotypes about Islam and Muslims. (3)

Abu-Lughod's statement shows how rhetoric surrounding the honor crime rests on harmful assumptions about Islam and Muslims that peddle in ideas of their danger and incivility.[45] Abu-Lughod's words bring into focus the racist underpinnings of an order whose proponents have adamantly denied their targeting of any particular group of persons or religious belief system and who have worked hard to remove from the records such evidence.

In a detailed and follow-up amicus brief focused on the inclusion of honor killings in the second version of the executive order submitted to the US Supreme Court, leading social scientists at American universities (including Abu-Lughod) carefully demonstrated the anti-Muslim animus of the text of the order in three central ways. First, they sought to dissociate honor killings from the crime of terrorism. They argued that the reprehensible acts of violence against women such as the honor killing remain statistically rare in their occurrence in the US and are not "harbingers or proxies for terrorism, and the government does not contend otherwise" (Anderson et al. 2017, 16). The authors contest the link between the countries that the ban targets and the honor crime, arguing that no credible links are to be found between national security, terrorism, and the honor killing even in government-issued documents on terrorism in the countries targeted by the ban, including in the US State Department Country Reports on Terrorism 2015. The authors also return to the text of the first version, showing that the revised version extends the same "hold over" rhetoric from the first one, revealing that the inclusion of the honor crime in the revised order is "an invocation of anti-Muslim animus" (18).[46] By focusing on the anti-Muslim bias of the text, the brief strikes at the exclusionary ban while exposing the rhetorical fallacies used as impetus for its issuance. As Gerald Neuman (2017) argues, the inclusion of honor killing in the text of the order offers the most obvious and compelling evidence that this "directive *has no conceivable relation to the alleged national security purpose of the travel ban,* and it continues to reveal the true underlying purpose of both orders" (emphasis in original).

A review of the language of Executive Order 13679 and its revised iterations helps demonstrate how the honor killing puts into use a "coded" language that traffics in racial associations between certain forms of gender-based violence and terror (Volpp 2019, 36). By lacing the two together, the order denotes particular forms of violence against women as violence that is attached to the marked bodies of foreign-born nationals who must be kept out of US borders, and if they are already in as legal residents, then their activities must be regulated, tracked, and reported on. The act of embedding honor killings in the rhetoric of terrorism rests on the elasticity of the concept of terror and the lack of definitional consensus about *what* constitutes terror and *who* engages in it. This definitional dilemma can be understood to reflect "the changing nature of terrorism, sloppy use of the term, and most importantly, the pejorative and subjective nature of the term terrorism" (Perry 2004, 254). What concerns me about the term *terrorism* and its linking to gender-based violence is not necessarily the quest for an agreed-upon definition (there is none) but rather the opposite: namely, how the lack of a definition helps buttress the concept's capacity to incorporate within it all (or even any) forms of violence, including gender-based violence, that it seeks to morally and legally condemn when convenient for its authors to do so. The power of this discourse rests less in its specificity and more in its rhetorical and political capacity to fold racialized acts of violence against women into the ever-expanding, antiterror security agenda of the state, an agenda in which gender-based violence has featured more prominently than previously imagined.

BEYOND EXCEPTIONALISM

In an astute letter submitted to President Donald Trump contesting the Muslim ban, members of fifty-five advocacy groups and organizations noted their disagreement with the order and its exceptionalized approach to violence against women. As groups specifically concerned with ending violence against women, they state that the order "not only promotes and inflames Islamophobia, but it further feeds into the false narrative that violence against women is specific to non-Western cultures" (CARE USA et al. 2017). They urge the president to recognize how the ban, by shutting out refugee communities from the six banned nation-states from the possibility of asylum and resettlement, works to further risk the lives of girls and women and renders them more vulnerable to violence, assault, exploitation, and sexual harassment at every stage of their journeys to safety. It reminds him that the women the order shuts out may themselves be fleeing experiences of gender and sexual violence in addition to their war-ravaged countries and communities. The letter works to instruct the president on the imbrications of gender violence and migration policy, delivering what is, in essence, an intersectional reading of violence against girls and women that refuses to spectacularize or exceptionalize violence, even in times of crises and war.

In this chapter, I showcased how exceptionalized and racialized forms of gender violence were interlinked with terror in the US context. My goal in reading these texts alongside one another and relationally is to show how this discourse, in its various historical manifestations and despite its subtle differences, has worked to target specific forms of gender-based violence, such as FGM and the honor crime, and to attach them to state agendas in historically and geographically specific ways. This reading is nonexceptional, bringing into view an analysis of the executive order that places it in a much longer history of anti-Muslim sentiment, policies, and practices and US state discourse that have regulated how gender violence is understood and confronted on both local and global scales. Without history, the Muslim ban's invocation of the honor crime appears to be an anomaly, a legislative piece that emerges out of nowhere. Instead, this chapter links the recent twinning of the honor crime with the crime of terrorism in the US and the political events unfolding in this country almost three decades before the issuance of Trump's order. In rereading Tina Isa's murder and its trying in two separate but interconnected courts, we see that Trump's executive order neither creates an unfamiliar worldview nor breaks juridical grounds for the linking of domestic violence with terror. Rather, when placed within a longer genealogy of gender violence as terror, it becomes clear that Trump's order formalizes the adoption of such rhetoric into the letter of the law and operationalizes an understanding of gender violence that has often attached these crimes to culturalized and racialized others existing within the US and those routinely and systematically kept outside of it.

Reading this order nonexceptionally attends to how it revives in new ways old and ongoing forms of surveillance, policing, and monitoring of racialized communities and racialized crimes that have been in force in the US before its issuance. This includes linking Trump's Executive Order 13679 to policies that have targeted Muslim, Black, and people of color communities in the US under more "liberal" forms of governance that laid the groundwork for the selective legal targeting and state management of exceptionalized forms of gender-based violence. In these policies and practices, Muslims and migrants and their bodies are tied to domestic and foreign terror in a way that legitimizes their banning and the invading of their privacy by "activating the invading, terrorist other narrative" (Al Samman 2017, 483). Reading Trump's executive order and its focus on gender violence in this way helps shed light on how certain forms of violence have been used to construct links between gender violence and racial terror in the service of US state interests. For feminist scholars concerned with the further racialization of this honor crime and its tying to border policing and control programs, a critical lens attuned to a historical, transnational, and multileveled analysis of both gender violence and terror that extend before and beyond the Trump presidency can help push against understandings of the honor crime's resurfacing that are constrained by the logic of exception.

CHAPTER 4

At the Limits of Legal Justice

Women's Organizing and Juridical Activism in Jordan

ON MARCH 16, 2017, the Jordanian government approved recommendations made by the Royal Committee for Reforming the Judiciary and Enhancing the Rule of Law. Formed under the auspices of King Abdullah II, the committee was empowered to amend old laws and to propose new legislation to entrench the rule of law in the kingdom.[1] In its 285-page report, the royal committee made specific recommendations that targeted legislative codes believed to provide legal sanction for violence against women, including article 308 and article 98 of the Jordanian Penal Code.[2] Commonly referred to as the "marry your rapist law," article 308 permits the pardoning of rape perpetrators who marry their victims and remain married to them for a minimum period of at least three years. Article 98, often referred to as the "honor killing" law, provides penalty reductions to killers who commit an act of murder in a "fit of fury" caused by "an unlawful and dangerous act" by a victim.[3] The committee's recommendations to amend these laws come after decades of lobbying and campaigning by Jordanian women's rights activists, who have long highlighted the discriminatory and harmful nature of such laws while positing national legal codes as significant sites for social struggle and political change.

Jordanian women rights activists were rewarded for their efforts on July 27, 2017, when the Jordanian Parliament voted to repeal article 308 of the penal code (Husseini 2017c). The intense debate surrounding the repeal of article 308 and other legal amendments divided the Jordanian Parliament (and along with it, Jordanian society) between those who argued that the existence of such laws was harmful to women's right to security and freedom and those who believed that their repeal posed a threat to Jordan's traditions and would, ultimately, lead to the undoing of the country's cultural codes and moral edicts. The parliamentary debates reflected wider divisions in Jordanian society itself, ones that spilled over to social media, on television programs, and in the local newspapers, where the two sides vigorously discussed the merits and follies of the proposed changes. While both parties repeatedly confirmed their loyalty to the crown, at stake in such debates are troubling binaries that depict struggles over the penal code as an ongoing battle between progressives and traditionalists, secularism and religion, culture and law. Despite these divisions that continue to mark the troubled terrain of rights in Jordan, the repeal of article 308 is a historic event in its own right. It reflects the conjoining of efforts by civil society organizations to amend or repeal laws they deem harmful to women with the desires of the kingdom's monarch to project the country as a modern and progressive Arab state in which both Jordanian men and women are granted equal rights and protections. These two constituencies posit the law as an effective tool in efforts to combat gender violence against women.

As is well known in feminist literature on the law in the Arab world, legal loopholes that exonerate men who commit acts of violence against women—such as article 308 and article 98 of the Jordanian Penal Code—are not unique to Jordan.[4] Efforts to confront these laws reflect a rising awareness of the importance of the law for the attainment of the equal rights of men and women. Contrary to popular depictions of such work, this wave of activism is neither new nor exceptional but is part and parcel of past and ongoing mobilizations of women's rights activists to reform the Personal Status Laws that began in Jordan as early as 1989 (Clark and Young 2008). Undoubtedly, calls for legal reform have been re-energized by the Arab uprisings and the various political upheavals that have swept the region. Across the Arab world in countries like Morocco, Lebanon, and Jordan, campaigns to repeal laws that discriminate against women have increased, and their success has been lauded at the local, regional, and transnational levels. They reflect, as a *New York Times* article argues, "a steady expansion of women's education in the region and a new kind of public activism spurred by social media" (Sengupta 2017). Celebratory accounts of these legal victories abound in media, powerfully wielded by state and nonstate actors to reflect the capacity of Arab governments to respond to citizen demands and to implement important legal changes that are framed in local terms (Merry 2006). They showcase, in other words, the growing will of the people to suture social problems through the apparatuses of the state itself, such as the law. Regardless of their immediate and long-term outcomes, however, such legal battles and women's juridical activism demand serious scholarly attention that neither exceptionalizes their occurrence nor overplays their significance but rather investigates the discursive practices and material politics that underpin them. While a study of the applications of the law by state apparatuses in actual legal cases is crucial, this chapter focuses primarily on activist calls for judicial reform.[5] In other words, it provides a discursive analysis of the texts of the law and the various arguments animating calls for its amendment or removal, recognizing a distinction between the law as text and the law as practice.[6]

In what follows, I attempt to provide what Cynthia S. Gorman (2019) describes as "legal archeology," a process of digging up the work of the law in shaping not only the juridical realm but also the social world. As she states, "Such an examination involves exploring how laws are constituted through contested socio-spatial ideas, but also the dynamic ways in which discourse is constituted through interactions within the legal process that are always spatially and territorially embedded" (1054). In tracing contemporary legal battles and contestations in Jordan, this chapter concerns itself with the mooring of antiviolence work to the law in Jordan. In this work, I map Jordanian women's efforts to end gender violence, and in particular crimes related to honor-based violence, showing how women's rights activists have negotiated a tricky political terrain that demands loyalty to the state while attempting to wrest power from it. I look at the discursive contexts in which recent legal mobilization efforts have taken place and the different positions adopted by opponents and proponents of the repeal of article 308. Through analyzing public discourses, I show how the article's removal from the Jordanian Penal Code reflects a culmination of the work of various actors and stakeholders, and I analyze the careful considerations, negotiations, and compromises that yield legal change invested in juridical forms of feminism. My aim is to explore how women rights activists in Jordan work to alter national legal frameworks about morality, justice, and honor. Drawing on the important work of Catherine Warrick (2009) on law and legitimacy in the Jordanian context, this chapter investigates the contemporary, multiple, and competing discourses that shape legal changes and challenges to the Jordanian Penal Code. My goal is to examine what women's organizing around juridical reform and activism can tell us about state-backed efforts to end gender violence in Jordan.[7]

MAPPING JORDANIAN WOMEN'S ACTIVISM

Although there is a long history of women's activism in Jordan, scholarship on the topic often takes the year 1989 as a starting point for the emergence of civil society organizations and political movements in the kingdom. This period is discussed in relation to democratizing and liberalizing trends initiated under the auspices of King Hussein that continued with the succession to power in 1999 of his son, King Abdullah II. This ten-year period is marked by the suspension of martial law, the drafting and issuance of the National Charter in 1991, the legalization of political parties, and the resumption of three rounds of parliamentary elections in 1989, 1993, and 1997 (Lucas 2008). Together, these initiatives, which are also characterized by a period of intense regional and global change, helped project Jordan as a state committed to a form of controlled democratization or restricted liberalization (Brand 1999; Nanes 2003; Robinson 1998). In this environment, civil society actors, including women's groups and organizations, often organized within the shadow of the state. They thus emerged, lobbied, and functioned in relation to the state's regulatory liberalizing aims and efforts and worked in tandem with its policed democratizing projects.

Significantly, calls for social and legal reforms were carefully calibrated in relation to the ability of the state to realize them while satisfying the desires of its various tribal and religious constituencies and guaranteeing the regime's own survival (Wiktorowicz 2000). Civil society groups therefore worked within an environment that ceded some ground to their demands while restricting their power to engage issues of a political nature through imposing restrictions on the press and civil liberties (Nanes 2003). As Peter Ferguson notes, "Civil society evolved in direct response to institutionalized state practices that granted calculated political freedoms, rather than emerging as a distinct and opposing actor" (2017, 60). These organizations continued to urge for reforms that the state actively or tacitly either encouraged, mitigated, or condemned.

Highly attuned to the political reality of limited reform that structures political and social change in Jordan, the women's movement has undergone significant developments in the past few decades. Writing on this history, Ibtesam Al-Atiyat (2012), a member of the National Committee for Jordanian Women's Affairs, divides women's activism in the kingdom into three overlapping historical and political phases: "the emergence phase" (1944–48), "the equality phase" (1954–70s), and the "'renaissance phase'" (1970s onwards). In her account, Al-Atiyat argues that the first phase of women's activism in Jordan was led by elite and upper-class women. In its early state-building phase, university-educated women from the middle and upper classes, who enjoyed important positions in the kingdom through their kin and marital relationships, advanced a "charity-oriented" approach to women's rights (135). This included the promotion of women's right to literacy and education, a goal that was achieved through providing literacy training to women from poorer socioeconomic backgrounds. As Nicola Pratt (2015), in her account of Jordanian women's activism, notes, "Women's involvement in charitable and welfare activities has been a socially-acceptable way for women to enter the public sphere, which historically has been reserved for men only."

Women's slow but steady entry into the public sphere and its inscription as a space that included women in sometimes reluctant and nominal ways ushered in the second phase of women's activism. In describing the tension between nominal inclusion and full participation and equal rights, Joseph Massad describes this history thus:

> On the one hand, political ideology seems to have led to and informed the codification of women's status as inferior in the private sphere with minimal state intervention, and a steady expansion of women's presence in the public sphere as nominally equal citizen-nationals with state protection. On the other hand, juridical rights (foremost among which are constitutional rights and personal status laws) inform an ideology of legal equality and expansion of rights, which many feminists and their state backers adhere to, and an ideology of traditionalization calling for circumscribing women's rights and their presence in the public sphere and keeping the state out of the home, which secular and Islamist antifeminists and their state backers adhere to. (2001, 98)

Jordanian women activists therefore situated their efforts to attain equal rights within a national framework that was, at times, attuned to the Palestinian liberation struggle and the spirit of Arab nationalism. While they were sometimes constrained by this nationalist agenda, women still lobbied for the right to vote and to run for public office. And although some of these demands were fulfilled in limited ways, such as the preliminary granting of the right to vote only to literate and educated women, activist campaigns sought to extend equal citizenship rights and privileges to both men and women regardless of education level in 1955 (Al-Atiyat 2012).

Building on two these preliminary stages that were marked also by various internal and external difficulties, Al-Atiyat shows how the third phase of women's activism in Jordan "witnessed a 'renaissance phase'" that was characterized by a significant growth in women's activism in more visible, sustained, and encompassing ways (2012, 138). In 1974 women officially gained the right to vote, a right they would not be able to practice until 1989 with the end of martial law and the resumption of parliamentary elections (Massad 2001; Pratt 2015). The founding of the Arab Women's Union (AWU) in 1954 was also an important milestone in this period of women's activism, with the union bringing together women from all over the kingdom to collectively call for their rights. Women's groups sought funding and recognition from the state while also forming connections with the global community through attendance at international conferences. In an attempt to limit the influence and reach of the women's union, the state set up the General Federation of Jordanian Women in 1981 to both coordinate and set the women's agenda during this period in ways that cast the kingdom in a positive and modern light. The regime thus aimed to monopolize women's issues and discussions surrounding them. The success of this effort was limited because of the structure of the organization and its inability to attract membership, as Al-Atiyat demonstrates. However, this move shows the desire of the state to "channel women's activism" away from civil society organizations and its grasp of the significance of women's rights issues for its own survival (Brand 2003, 165).

An important feature that also characterized this period (and that continues to shape women's politics in Jordan today) is the royal family's support of particular women's issues. This includes leading women's organizations, as in the case of Princess Basma Bint Talal (the late King Hussein's sister), who has served with a number of women's organizations in Jordan, including as chairperson of the Jordanian National Commission for Women (JNCW), as president of the Jordanian National Forum for Women (JNFW), and as honorary president of the General Federation of Jordanian Women (GFJW).[8] Similarly, Queen Rania plays a visible role in a select set of women's issues, including a focus on education for girls and teacher training. In an effort to promote women's right to work, the queen has set up organizations that train professional women as teachers and as craft makers. She has also focused on issues of family health, domestic violence, and children.[9] The queen's agenda often oscillates between a neoliberal and developmental focus on women's empowerment and discourses of political and economic inclusion and sporadic efforts to create change in areas that provoke debate and contestation in the country, such as reforms to the Personal Status Law and the Nationality Law.[10] The involvement of royal family members in the women's movement in Jordan can be understood as a form of "embryonic Hashemite state feminism" and as an extension of the regime's efforts to take a leading part in simultaneously defining, setting, and limiting the agenda for women's activism in the country (Brand 2003, 165). They are also, often, staged spectacles that demand recognition of Jordan's efforts to comply with international law and displays of Jordan's commitment to modern and yet traditional values that align with Islamic teachings. Importantly, women's organizations have sometimes actively sought royal support in order to guarantee the state's backing of their agendas and to minimize its intervention in their affairs. In a state like Jordan, where the dividing line between the regime and the crown is thin, royal support ensures a form of legitimation for women's issues that are deemed divisive or sensitive.

Despite the difficult political terrain around women's rights, royal family members have made public stances against gender violence and crimes that are known as honor crimes. In 2000 Prince Ali (the half-brother of King Abdullah) and Prince Ghazi (the king's cousin) led 5,000 demonstrators in a protest against honor killing laws. Prior to this protest, Rana Husseini reports that the late King Hussein and his wife Queen Noor had voiced their opposition to this crime, arguing that it is "foreign to Islam" (2000, 20). Queen Rania and King Abdullah have also spoken against the honor crime publicly. In an interview with the *Daily Telegraph,* where she was explicitly asked about her position, the queen stated, "Honour killings are a terrible and totally unacceptable and unjustifiable practice. We still see cases every year in Jordan, and it is an issue we take extremely seriously" (qtd in James 2016). The queen's stated opposition against the honor crime in international media comes at a time when international attention has uncritically attributed this form of violence to the "traditional" or "Bedouin" character of Jordanian society. While internationally the queen has used her fame and power to articulate her clear opposition to the crime, she and the royal family at large have carefully negotiated their positions at home for fear of angering conservative members of Jordanian society who reject such state-led interventions, including tribal and religious sectors of society that the monarchy has relied on for support. Writing on the women's movement in Jordan and Palestine, Frances Hasso notes that "the regime also legally and discursively reinforced a form of patriarchal social organization that subordinated men to women in their socioeconomic and religious groups because its stability partly relied on alliance with conservative tribal and religious forces" (2005, 18).

This truncated account of women's activism in Jordan demonstrates that, from its inception, the women's movement sought to define an agenda that advocated for social change by securing citizenship rights for Jordanian women and men. Women who organized in Jordan came from different class backgrounds, but the movement has also been dominated by women from privileged socioeconomic backgrounds who have pushed for social changes that have sometimes alienated segments of the Jordanian population.[11] Never completely homogenous, the women's movement sought to alter the status of women by working in collaborative and creative ways with the state. It thus set its agendas around certain legal, social, and political benchmarks that it sought to reach incrementally. Caught between attaining state-backed reforms and the risk of alienating conservative elements within Jordanian society, women's activism in Jordan has operated in an environment where negotiations with the state are a constant part of everyday politics and where state feminist projects are the norm and not the exception.[12]

Historical records of women's activism explore these imbrications, showing how women's organizations have worked together with the state to gain particular rights and privileges that include, for example, the establishment of a parliamentary woman quota, the gaining of the right to divorce (or *khulu'*), and the right to be informed of a husband's decision to remarry or to take a second wife.[13] In addition to these gains, in 2003 the state raised the marriage age from fifteen for girls and sixteen for boys to eighteen for both sexes, a decision it would reverse in 2017 at the same time that article 308 was repealed.[14] Through long-term investments in the education sector, the state was able to halve illiteracy rates of girls and women throughout the kingdom, an achievement that is often assumed to indicate Jordanian women's true integration into the labor force and achievement of economic access and equality (Adely 2009). Occurring in a short two-decade period, these local reforms were also backed at the international level in Jordan's signing of the Convention on the Elimination of All Forms of Discrimination Against Women (CEDAW) in 1992. Like many other Arab states, however, Jordan placed a number of reservations on some articles of the convention, including ones pertaining to equal rights on nationality, movement, and marriage decisions (El Muhtaseb, Brown, and Kayyali 2016). The state's delayed publication of the convention in the *Official Gazette* until 2007 gestured toward the complex terrain that the issue of women's rights occupies in Jordan and the government's desire to balance competing local claims of authenticity and tradition with global calls for human rights and women's equality.

As state-backed reforms, these changes were (and continue to be) of immense importance to Jordanian society, having contributed to the reshaping of the state's policies and practices and the day-to-day lives of its citizenry. Undoubtedly, many of the achievements of the women's movements such as the right to work and the right to vote impacted both Jordanian men and women and the workings of the Jordanian state, and yet their adoption did not automatically translate into calculable or immediate gains for Jordanian women from all socioeconomic backgrounds. While the women's movement in Jordan has succeeded at fulfilling aspects of its agenda that align well with the Jordanian state's national efforts, these changes have not cured the various social, cultural, and legal problems that Jordanian women—and Jordanian society at large—continue to face. My aim in listing these reforms is not to romanticize their occurrence or to overstate their significance in reconstituting or transforming the position of Jordanian women as subjects of the Jordanian state. Rather, I wish to show how legal reforms and celebratory accounts of rights-based and juridical gains underpin the structuring logics of women's activism in Jordan. They are the benchmarks against which women's activism in Jordan measures both its successes and failures and through which it both defines and calibrates its relationship with the state.

THE TRANSNATIONAL TERRAIN OF RIGHTS AND LEGAL CONTESTATIONS

Women's rights and legal contestations are central features of women's organizing and activism in Jordan. While it is true that the women's movement in Jordan was never "counterhegemonic" to the state, the movement has grappled with the legal status of Jordanian women since its inception (Warrick 2009, 31). Women from all over the world have struggled to attain equality before the law, and legal contestations have marked feminist struggles to secure a variety of personal, national, and political rights, including the right to vote, the right to work, the right to citizenship, the right to movement, and the right to marry. Advancements in human rights in general and women's rights in particular have long been used as instruments that record and measure the commitment of developing nation-states to the projects of modernity, liberalization, democracy, and equality. As indexes of modernization, women's rights function within a transnational regime of governance that enables the regulatory functions of the nation-state.

Scholars such as Inderpal Grewal (2005) have explored the ways in which human rights discourses have been deployed in a number of struggles. Grewal traces the genealogies of these struggles, reading the uptake of human rights and women's rights discourses across transnational geographies of state power. Grewal demonstrates how "human rights instruments when applied to women's issues could break down the distinction made by patriarchal states between public and private domains and thus address the violence and subordination of women within the private sphere" (127). In other words, women's rights become viewed as mechanisms with the capacity to undo the rigid binaries of the private and the public on which the patriarchal nation-state relies and in which violence against women is often enacted. Laws that protect women from violence are thus expressed through the discourse of women's rights to life, liberty, and safety in both the public and the private spheres. In the (trans)national rush for rights, the efficacy of the law and the discourse of rights as instruments of change, along with their ability to seed cultural and social transformations, are often overemphasized. More dangerously still, the ability of states to both absorb and imbibe rights discourses in their modernization bids, while restricting more radical forms of change at the structural levels, is also underplayed in celebratory rights accounts and discourses.

In a counterpart to exultant accounts of rights, Mervat Hatem shows how the Arab state has utilized women's citizenship rights in ways that reified its power and served broader national and international interests. Significantly, Hatem's rich analysis demonstrates how women's bid for citizenship rights did not automatically translate into political gains but rather allowed Arab states to extend their control over women whose "status as dependent citizens of the state" were confirmed through appeals to rights (2005, 26). Women's engagement with the state, and their efforts to expand citizenship rights in this context, "was a potential double-edged sword" that reified the status of women as state subjects whose rights-based victories would not "challenge the state's class and gender interests" (27).

The writing and publication of the *Arab Human Development Report 2005: Towards the Rise of Women in the Arab World* is an example of a work that measures women's progress in a number of arenas, including the domain of legal rights. The 335-page report, published with the backing and funding of the United Nations Development Programme (2006), provides an extensive overview of the status of women in the Arab countries. It focuses on Arab women's achievements and struggles in cultural, social, educational, and legal sites. The work offers an in-depth analysis of the various challenges and successes that women have experienced in the region while providing a sober view of impediments that continue to prevent women from attaining equality in Arab states. Rife with legal explanations for the lagging status of equality of women in Arab states, the report identifies a number of discriminatory "provisions and practices that reveal the bias of the Arab legislator against women" (17). The report also states that juridical equality flounders "on the reservations of Arab judiciaries, a resistance fueled by the growth of fundamentalist trends and their increasing impact on the legal consciousness of Arab judges" (19). Although the report makes the important distinction between the existence of laws on paper and in national and international conventions and their applications, it readily ties Arab women's advancement to the realms of rights, laws, and legality.

The focus of the report on reforms to the Personal Status Law, Arab Family Law, and the Nationality Law highlight its authors' support of legal change. The report identifies key areas in which discriminatory laws impact the lives of Arab women while hailing the Tunisian Personal Status Code as a "model for promoting the principle of equality in marital relations in law" (193). In their effort to identify discriminatory legal codes in Arab contexts, the report's authors repeatedly state their commitment to "sustainable and wide reforms in the law" that require the development of a civil-society-based "culture favourable to gender equality" (200). Elsewhere, Lila Abu-Lughod has critiqued the report for the "political dialect it deploys" (2009, 91). Abu-Lughod rightly identifies "the liberal language of human development and the neoliberal discourses of structural adjustment and global markets" that structure possibilities and limits of the horizon of change in the Arab world as envisioned through this report (91).

While Abu-Lughod focuses on the liberal underpinnings of political reform that the report calls for, I also find it interesting that the report valorizes the law as a crucial site for change and for the protection of women. Nowhere is this discourse more apparent than in the report's discussion of gender violence in the Arab world. In the section pertaining to forms of violence against women, the report specifically names honor crimes, domestic violence, and female circumcision as forms of violence that Arab women experience. The report attributes the occurrence of gender violence to both tribal customs and the presence of laws that sanction the killing of women by offering reduced sentences to men who kill. The report faults both the judges who exonerate these men and the state that allows certain forms of violence to be practiced in its "full view" (117). What goes missing from such an account are the structural and systematic conditions that give rise to violence against women, such as the socioeconomic conditions that cannot be altered through a focus on the law alone.

In itineraries of women's rights, progress is often measured in relation to women's ability to gain rights that do not already exist, to alter laws that are discriminatory toward women, or to introduce new legislation believed to have a potentially positive effect on women's lives. Legal progress is thus calculated linearly: if women gain particular rights, they move closer to gender equality. If they lose said rights or are unable to achieve them, they move further away from succeeding in creating parity. When the quest to attain legal victories falters, the women's rights movement is assumed to be stalled or at a standstill. As a *New York Times* article lamenting the state of women's rights in Jordan in the Arab revolution period states, "Women's rights have played only a limited role in demonstrations. Some female demonstrators have called for children they have had with non-Jordanian husbands to gain citizenship. While some women have been active in street protests, they have mostly focused on calls for broader economic and political changes" (Sweis 2012). In this account, calls for citizenship rights for women and children are seen as evidence of the continuing existence of women's activism. Here we see how activism that seeks women's full citizenship rights is imagined to be at odds with women's efforts for broad and systemic political and economic change. In such accounts, women, as a legal category, become essentialized and their needs become uniform, coalescing around preconceived notions of equality and reform that are restricted to the realm of the law. Their struggles for equal citizenship become divorced from various sites of struggle in which citizenship difference is deployed and enacted and in which it becomes meaningful.[15]

Thus, women's encounters with legal violence and their differential structural relationships with both citizenship and the juridical system that manages it are also homogenized (Razack 1998). Through this logic, the law appears progressive and violence-free. Gains made through the law are thus sanctioned and legitimized whereas failures to secure rights are constituted as major setbacks. Read against this critical backdrop, how might the Jordanian women's movement push for rights, legal recognitions, and legal adjustments be understood? And how has the law functioned as both a goal itself and a limit point for women's rights activism in relation to gender violence in Jordan? To address these questions, I turn to women activists' most recent encounters with article 98 and article 308 of the Jordanian Penal Code.

JURIDICAL ACTIVISM AND THE POLITICS OF MANAGED CHANGE

On October 16, 2016, King Abdullah II released his "Sixth Discussion Paper: Rule of Law and Civil State."[16] The document outlines the king's vision for political reform in the country. In this paper, the king made a connection between development, modernization, and the law, urging for the adoption and strengthening of the rule of law in the country. Shortly after the publication of this paper, he called for the forming of the Royal Committee for Developing the Judiciary and Enhancing the Rule of Law. Tasked with the role of reforming the judiciary and enhancing the rule of law in Jordan, the committee was headed by former prime minister Zaid Al Rifa'i and thirteen members-at-large selected by the king. Their main role, according to the king's appointment letter, was to devise "a comprehensive strategy to address challenges and continue efforts of development and modernisation to elevate the performance of the judiciary" (qtd in Jordan Times 2016). Four months after its royal formation, the committee submitted to the king its 282-page report, which included forty-nine specific recommendations intended to improve the judiciary and the criminal justice system, changes to thirteen laws, and four new draft laws and regulations (Human Rights Watch 2017a). In response to the report, the king vowed a swift follow-up and implementation of the submitted recommendations, claiming the judiciary to be a "'red line'" (Petra News Agency 2017).[17] Among the recommendations made by the committee regarding the Jordanian Penal Code are the repeal of article 308 and the amendment of article 98 (Report of the Royal Committee 2017). Some of the recommendations put forth by the committee were "key demands by advocacy groups and activists for decades" (*Jordan Times* 2017a).

Both article 98 and article 308 of the Jordanian Penal Code have long been subject to calls for reform from Jordanian women activists and central sites for active civil society and women-led efforts for legal change.[18] They are also the concern of a large body of scholarly inquiry that investigates the relationship between gender violence and the law.[19] While article 308 concerns itself with the crime of rape, article 98 focuses on extenuating and mitigating circumstances in a crime. Both laws have their origin in colonial French and British legal codes and have also been transplanted across the Arab world through the Egyptian Penal Code.[20] Because of the central place that these two legal statutes occupy in reifying notions about social order, honor, and morality in Jordan, they have often been lumped together in discussions of discriminatory laws and legal loopholes in the Jordanian Constitution.

Women's relationship to the law in Jordan is complicated by the fact that Jordan uses two legal systems: one drawn from European legal codes and the other from Islamic law.[21] Thus, the civil and criminal codes exist apart from Personal Status Law or codes that regulate the affairs of women in issues such as marriage, divorce, and inheritance. This distinction does not mean that the two codes operate separately from one another but that legal challenges must contend with the different sources of the law and the state's complex relationship to them. The Jordanian dual legal system, like its counterpart in other Arab nation-states, brings together "modern" law and Islamic law or *Sharia*.[22] As Catherine Warrick demonstrates, the state's implementation of these two systems is purposive, enabling it "to meet particular political ends" (2009, 44). Thus, the adoption of certain laws and their abrogation are never purely legal or political matters; rather, the law—and its inscriptions—is an ongoing process of negotiation that reflects past and ongoing struggles over social, cultural, and religious meanings and values. In Jordan, these struggles are not only the purview of civil society actors and their activist-led agendas. They are, at times, also the domain of the state and the site through which the state legitimates itself and expresses its sovereignty (Warrick 2009).

Article 98 of the Jordanian Penal Code occupies an important role in conversations about honor-related violence and is believed to be part of a trifecta of laws that include articles 340a and 340b of the penal code that collectively work to sanction the murder of women in Jordan (Sonbol 2003, 190). Article

98 of the Jordanian Penal Code states: "He who commits a crime in a fit of fury caused by the unrightful and dangerous act on the part of the victim benefits from a reduction of penalty" (No. 16, 1960). There are two important aspects to this article that are relevant to discussions of gender violence and are useful for understanding how it has been used to sanction murder in the name of honor: (1) the article provides a generalized state of anger and fury as legitimate rationale and extenuating circumstance for crime, and (2) the article employs a reversed logic of crime. Rather than placing the responsibility for the act on the person who has committed the crime, the article places the motivation of the crime on the victim for committing an undefined but nevertheless "unrightful and dangerous act." As Catherine Warrick explains, "The murder victim is essentially redefined by this law as a guilty party herself" (2009, 85). The article's vagueness around the issues of time lapse between the fit of fury and the crime's occurrence, the nature of the victim's unlawful act, and the article's gendered language have all contributed to its frequent application over more specific legal statutes such as article 340, which requires that a man catch a woman in an unlawful bed or *in flagrante delicto* in order to be eligible for a reduced sentence, a standard that is exceptionally difficult to achieve (Warrick 2009). In her work on honor crime laws, legal scholar Lama Abu Odeh argues that, because of its more general nature, article 98 has been applied to honor killings since 1964 and that it has "[paved] the way to a body of decisions that have since then come to define the parameters of the crime of honor until our present day" (2010, 925). While article 98 does not single out those who commit honor crimes to be beneficiaries of reduced sentences, it has been used to exonerate men who murder women.

In her influential writing on the honor crime in Jordan, Abu Odeh (2011) argues that the locus of the honor crime in the Jordanian Penal Code exists in article 340. Abu Odeh provides a genealogy of this code, tracing its roots to both the Ottoman Penal Code of 1858 and the French Penal Code of 1810. Abu Odeh shows how this article works to provide a "legal intervention" on the part of national legislators to regulate the "private violence of honor killings" (17). As Abu Odeh demonstrates, the mitigating excuse in article 340 provides a husband who surprises his wife or a close female relative in an "unlawful bed" with another person, and kills, injures, or harms either or both of them a reduced sentence for the specific reason of adultery. Abu Odeh notes the specificity of the mitigating circumstance delineated in the article and likens the killing of a woman *in flagrante delicto* to a crime of passion. She then shows how Jordanian legislators ignored this article in favor of article 98, which provides a "general provision" to men who commit what are known as crimes of honor (22). Under this provision, reduced sentences are provided to men who harm or murder women "in a fit of fury caused by an unrightful and dangerous act on the part of the victim" (qtd in Abu Odeh 2011, 19). This switch from the specific legal provision against the crime of passion to the general legal provision of the crime of honor is historicized in careful ways in Abu Odeh's work. Her argument favors the return to the specific legal provision of article 340, writing that "if indeed the demand to completely abolish crimes of honor by severely punishing their perpetrators is unrealistic, this article argues that these crimes, in so far as their legal sanction is concerned, should be reduced to those of passion" (2011, 3).

Challenges to article 98 have a long history in the country and are part and parcel of decades-long efforts to end gender violence and crimes of honor in Jordan. Stefanie Eileen Nanes (2003) traces political activity against honor violence in Jordan back to the 1980s. She commends the work of journalist Rana Husseini in the *Jordan Times* for bravely and diligently reporting on honor-related crimes in the country since 1994, work that she continues to do today.[23] In her article, Nanes shows how both state and nonstate actors collaborated to confront these crimes, demonstrating how the king, as early as 1998, had instructed his then prime minister 'Abd al-Ra'uf Rawabdeh to amend any law "that discriminates against women and inflicts injustice on them" (qtd in Nanes 2003, 119). This led the government, with the help of women's organizations such as the Jordanian National Commission for Women (JNCW), to embark on a campaign that calls for the cancellation of article 340.[24]

At the same time that state-backed efforts to end violence against women were proceeding, the women-led Campaign to Eliminate So-Called Crimes of Honor was formed and began to collect signatures of Jordanians who endorsed the call to cancel article 340. The campaign managed to collect 15,000 signatures by November 1999, while the state, at the urging of the king, formed a legal committee that examined article 340 and proposed amendments to it that allow wives who catch and kill adulterous husbands to benefit from similar mitigating circumstances. In other words, rather than altogether abrogating the law, the committee embraced a "gender-equal" reformulation that expanded the license to kill those who commit sexual acts outside the bounds of marriage to both men and women. While the cabinet endorsed the suggested amendments to the article, the lower house of Parliament rejected them twice by 2000 (Clark 2006). Opponents of the amendments to article 340 believed that calls to amend the Jordanian Penal Code were a result of Western-backed efforts to control the woman's agenda in Jordan, efforts that would eventually lead to the dissolution of the Jordanian family and its honor-based culture. As Abdul Latif Arabiyat, then secretary general of the Islamic Action Front Party, would state: "We feel that whoever is leading all these campaigns to change is aimed at demoralizing our society, and the women's issue has been used by the West against the Arabs and the Muslims to push Arab women to abandon their honor and values and start acting like animals" (qtd in Nanes 2003, 125).

Echoes of this discourse would again be repeated in 2016, when women-led organizations, emboldened by the king's royal support, began calling for the repeal of article 308, which appears as part of a chapter titled "Offences Against Public Ethics and Morality." Article 308 of the Jordanian Penal Code consists of two clauses that state the following:

> 1. If a valid marriage is concluded between the perpetrator of one of the crimes provided in this Chapter and the victim, the prosecution shall be discontinued, and the execution of any sentence rendered against the perpetrator shall be stayed.
> 2. If the marriage ends with the divorce of the woman without a legitimate reason, the Prosecutor General may, before the lapse of three (3) years starting on the date of the commission of a misdemeanour, or five (5) years starting on the date of the commission of a crime, resume the prosecution of a case, and the execution of a sentence. (No. 16 of 1961)

This article sanctions legal exoneration of men who marry (and stay married to for a specific period) women they have sexually assaulted and/or raped. Purportedly intended to protect women who have been assaulted or raped, the time limit imposed by the law ends up further harming them by compelling them to remain married to the perpetrator-turned-husband for a minimum of three years from the date of the assault. The problem with this law is that it puts female survivors of assault and rape in a difficult place: they are pushed, by the very existence of this law, to accede to marriage proposals from men who have harmed them—often with disastrous results, as the tragic case of suicide by Amina Filali, a Moroccan teen who was forced to marry her rapist under a similar article in Moroccan law, clearly demonstrates (Hayoun 2013). On its surface, the law presents itself as protective of girls and women who are harmed or violated. In reality, the law protects the perpetrators who are now, through marriage, turned from rapists to husbands (Warrick 2009). Thus, the social problem of rape and sexual violence is concealed by the cloak of timed (and timely) marriage unions.

In 2015 the Sisterhood Is Global Institute (SIGI) conducted a study that found that 70 percent of Jordanians opposed the existence of article 308 (Husseini 2015). The study's findings helped back the growing momentum of civil society and women's rights activists to call for the law's repeal. In 2017, fifty-two women's and civil society organizations banded together to support the repeal of the law. Arguments favoring the repeal of the article centered on its blight on Jordanian women's rights and its tarnishing of Jordan's reputation as a modern nation-state. Support for activism against honor-based violence was inspired, in part, by the publication of a quantitative study measuring the attitudes of Jordanian adolescents toward honor killings in 2013. Conducting their study in a number of schools, researchers Manuel Eisner and Lana Ghuneim reviewed responses from 856 adolescent boys and girls studying in private and public schools in the capital Amman and measured their views on the topic. The researchers asked respondents to assess whether it was "OK for a man to kill his sister, his daughter, or his wife in the name of honor, and whether they believe that killing for honor is OK" (2013, 409). The responses they received revealed that 33.4 percent of respondents strongly agreed, showing a supportive attitude toward honor-based violence among adolescent male populations. Reproducing a troubling assumption that readily associates higher rates of violence with tradition and lesser privileged socioeconomic contexts, the study also found that boys were more likely to support the practice than girls and "that support for honor killings is more widespread amongst adolescents from poorer and more traditional family backgrounds" (413). The study's findings were reported in various international media outlets, casting a negative light on the country and adding further international pressure on Jordan to confront gender-based violence and oppose the traditional ideologies that reportedly sanction its occurrence.

In explaining his support for the repeal of the law, Member of Parliament Saleh Armouti argued that the law "contradicts the dignity of women and their humanity in our society" (qtd in Husseini 2017b). Presenting an argument in favor of the law's cancellation, Mustafa Khasawneh, Member of Parliament and Head of the House's Legal Committee, stated that "the Legal Committee supports the annulment of Article 308, because we believe there has been so much injustice caused and because we know that many criminals have been secured undeserved freedom because of it" (qtd in Al Tahat 2017). Significantly, efforts to repeal these laws received support from the government when the Jordanian General Iftaa' Department, the state branch that oversees religious issues, issued a *fatwa,* or religious opinion, against honor-based violence. The government-sanctioned statement not only declared such crimes contradictory to religious law but also went so far as to support the campaign to remove laws that offer perpetrators of the crime reduced sentences. As the document states, "Anyone who kills his relative claiming that he wants to cleanse the [family] honour is committing an act against *Sharia* and should be held accountable" (qtd in Maayeh 2016). The *fatwa* also emphasized

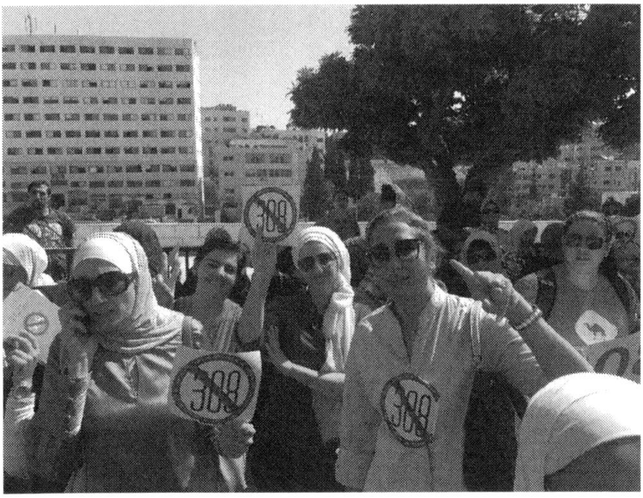

FIGURE 4. Jordanian activists protesting in Amman and calling for the abolishment of article 308. Photo provided by Samar Dudin.

the importance of the law in adjudicating such crimes, language that echoes the king's stance by insisting that "there should be no reduced sentences for a relative [who commits the crime] or if he based his actions on suspicions . . . because the judiciary is the only authority that is entitled to issue verdicts and enact them" (qtd in Maayeh 2016).

Beyond official and state-sponsored support for the cancellation of the article, it is important to note that its proponents worked collaboratively together to create the Civil Coalition to Abolish Law Article 308, which included both SIGI and the Jordanian National Commission for Women and another 100 civil society organizations from across Jordan (Al-Atiyat 2019). This coalition was buttressed by a growing movement of young, urban, and well-educated Jordanian girls and women who also endorsed this legal move. These activists and protesters form the backbone of a new and cross-sectional women's movement committed to challenging cultural conceptions of the body, honor, and morality in Jordanian society (see figure 4).

Activists protesting article 308 held signs declaring their bodies a red line, and their honors as theirs alone. They also called for legal changes that refused to appeal to notions of culture. Those who called out against the law's cancellation accused the law's opponents of representing the interests of middle-class, urbanite, and educated women divorced from the socioeconomic struggles and social pressures that victims of assault from poorer class backgrounds experience. In an argument in favor of keeping the law to protect underage victims of assault, Reem Abu Hassan, former minister of social development, argued that "'repealing the article altogether would cause a risk to the lives of women between the ages of 15 and 18 and would result in children being born without fathers in the cases of pregnancy'" (qtd in Husseini 2017c).

Echoing such concerns, Ibtesam Al-Atiyat argues that the Jordanian women activists' focus on the article's removal ignored how the existence of the law helped "couples who engage in premarital sex escape social stigma and legal persecution" (2019, 101). Al-Atiyat's position is informed by a recognition that the existence of the article had helped couples who engaged in consensual premarital sex and who wished to be married but who did not have their guardians' approval to use the law to make such marriages possible. Al-Atiyat argues that the existence of the law allowed women to compel men who impregnate them (and later on refuse to marry them) to marry them and thus guaranteed their children a legitimate future, a patriarchal lineage, and a personal status identification number in accordance with Jordanian law. Because the Jordanian Personal Status laws recognize only children born in wedlock and provides them their father's last name, lineage, and citizenship, rights foreclosed to women and their offspring, article 308 was a venue through which women could "exercise a degree of autonomy in regard to paternal authority and to marry their chosen partner, resolved children's legitimacy problems, and above all to avoid the threat of honor killing" (108). Al-Atiyat's position centers the socioeconomic context in which the existence and the removal of the law become hotly contested issues.

Here it is important to state that the efforts to repeal article 308 were mounted in tandem with a multipronged campaign that brought to the fore a discussion of gender violence and compelled a discursive and educational shift in societal views around these issues. Multiyear calls for legal change in Jordanian society could not be compelled without a broad and strong campaign that unfolded on a variety of educational platforms and that brought public attention to the potential harms of such laws and their abrogation of women's rights. For example, in *Room 308,* an educational short film supporting the cancellation of article 308, developed by SIGI and funded, in part, by USAID, societal understanding of issues of honor, reputation, and consent are examined in bold and potentially transformative ways.[25] In the short film, a young girl attending high school finds herself in a dilemma when a rejected neighborhood admirer attempts to force himself into her family's house in the absence of parental guardians. In the process, the girl prevents the man from physically entering her home, but, in an effort to compel a conversation between them, he rips her school dress. Alerted to the commotion caused by the encounter, an elderly neighbor and some young women rush to investigate the incident. Repeatedly asserting that nothing had happened and that the girl had simply misunderstood him, the man is taken aside and beaten by men in the neighborhood while the girl is dragged to the hospital against her will by the concerned neighbors. There, the elderly woman neighbor insists that she be examined by a doctor to confirm whether a sexual encounter had taken place between the girl and her assailant and whether the girl had retained her virginity. This is done in spite of the girl's repeated pleas against the examination and her insistence that she was a virgin. In the hospital, while the girl undergoes the physical virginity examination, the girl's uncle and a lawyer representing the man's family meet to discuss a possible resolution to the problem; the lawyer reminds the girl's uncle, who is seeking his "right as stated by law," that article 308 states that the "girl gets wed and the man gets out of jail." The lawyer uses the language of *sutr* instead of marriage when speaking about the girl's impending nuptials, implying that her honor and reputation would be restored through the act of marriage. The deal is sealed between the lawyer and the girl's uncle, who agrees on a *mahr* amount of 25,000 Jordanian Dinars in order to "disarm the whole situation."[26]

While the girl's virginity is corroborated by her mother and the examining physician, she is nevertheless compelled to marry her rejected suitor in order to preserve her family's honor and thus her own. The film ends in a scene that takes place a year after the incident, where the girl, lying on a bed and visibly pregnant and alone, daydreams about her former life as a schoolgirl while her aimless husband continues to chase women on the street. The short film, which was shared online and viewed by over 11,000 people on YouTube, represents the unfairness of such laws and their impact on girls and women from impoverished social backgrounds; it demonstrates, through an example drawn from real life, how the law can work to pressure girls into matrimony against their wills and best interests. The film thus visually represents a central slogan in the campaign launched by SIGI against article 308, which states, "Article 308 does not protect honor; it protects the perpetrator" (see figure 5).

While I am unable to assess audience reaction to the film or its broad impact on societal views on such topics, what its creation makes clear is the breakdown of certain social taboos: the film boldly represents the young girl as a victim of a rejected suitor who is also cast as an indolent youth, a young man who has no goals except the chasing of girls and women and their pursuit and sexual harassment. This casting helps establish the girl as an innocent victim of both social circumstance and the law. The girl's uncle, who violently slaps her, and makes a financial profit from the situation, and compels her to marry the man she has refused, is also presented in a negative light. In

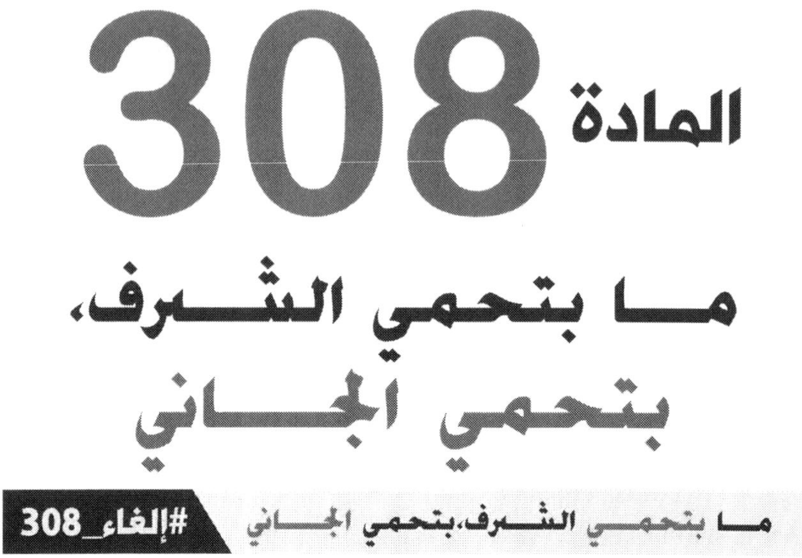

FIGURE 5. Banner from Abolish 308 Campaign. Image courtesy of the Jordanian National Commission for Women.

showcasing how the law can be used to compel an undesirable future for the young women, the film's creators highlight the law's capacity to cause social harm and ill. These facets index a conversational shift that, without directly confronting the various patriarchal logics that curtail a woman's freedoms and subject her to social and physical harm, takes aim at such resolutions and their buttressing through the site of the law. In that way, the film offers a social critique that brings to the fore the dangerous entanglements of the legal and social domains, especially in relation to sex and sexuality. Although the film skirts the issue of consensual sex versus rape, the filmmakers nevertheless emphasize the law's removal as a potential remedy to the social problem it presents.

Despite the film's support of efforts to revoke the law, it is important to remember that the debate surrounding the law's removal has reinforced what Lamis El Muhtaseb, Nathan J. Brown, and Abdul-Wahab Kayyali describe as a sharp "polarization of politics in many Arab societies, on full and even violent display since the uprisings of 2011" (2016, 721). As the authors demonstrate, these divisions are most visible around issues surrounding women's rights, where, they argue, two camps exist. On one side of the debate are those who "anchor their arguments in Islamic legal thought" and, on the other, are "those who turn instead to liberal conceptions of rights, sometimes relying on international human rights instruments" (721). Although I agree with the authors on their characterization of the polarized discourse that exists in Jordan in relation to gender issues, I want to suggest that the debates surrounding article 308 do not simply create neat divisions between Islamic law and international law that position their respective champions and adherents into two distinct and separate camps. Rather, these debates reassert the centrality of the law as an arbiter of Jordanian women's rights and guarantor of their safety for members on both sides of the political aisle whose difference in opinion, while strong, is sutured through their attachment to the law as a source of justice. In other words, these debates stake for the law (and thus the state) an unparalleled power to determine the course of women's political, social, and cultural struggles against gender violence in Jordan. How does this turn to the law re-empower and reify the state's significance in everyday life? In what ways does the regulation of gender violence become yet another domain in which the Jordanian state gets to remake itself as modern, enlightened, and prowomen?

JURIDICAL REFORM AND STATE-CENTRIC ACTIVISM

In their efforts to combat honor-related violence, women's rights groups have repeatedly called for the removal of article 98 from the Jordanian Penal Code (Faqir 2001). Adopting a tough-on-crime approach, women's groups have linked the frequent rates of occurrence of honor-based violence to the leniency of Jordanian penal codes used to prosecute these crimes. In particular, women's rights activists have maintained that legal codes that offer reduced sentences to perpetrators of such crimes (such as articles 340 and 98) effectively embolden men to harm or kill women and are thus to blame for the rising rates of violence against women in Jordanian society. To address the problem of gender violence, activists have thus focused their efforts on targeting state legislations to put an end to violence against women.[27] In Jordan, this view is often represented by leaders in women's rights organizations. Commenting on the frequent occurrence of honor-based violence in Jordan, Aseel Abu Albandora, a project coordinator at the Jordanian Women's Union, states that ending honor-based violence is "a matter of changing the law. If 'honour' crimes are clearly illegal then it will raise awareness and people will know they can't get away with it" (qtd in Cuthbert 2017). Here, ending violence against women is attached to the site of the law, which is configured as the marker of both what is legal or illegal and what is socially right or wrong. Legal changes are assumed to automatically signal to would-be perpetrators that the crimes would be dealt with severely in the courts and that fear of legal consequences would thus inhibit men from committing violence against women. Absent from such consideration is the social context in which these crimes occur and are sanctioned.

In 2017, in a landmark ruling against two brothers who had poisoned their sister and then claimed she had committed suicide, the Jordanian Cassation Court effectively doubled their jail sentences, increasing them from seven and ten years to fifteen and twenty years. In explaining his decision, Judge Mohammad Tarawneh stated, "We want to send a strong message to the people that killing women in the name of family honor will no longer be tolerated by our court and we chose Mother's Day to send this message" (qtd in Husseini 2017a). In response to the verdict, SIGI said that "it was a victory for women who are victims of violence and murder" (Husseini 2017a). The legal changes introduced have also authorized the adoption of tougher sentences for repeat offenders. Celebrations of legal reforms that focus on increasing the length and severity of punishment demonstrates the limits of a feminist framework that aligns itself with what Bernstein has named a "carceral worldview" that seeks juridical and punitive remedies to social problems (2012, 237).[28]

In an interview focused on the meaning of the repeal of article 308 and the revisions to article 98, Member of Parliament Wafa Bani Mustafa celebrated these accomplishments, commending their ability to deny "legal cover to perpetrators" and to send a strong message to Jordanian society:

> I think that changing the legislation is a vital part of changing society . . . The message we're sending to society is a correct one, that builds on the issue of equality—that equality is the right of the whole society. If they are not punished, they will do it again. We have managed to protect women and now it is the job of the state to protect and support these women, to provide care and empowerment for them and to work on accepting them into society as victims and survivors and not as being guilty. (qtd in Tahhan 2017)

Bani Mustafa's linking of social change to legislative reform advocates for tougher-on-crime policies but does so through appeals to the liberal discourses of equality and empowerment which are central to the operations of the modern Jordanian state. As Frances Hasso has shown, such an analytic framework reflects a longer history of women and women's rights activism that "often invite[s] and appeal[s] to male-dominated states to regulate, intervene, or change the rules in sexual and family life in order to address a range of problems and challenges, including lack of economic and other resources, political and citizenship exclusions, or intimate violence" (2014, 108). Hasso's work makes clear that such alliances always come at a certain cost, which women and marginalized constituencies from the most underprivileged socioeconomic backgrounds ultimately bear.[29]

Although Jordanian women's rights organizations celebrated their success in altering the law to support women's rights and promote equality, much less critical attention has been paid to the aforementioned changes and their role in granting the state further authority and power, including extending the ability of the state to fight gender violence through expanding its carceral state apparatuses. In a report lauding Jordan's reforms, Human Rights Watch positively described the legal changes, seeing them as a sign that Jordan was beginning to fulfill promises to deliver what Sarah Leah Whitson, Middle East director at Human Rights Watch, has labeled "real change on important issues" (qtd in Human Rights Watch 2017b). Nowhere in this celebratory account of legal reform is there a critical nod to the Jordanian state's use of women's rights to push forward the state's own political agenda, an agenda that fights gender violence through the enshrining of tough on crime legislation that expands police enforcement powers, rewrites the definitions and laws around criminality, and emboldens the state's capacity to curtail rights and freedoms. In here and elsewhere, tough on crime legislations secured by the state are automatically assumed to guarantee women's rights and safety and are thus used to shift women's understanding of justice and ability to confront gender violence away from community-based activism and other justice practices that have the potential to both exceed and potentially challenge the state.

In October 2017 the UN Human Rights Committee met to discuss Jordan's periodic report and its implementation of the provisions of the International Covenant on Civil and Political Rights (2017). Speaking to the committee, Saja Majali, the Permanent Representative of Jordan to the United Nations Office at Geneva, noted her country's commitment to comprehensive legal reforms and its intention to "promote human rights in all fields of life." While lauding the many achievements of the government in areas of human rights, including the removal of article 308 from the Penal Code, the committee of experts responding to the Jordanian report questioned the efficacy of law enforcement officials in dealing with cases of domestic violence. They also noted that the practice of "protective custody" of women "had not ended, leading to administrative detention of women threatened with marital or family violence" (2017). In response to the questioning by experts regarding Jordan's commitment to ending gender-based violence and protecting women who are at risk of it, the Jordanian representative noted that "the Government aimed to strengthen shelters for women and the provision of legal aid to victims of domestic violence or trafficking. Shelters did not entail any form of administrative detention" (2017).

The issue of protective custody has been central to discussions of legal reforms pertaining to gender violence in Jordan. *Protective custody* refers to the government practice of remanding to indefinite custody in Jordanian jails women who are at a risk of or who fear family retaliation in the name of honor. Jade Glenister argues that the key features of protective custody

> are detention in prison: not in accordance with national law; following the determination of a non-judicial state authority that a woman is at risk of harm; which may be prolonged and is likely to be in definite; and which may lead to severe feelings of despair and hopelessness because of the inability to be released, the lack of control over the risk of being released to the possibility of harm and due to the fact of being detained itself. (2016, 20)

Protective custody is a practice that is in contravention of international agreements and one that is applied in accordance with the will of a state-appointed employee with unchecked power to interpret and implement the law. In 2004 Human Rights Watch reported on the practice of protective custody by interviewing police, government officials, and four women held in the Jordanian Jweideh Women's Correctional and Rehabilitation Centre. The report sought to shed light on gender violence in Jordan and paid particular attention to the period of imminent danger and threat that precedes honor-based violence or an honor killing and in which women at risk of this violence typically resort to the state for protection from their male relatives. This period has been described by Nadera Shalhoub-Kevorkian as "living on death row, always in fear of execution," a condition that "results in an inability to live and is a major part of the death process" (2003, 581). In response to such fears, the Jordanian state resorted to the practice of detaining the women who live in fear of violence and murder, moving them to spaces of indefinite carcerality and imprisonment.

Jordanian officials interviewed about this practice rationalized the move to imprison women who fear being harmed or killed rather than detaining the men they fear by stating that the government responds to a woman who is threatened and that they want to do something to help protect her from the threat of potential harm. While they recognize that issuing threats against a woman's life could be considered illegal, they nevertheless maintain that the police "cannot arrest a man because of his intentions" (qtd in Human Rights Watch 2004, 12). Even if the threats appear credible in the eyes of state officials, the move to imprison women into safety is rationalized by a concern that imprisonment of a male relative who has threatened to harm a woman may increase the likelihood that she will be harmed or killed after his release. The state thus uses the fear of retaliation to deny women their right to freedom. This situation has led the Jordanian government to place women at risk of gender-based violence in prisons, where they are held in periods of indefinite detention that can stretch for as long as thirteen years in one reported case (Baker and Søndergaard 2014). In one case, reported in interviews with women held in custody, one formerly incarcerated woman stated that she was held in custody for twenty-two years after witnessing the murder of her sister by members of her family.[30]

Protective custody has received ample attention in media accounts of gender violence in Jordan. Reports of its occurrence and frequency vary, with some suggesting that "an estimated 65 percent of more than 1,700 female inmates in Jordan's prisons" are being held under administrative detention (Thompson 2017). Administrative detention is sanctioned under Jordanian law by reference to the 1954 Crime Prevention Law. This law allows a state representative to initiate legal proceedings against someone who is "about to commit a crime or assist in its commission" or someone whose freedom constitutes a danger to the public (Human Rights Watch 2009). In the case of detaining women fleeing potential cases of gender-based violence, the law is activated in the name of maintaining the woman's personal safety. This form of mandatory protection is administered by a government-appointed official (a governor) who has the authority to reprimand and remand women to custody. When a woman seeks protection from the state, the governor stipulates that the woman either agrees to leave the prison or jail in the company of her male guardian (usually a father or a brother or an uncle) or, in a less frequent scenario, agrees to an arranged marriage to an appropriate male suitor of the governor's choosing (Rimaz Musa 2015).[31] The troubling options put before women often lead them to choose remaining "voluntarily" in jail over the risk of being released into the custody of male guardians who may harm them in the future or who have threatened to harm them in the past.

The issue of extensive and unchecked power that the administrative governors hold over women's lives in these cases is explored in an interview conducted by Rimaz Musa from the online Jordanian website *7iber* with Hijazi Assad, a Jordanian governor.[32] In the interview, Musa inquires about the mechanisms that the governor uses in determining whether a woman can be safely released to male guardians. Before a woman who is held in protective custody is released to a male guardian, the governor insists on having the guardian sign an agreement that guarantees that he will pay a certain financial penalty if the girl or woman is harmed after her release. Despite tying a person's safety to a financial guarantee that is hardly ever recuperated even in the event of a woman's murder, the governor states that when a person is determined to harm a woman, such guarantees will not prevent him from doing so. The governor explains that he uses his hunch, ferocity, and guidance from God to assess whether a person intends to harm a woman or not and that he correctly assesses whether to release a woman to her male guardians or not about 99 percent of the time. The governor also explains that removing protective custody will harm society and that ending such practices at the urging of international human rights organizations would make it unsafe for everyone to leave their homes. In the governor's language, women who are at risk of being violated are themselves reconstituted as a threat to the communities in which they live. Their removal, therefore, is configured as a guarantee of their safety (Musa 2015).

Writing on protective custody in Jordan, Afaf Jabiri notes that "by failing to protect women from crimes or abuses, the state defines the notion of protection according to the normative framework of gender order that favors protecting family and kinship relations over women's interests and protection" (2016, 163). Jabiri explains how patriarchal codes work in tandem with state interests in maintaining order to produce a concept like "protective custody," a notion that safeguards and enables men's ability to manage women's futures through the legal domain. In her study on guardianship in Jordan, Jabiri interviews both government officials and women held in custody in Jordanian jails to better understand this phenomenon. Jabiri finds that the imprisoning of women in the name of honor "complicates their release, places them in more vulnerable positions, and also draws attention away from the state's involvement in protecting male authority over women" (166). In an interview conducted with Nadia Shamrouk, the General Director of Jordanian Women's Union, Jabiri learns that "the government is not serious in finding a solution for those women because it does not see them as victims but rather criminals of the social values" (qtd in Jabiri, 167). Women who fear gender violence are stigmatized by the law as criminals who must be separated from an otherwise healthy society that, if they are released into, they may harm and infect.

Jordanian women activists have publicly denounced the practice of protective custody, drawing attention to both its illegality and its inhumane consequences for women who are detained. In 2016 Eva Abu Halaweh, the executive director of Mizan Law Group, an organization that has spearheaded the efforts to end this practice, argued that "administrative governors violate the law when they detain women who are under the threat of murder by their families, those who are tortured at home or those who flee their homes" (Al Emam 2016).[33] In response to growing local and international pressure against administrative custody, the Jordanian government established a center to house women who are fleeing gender violence. Speaking on the government's decision, Mohammad Ensour, a representative from the Ministry of Justice, stated that "we all know that there are some women whose lives are under threat by their families for reasons related to 'family honour,' and we are committed locally and internationally to finding an alternative and a dignified solution for them" (qtd in Husseini 2016a). At the time of its opening, the center housed a maximum of fifty women, and the women who were admitted had to have no prior criminal record. Deploying a securitized discourse, Ensour states that the center will "mainly receive new cases, mostly of women who are absent from home, and anyone wanting to visit them will need a special security permission" (qtd in Husseini 2016c).

In late 2018 the Ministry for Social Development, with the support of various local and transnational non-government organizations, opened *Dar Amneh,* the House of Safety, to help women at risk of violence find temporary refuge and build new lives. The project has received positive media attention and is the result of civil society efforts and government commitment to reform laws pertaining to gender-based violence (Luck 2018). Women admitted to *Dar Amneh* are free to leave after being made aware of the risks associated with their voluntary departure. At the center, women receive assistance from social workers and may also use their time to develop skills they can use after their release in order to gain employment and income. Responding to the news that the government would open the center, executive director of the Sisterhood Is Global Institute (SIGI), Munir Idaibes, stated that "protective custody is a method that compounds the suffering of these women" and that contributes to "the deprivation of their freedom and their exposure to many risks, including intermingling with inmates with different criminal records" (qtd in Prieto 2018). At stake in such statements is an investment in a carceral logic that distinguishes vulnerable citizens from criminalized ones. As Raghda Azzeh, the social worker in charge of the center, stated, "Our aim is to ensure a temporary residency for these women and for them to be independent" (qtd in Husseini 2018). Such discourse reveals a desire to save *good* victims of gender violence from *bad* and criminalized women and to reconstitute the former in the service of socioeconomic reform and social development through the social apparatuses of the state.

CONCLUSION: JUSTICE AT ITS LEGAL LIMITS

The context of managed legal reform and activism around the site of the law discussed above is crucial for understanding the relationship between the realms of the law and women's activism in Jordan. To further demonstrate how struggles over rights that hinge on legal change can sometimes falter in attaining justice for women, I return briefly to the latest legal reforms to repeal article 308 in the Jordanian Penal Code. As previously discussed, article 308 exists as part of a chapter that identifies a number of "offences against honor." Together, this chapter defines and limits the meaning of rape to an act against "Public Ethics and Morality." Article 292 in the chapter describes rape in the following way: "any person who has forced sexual intercourse with a female, other than his wife, shall be sentenced to at least five (5) years of temporary hard labour." As currently written, the law thus exempts forced intercourse within marital relationships from the charge of rape.

As a report by the Arab Renaissance for Democracy and Development (ARDD) argues, the law renders rape occurring outside the bounds of marriage to be a societal crime, "an attack against *public ethics* and *honor* rather than a violation of the *bodily integrity* and *sexual autonomy* of the victim" (2017, 2; emphasis in original). The law takes issue with forced sexual intercourse because it threatens the "honor" of the community at large. Nowhere in its current wording does the law discuss the coercive nature of rape, nor does the law discuss the right of the survivor herself to a fair or just trial. Instead, the law creates a discursive condition that renders rape beyond the pale of the socially imaginable by "vanishing" its victim through marriage (Warrick 2005). Understood this way, it becomes clear that article 308 is an extension of a legal system that prizes social order over the rights of women by disappearing "the crucial distinction between rape and sexual intercourse with consent" (ARDD 2017, 2).

While the removal of article 308 certainly ensures that "such crimes can undergo proper investigation, prosecution and punishment of perpetrators," the exact impact of its removal will not be determined quickly or easily (ARDD 2017, 2). Its champions' stated goals to have rape charges be properly investigated, prosecuted, and punished are worthwhile and may even lead to a broader discussion about the meaning of forced and nonconsensual sex in Jordanian society. It could also lead to a rethinking of the meaning of terms such as *honor, culture,* and *the body,* terms that the law inscribes through its various stated and hidden assumptions about sexuality and social order. It is important also to recognize that, in addition to exercising the state's right to define rape and sexual assault in ways that are both limiting and limited, the law requires its own sets of proof of physical violence. Evidence that, once demanded, may place additional burdens on women who have been raped and sexually violated, especially those unable to acquire adequate legal representation or to come forward for fear of community reprisal and public shaming.

Simply stated, my work contests celebratory accounts of legal victories that readily moor women's struggle against gender violence in juridical change that is administered by state officials and that is tied exclusively to the domain of the legal. It argues that efforts to end gender violence in Jordan, including rape and honor-related violence, cannot only be fueled by activism that begins and ends at the site of the law. What happens to victims of gender violence who cannot avail themselves of the law, its legal instruments, and its discursive practices? What happens to their right to justice outside the domain of the legal? While efforts to confront discriminatory laws are significant in shaping the current wave of the women's movement in Jordan and its ability to reform state law, I am reluctant to believe that hinging such struggles on the law alone, especially when the law is so carefully administered and managed by the state, can bring an end to gender violence against women. This critical view of the law seeks neither to admonish its champions nor to diminish the significance of their historic successes. Rather, it seeks to bring attention to a historical conjuncture in which the fight against gender violence in general, and the so-called honor crime in particular in its different manifestations, has been annexed in the service of the state.

AFTERWORD

Intersectional Feminism and the Politics of Hope and Solidarity

THIS BOOK presented a genealogy of honor crime discourse, tracing how it emerged and the shifts and turns it has taken in the past few decades. My study has sought to show that the honor crime discourse, as a governing rhetoric, travels from one place to another in ways that are not controllable and that are attached to laden rhetorics and to distinct but overlapping materialities. In their travels from one place to another, honor crime discourses construct meanings and shape local and transnational debates surrounding a variety of issues such as migration, citizenship, and nation-state building. I have focused my analysis on the multiple and competing narratives that underpin our conception of this crime, its scale, and its magnitude in order to explore how the singular focus on honor-based violence has restructured how we think about violence and its various manifestations at the physical, psychological, structural, and rhetorical/discursive levels. In tracing the workings of this discourse in a number of geopolitical contexts, I have shown how its movements contribute to the shaping of our understanding of gender violence, the development of antiviolence strategies, and the structuring and delimiting of what can and cannot be done to end gender violence.

Gender Violence and the Transnational Politics of the Honor Crime provides an interdisciplinary approach to the discourses of honor-based violence. I have specifically chosen to focus on a number of interconnected geographic contexts in order to tell a more complex story about the intricacies of defining and contesting gender-based violence. These stories are inherently only partial and neither cover the multiplicity of stories that exist within each of these specific contexts, nor do they exhaust the range of possible interpretations. In discussing multiple, intersecting, and even competing approaches to gender violence in distinct but interconnected local contexts, this book charts how particular forms of violence come into focus in certain historical conjunctures, how attention to the honor crime rises, shifts, or wanes. In attending to the ebbs and flows of this discourse and its circuitries and circulations, I have also explored the various meanings that the honor crime constructs to narrate a story about violence that attends to its multiple iterations. The book thus examines honor-based violence as a modern form of violence that is immersed in particular political and historical contexts, refuting ahistorical claims about its occurrence, scope, or frequency. Rather than read the honor crime as a set, given, or determined form of violence, I have sought to show how it emerges as a legal, social, political, and discursive category whose meaning shifts and alters over time and space. In this work, the honor crime is read in relation to, and not apart from, other forms of violence, including the violence of migration, colonialism, imperialism, and modernity.

In her writing on the politics of sex trafficking, Jennifer Suchland suggests that we read the category of "violence against women" in a way that allows us "to see the inherent incompleteness of the term in order to contextualize violence and strike at the multidimensionality of racial, class, sexual, gendered, able-bodied, and national hierarchies" (2015, 188). Suchland argues that while the category of violence against women does convey particular meanings, "it should not convey a set understanding of why that violence happens, how it is constituted, what remedies are appropriate, and how to prevent it" (188). In tracing the various meanings and genealogies of honor crime discourses, I have similarly sought to unsettle the set understandings that have been attached to the honor crime discourse and thus to reveal the wide range of political, social, and legal work that has been done in its name. I have worked to trouble its representations in public and official discourses and to analyze the confrontation circuits it has generated and continues to produce. Unsettling the dominant stories of honor crime discourses requires (dis)assembling and analyzing a multiplicity of texts that help construct and buttress them, to trace the many actors who narrate them, and to uncover some of the preset assumptions they emphasize or downplay. It also requires recognizing one's own complicity in the discourses that are produced and cohered around this form of violence. This is why this work has brought together ideas, representations, and practices that are not often read relationally and that are seldom put in conversation with one another.

In her discussion of honor-based violence and the dilemmas it poses to feminist scholarship and activism, Lila Abu-Lughod argues that "the honor crime poses perhaps more starkly than any other contemporary category the dilemmas of feminist scholarship and rights activism in a transnational world" (2011, 17). My study of honor crime discourses in the four contexts of the US, Canada, Palestine, and Jordan reveals precisely why the honor crime's classification as a singular and exceptional form of violence is beset with difficulties and how it continues to both inspire and regulate how we can speak on and contest gender violence in its various manifestations. Studies on the honor crime seldom attend to the transnational circulations of these discourses and instead focus on how they operate in singular locations and contexts. Thus, we often miss how the singularized discourses surrounding the honor crime travel from one place to another and how the arguments they present "network to wider contexts such as historical discourses, geopolitics, global economics, and cultural expectations" (Dingo 2012, 145). By analyzing the circuitous travels of these discourses from and in between different sites and the various politics to which they become appended, I use a transnational and intersectional feminist analytic framework that troubles distinctions between what is local and what is global, revealing both the emplaced and the displaced effects of dominant representations of the honor crime.

Because the category of the honor crime is changing and often eludes definitional consensus, my work focuses on the varieties of violence that are invoked under its name. In this work, I view the category of the honor crime as a set of signs and practices that carries multiple referential meanings and that, through its deployments, constructs particular material realities that travel from one place to another. As Laura Shepherd has observed, "Discursive practices maintain, construct, constitute, legitimate, resist and suspend meaning" (2018, 21). Over the past few decades, dominant discourses on the honor crime have solidified, treating this violence as a particular kind of violence against women and a marker of a unique or excessive form of gender violence. This process encodes (and is in turn encoded by) a set of interlocking racialized and classed discourses and assumptions. As a result, the violence of the honor crime has been scripted as the violence of the other or as an othered violence. The excess of signification underlying dominant honor crime discourses renders it co-optable by a wide variety of political formations, and the discourse's othering function dovetails with demands that bolster the regulatory powers of nation-states, as we have seen in the context-specific analysis provided in this work. In shifting my focus to a multisited and multitextual discursive analysis of the honor crime, I reveal both the obvious, immediate effects of these discourses and the hidden, long-term consequences of their circulations. While this analysis helped broaden my understanding of the diffuse and transnational grammars of dominant honor crime discourses, this study does not purport to cover all its manifestations or to anticipate the new ways in which it will operate in the future. Needless to say, my discussion of honor crime discourses in the four separate but interconnected sites that this book has examined does not exhaust the ways in which this discourse continues to circulate within the particular sites of analysis and beyond them and how its circulations exceed the mappings provided herein.

Attending to the transnational iterations of hegemonic honor crime discourses requires acknowledging the concept's constant ability to gain new meanings, to reshape how we think about gender violence and how we come to envision and enact an end to it. In assessing the multiple uses of the honor killing and honor crime discourses, I do not refute the existence of gender violence; nor do I contest that certain physical, emotional, and psychic violations are planned, executed, and invoked under the name of "honor." Instead, I point to the difficulties that the hegemonic honor crime discourses give rise to and the ways in which they serve to constrain intersectional analyses of gender violence that can attend to its economic, social, political, and racial imbrications. At stake in this study is not simply how gender-based violence is defined but also how certain definitions, and their embrace and uptake, inform what is recognized as violence and how it is contested. If our goal is to end gender violence in all its forms, then we may need to envision activism against violence that attends to the imbrications of this discourse in different and interconnected forms of violence. We may wish to develop an alternative language or discourse more capable of attending to the overlapping—and also the competing—interests of communities across national and transnational divides. This new language must constantly be grounded in what Nadje Al-Ali has described as a "historical approach" that acknowledges and troubles the politics of positionality and "reveals the complex interplay of inter- and transnational, regional, national and local factors in shaping the specific political economies and socio-historical contexts in which sexual violence might become more widespread" (2018, 23).

In seeking ways to confront gender violence that do not reproduce the troubling limits of dominant honor crime discourses, I turn to a recent and contemporary example of activism against gender violence that enacts politically conscious and radical feminist praxis. In late summer 2019, the story of Israa Ghareeb's murder went global, eliciting wide condemnation from various groups and constituencies and calls for the ending of violence against women. A twenty-one-year-old Palestinian makeup artist, Israa was beaten to death by members of her family. The supposed crime that led to her violent murder was her sharing of a selfie with her fiancé on social media that affronted her family's "honor." Outraged by her ostensible social trespass, members of Israa's family beat her, rendering her immobile from a spinal injury that may have paralyzed her. While recovering at the hospital, she was again attacked, and an audio recording of the incident was captured by a worker there and later shared on social media (Hawari 2019). Israa died at her family's house, reportedly from a stroke (Abueish 2019). In response to the media outrage over Israa's murder, her family claimed that her spinal injuries were caused by her falling from a building because she was possessed by *jinn,* or evil spirits, or because she struggled with her mental health. The family claimed that her death was not caused by any wrongdoing on their part but was the result of "natural" causes of voluntarily falling from a building. With mounting pressure on the Palestinian Authority to investigate the crime, its attorney general, Akram Al-Khatim, held a news conference on September 12, 2019, to report on the reasons for Israa's death, which he claimed was caused by "respiratory failure as a result of serious injuries from domestic violence" (Begum 2019).

The public and broad condemnation of Israa's murder has rendered apparent a Palestinian refusal to either normalize or exceptionalize such violence under the guise of "honor." By rejecting the family's claim to innocence and their attempt to demonize Israa as a possessed or deranged youth, Palestinian society at large interrupted a narrative framework that blames survivors and victims of gender violence for their experiences and encounters with patriarchal violence (PC 2019). Palestinian society also refused to take for granted the findings of the Palestinian Authority regarding Israa's murder, pointing instead to the complicity and imbrication of state apparatuses under colonial rule in exacerbating and enabling violence against Palestinian women. In simultaneously denying both Israa family's and the Palestinian Authority's claims to innocence and by refusing their explanatory frameworks, Palestinian society showed its understanding of the imbricated workings of patriarchy at the familial and the national levels. Instead of normalizing these narratives, activists chose to celebrate Israa's life, her dreams of becoming a famous makeup artist, and her resilience in the face of physical beatings and family oppression that was either ignored or concealed by authorities. By registering their collective and national outrage, Palestinians were united in their opposition to acts of violence that target the lives of girls and women. This communal stance extended a recognition that gender violence is a social and a political problem impacting Palestinian society as a whole, one that cannot be silenced, tolerated, or ignored. On social media sites, an image of Israa Ghareeb was repeatedly shared within Palestine and transnationally, calling for justice for her murder and insisting that "We Are All Israa" and demanding "Justice for Israa." Despite the limitations of such claims to the oneness of embodied experience or a shared commonality, they nevertheless register acknowledgment of the importance of collective confrontations of gender violence in all its manifestations.

The collective condemnation of the murder of Israa Ghareeb would mobilize thousands of Palestinian women from across Palestinian cities and in the diaspora to march against gender and patriarchal violence in occupied and colonial contexts. This action took place in response to a call issued by *Tal3at,* a collective of nonpartisan and cross-generational Palestinian feminists from across historic Palestine determined to end gender violence and to reclaim public space. The name of the movement can be translated as "rising up" or "coming out," implying a refusal to read such violence as primarily private matters, separate from the public sphere, and the centering of an intersectional and grounded analytic framework of gender violence. The call they issued thus invited Palestinians from all walks of life to march in feminist solidarity under the collective banner "No Free Homeland Without Free Women" and against the fragmented archipelago of Palestinian life (Marshood and Alsanah 2020).

In their broad calls for mobilization and struggle, the *Tal3at* collective centers an analytical framework that readily places violence against women within a historical framework deeply attuned to the structures of patriarchy and colonialism and their intersectional imbrications. This approach neither separates the national struggle from gender politics nor reproduces a troubling hierarchical order of decolonial priorities. Rather, it foregrounds issues of gender violence as intimately linked to liberatory struggles not only in the public and the legal spheres but also in the spaces of the intimate and the personal. As Hala Marshood (2019) rightly notes, *Tal3at* insists that the murder of women and the politics of patriarchy that enable such acts are not "personal matters or isolated criminal cases; they are part of a deeply rooted social condition embedded in entire systems of violence and corruption, and in turn, they should matter to every Palestinian woman and man."

At the demonstrations that took place across Palestine, activists from a range of political and social backgrounds carried signs denouncing all forms of violence directed toward women. Linking Palestinian anticolonial and national liberation with the freedom of women, demonstrators called for the end of gender violence, carrying signs that celebrate women as revolutionaries and that confront men's silence in the face of increased attacks on women's bodies (see figure 6). Defiantly reclaiming the public space as a site of radical protest where women's issues are made central to the Palestinian struggle, the demonstrators brought to the fore a type of analysis that rejects the siloing

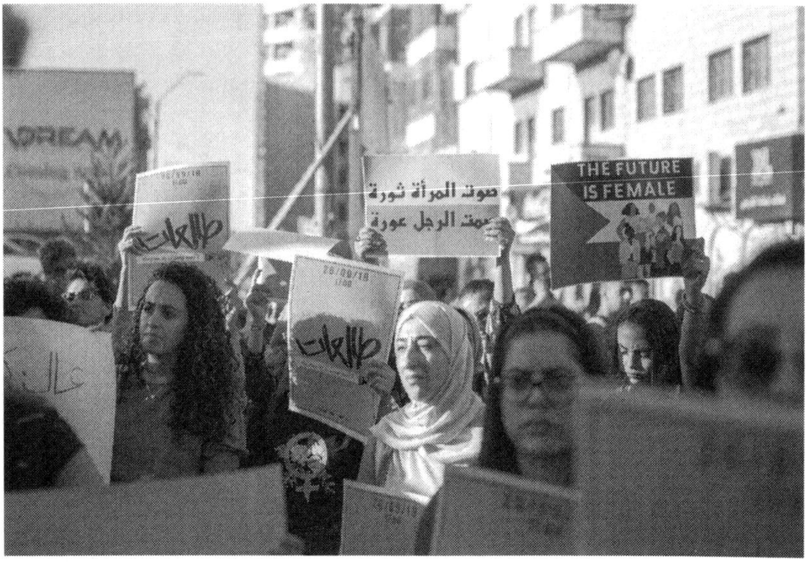

FIGURE 6. Image from *Tal3at* March in Ramallah on September 26, 2019. Photo courtesy of Sharif Mosa.

of gender struggles and oppressions and their unbinding from the socioeconomic and political national contexts of their occurrence. In this way, the movement does not call for superficial or cosmetic legal reforms or policy changes. Instead, it seeks a radical rethinking of the antiviolence agenda that readily identifies the links between multiple forms of oppression and separate but inextricable and interrelated forms of colonial and patriarchal power. Writing on what the *Tal3at* movement means for Palestinian liberation struggles, Soheir Asaad (2019) insists that it is primarily a movement that refuses fragmentary politics and analytics; it is a movement about the right to reclaim the site of the political by centering people's lived experiences. As she states, "In the dominant and crude conceptualization of national politics, personal and private injustices are afterthoughts. However, people's lived experiences are the essence of liberation and should be at the core of any political thought and action that is authentic, just, and liberatory. We should transform these scattered personal stories into a collective story of oppressive matrices that engenders a political analysis to simultaneously understand and fight against these systems." Asaad's inspiring call to action and accountability from men and those who separate the political from the personal reminds us of the power of a feminist movement premised on notions of justice that far exceed the domains of the legal and that seek, instead, "a new definition of national liberation in Palestine" (2019). Without exonerating Palestinian society of its responsibility to oppose gender violence, this activism demands an intersectional and transnational feminist analysis of gender violence informed by an attention to the politics of place and space.

I want to end this book with the feminist activist efforts of the *Tal3at* movement because they offer a concrete and hopeful example of how to contest iterations of gender violence rooted in social, moral, and cultural patriarchal codes. In this example, activists present a complex understanding of gender and sexual violence that attends to its specificities, that takes collective responsibility for its occurrence, and that refuses state co-optations of such efforts. This activism helps put into place an antiviolence agenda attuned to the violence of discourse and the discourse of violence. It shows how communities define their own agendas for fighting violence and how they work collectively to develop a politics and an ethics for confronting gender and sexual violence in ways that are informed by their own experiences, commitments, and encounters. Their work exemplifies how a political approach to ending gender violence, including violence that targets women and those whose lives exist at the sites of multiple marginalities, can attend to both the intimate and the structural conditions that cause it. By centering a politics of feminist solidarity in antiviolence agendas and campaigns, such activist efforts remind us of the power of collective action and the urgent need for transnational praxis that crosses the borders of the nation-state and challenges its assumed centrality to gender justice agendas, thus making communities between and among people from different and varying experiences, positionalities, and political orientations. My hope is that ongoing intersectional contestations of gender violence, including violence carried out in the name of honor, becomes identified as honor-based violence or the honor crime, can similarly hold together such material, political, structural, and discursive tensions, complexities, and im/possibilities.

NOTES

NOTES TO INTRODUCTION

1. In her 2000 report to the UN Commission on Human Rights, Asma Jahangir, the United Nations Special Rapporteur on extrajudicial, summary, or arbitrary executions, speaks directly about the practice of killing women in the name of honor and specifically mentions the role of governments in protecting women from such violence and in ensuring that all appropriate measures are taken at the legislative level to end practices that are in violation of women's human rights. The report is available here: https://digitallibrary.un.org/record/408173?ln=en#record-files-collapse-header.
2. The network describes itself as "an international digital resource centre working to advance understanding of HBV (honour based violence) and forced marriage through research, documentation, information and training for professionals who may encounter women, girls and men at risk of these forms of abuse in order to suggest good practise in responding to their needs." See http://hbv-awareness.com/about/ for more information about its goals. For access to its statistics and data section, see http://hbv-awareness.com/statistics-data/. In addition to the UN-based statistic, the organization also states that 1,000 honor killings occur in India (no given year), 1,000 honor killings occur in Pakistan (no given year), and twelve honor killings occur per year in the United Kingdom. It is not clear whether these numbers are in addition to the 5,000 honor killings per year or are part of the same estimate. As with the 5,000 UN number, no sources are offered to document these figures.
3. In the past few years, US media and US government officials began to report that twenty-three to twenty-seven honor killings occur in the country per year. This number, as Volpp's work has shown, is often wrongly attributed to a report that was funded by the Department of Justice and thus claimed to accurately reflect the rates of the crime's occurrence. Volpp traces the number to an unpublished study by nine authors under the title "A Comparative Approach to Estimating the Annual Number of Honor Killings in the United States among

People from North African, Middle Eastern, and Southeast Asian (MANASA) Countries." Volpp (2019) details the abundant methodological issues with the research and its findings, questioning the validity of the research and uncovering the political workings of its numerical evidence.

4. Volpp draws on Sherene H. Razack's configuration of the three allegorical figures that "dominate the social landscape of the 'war on terror' and its ideological underpinning of a clash of civilizations: the dangerous Muslim man, the imperiled Muslim woman, the civilized European, the latter a figure who is seldom explicitly named but who nevertheless anchors the first two figures" (Razack 2008, 5).
5. Various feminist scholars have explored the difficulties of creating a generally accepted definition of the honor crime, arguing that the term is now beset with an overdetermined discourse that curtails and undermines, rather than enables and supports, the work of antiviolence activists and practitioners.
6. Because of the linking of Islam with honor-related violence, Muslim associations and Muslim clerics have been called upon to denounce this form of violence as un-Islamic. Religious and clerical disavowal of honor-related violence is now quite common. In 2016 the Jordanian General Iftaa' Department's Director of Public Relations and Cooperation, Hassan Arquoub, issued a *fatwa* on behalf of the Jordanian government stating that honor crimes were against *Sharia* law and that anyone who kills a female family relative should be held accountable for their crime. See Rana Husseini's "Honour Crimes Anti-Islamic—Fatwa" (2016b). In 2011, during the highly publicized Shafia murder trials, the Islamic Supreme Council of Canada issued a public statement that denounced these crimes. Speaking to Canadian press, Imam Syed Soharwardy stated, "Domestic violence is very un-Islamic. It's a crime in the eyes of the law, it's a crime in the Islamic teaching" (qtd in McQuigge 2011). Such disavowals are important for a number of political, rhetorical, and symbolic reasons not only because of what messages they send to the Muslims whom these organizations represent but also because of what messages they send to general audiences in local and host societies. In Canada, response to efforts by leaders of the Muslim community has been celebratory, with liberal and conservative national media commending the steps taken by the Muslim leaders to speak against difficult but crucial issues such as honor crimes. The *National Post*'s Jonathan Kay (2011) described the imam's efforts as "a genuinely useful gesture." In explaining its significance, Kay writes: "The millions of Canadians following the Shafia trial generally need no lectures to instruct them on this subject—their revulsion at the details being disclosed in court provides more education on the subject than they needed. But many recently arrived Muslim immigrants, or those who merely have not yet integrated into Canadian society, do not get their news from mainstream news outlets like this one. The sermons they hear on Fridays may be one of their only regular ways of learning about the outside world." Here we see how the denunciation of the honor crime as an un-Islamic practice becomes an imperative for Muslim communities seeking belonging and integration in Western national contexts or those desiring to be seen as members of modern and progressive religious communities in Arab and Muslim nation-states.
7. In subsequent appearances of the term "honor crime" in my work, and throughout the text, I will be problematizing its usage but will not be using quotation marks to indicate this.
8. Two important scholarly works have studied this phenomenon and the politics of its naming in the European context. Katherine Pratt Ewing's *Stolen Honor: Stigmatizing Muslim Men in Berlin* (Stanford University Press, 2008) explores how honor-based violence is configured in relation to Muslim migration to Germany. Its analysis of stigmatized masculinity, national abjection, and racial injury helps inform my own critique of the deployment of honor crime discourses in the multiracial and multicultural states of Canada and the

US. See also Beverly M. Weber's *Violence and Gender in the "New" Europe* (Palgrave Macmillan, 2013), where the author deconstructs the essentialized relationship between Islam and gender and cultural violence. Among other social phenomenon of gender violence, Weber analyzes how honor crime discourses, as well as hijab controversies, construct Muslim women's place in European nation-states. The author attends to the honor crime in relation to European investments in discourses of peace, security, and secularism. This work provides important evidence of the weaving of the honor crime into national and public life in Germany and resonates with the transnational discussions raised in my work.

9. See https://clarionproject.org/films/honor-diaries/.
10. See the "About" section of the organization's website: https://clarionproject.org/about-us/.
11. Prominent Muslim American activist Linda Sarsour argued on Twitter that *Honor Diaries* is "#DisHonorDiaries because it's disingenuous when it's funded by representatives and organizations labeled hate groups." Similarly, writing for the Canadian *Globe and Mail*, Sheema Khan (2014) argued that ending honor crimes is possible "but not with films by anti-Muslim zealots."
12. In 2003 Norma Khouri published her memoir titled *Honor Lost: Love and Death in Modern-Day Jordan*. The memoir purported to tell the true story of a young Jordanian Muslim woman named Dalia who was killed by her brother for the crime of falling in love with a Christian man named Michael. Shortly after its publication, Khouri's memoir was revealed to be a hoax and, due to pressures from Jordanian activists Rana Husseini and the former secretary general of the Jordanian National Commission for Women, Amal Sabbagh, was reclassified by its publisher from memoir to fiction. See Gillian Whitlock's "Tainted Testimony: The Khouri Affair" for an important discussion of the literary hoax and its ability to garner empathy from Western audiences as well as how such texts work and what they "can tell us . . . about readers, their communities, and the politics of reading" (2004, 173).
13. Feminist scholars have long written against the opportunistic uptake of feminist causes in general and the violence against women agenda in particular in politically charged times. As early as the 1990s, Leila Ahmed wrote about colonial feminism or the support of feminist causes by colonialists who sought to destroy the patriarchal orders of the societies they colonized (1992; 2011). After September 11, 2001, and George W. Bush regime's tying of the "War on Terror" to the liberation of women, this body of scholarship served to chart links, similarities, and disjunctures between the discourses and practices of colonialist feminists both past and new. See Abu-Lughod (2002, 2013), Razack (2008), and Thobani (2007b, 2015).
14. Debate around the pressure to cancel a 2015 screening of *Honor Diaries* at the University of South Dakota closely mirrored these terms. In support of the right to screen the film, Miglena Sternadori, a professor of media and gender studies, argued that it is "just the wrong thing to do to censor a movie" (qtd in Ellis 2015). The exchange between supporters and detractors of the film is framed by Ellis's article as one about a tension between calls for censorship and tolerance. Importantly, the debate around documentaries like *Honor Diaries* is part and parcel of a longer discussion taking place in the US regarding academic freedom and freedom of speech on US university campuses. In 2019 President Trump signed the "Executive Order on Improving Free Inquiry, Transparency, and Accountability at Colleges and Universities," which required university campuses to engage in free and open debate or risk losing federal funding opportunities. The order responds to right-wing claims that US university campuses have foreclosed open debate and shut down conservative viewpoints in academic curricula and university spaces.
15. See Coomaraswamy's report "Violence Against Women in the Family," which was submitted to the United Nations Commission on Human Rights 55th Session on March 10, 1999. The full text of the report is available here: https://undocs.org/pdf?symbol=en/E/CN.4/1999/68>.

16. See "Cultural practices in the family that are violent towards women" (E/CN.4/2002/83) which was published on January 31, 2002, and is available here: https://undocs.org/en/E/CN.4/2002/83.
17. The crime of passion is distinguished from the honor crime primarily because it is understood as a crime that takes place during a temporary loss of sanity or reason and in a moment of heated anger towards an act of sexual betrayal by a partner. In "Comparatively Speaking: The Honor of the East and the Passion of the West" (1997), Lama Abu Odeh notes that "*flagrante delicto* and that the killing should be immediate" are central characteristics of the classic definition of the passion crime (304). The honor crime is seen as premediated act, a crime that is primarily committed by brothers and fathers rather than by a husband. I return to this distinction later in this introduction.
18. See "Third Committee Adopts Two Draft Resolutions on Crimes Against Women—Urging Elimination of 'Honor Crimes' and of All Forms of Violence." Full text available here: https://www.un.org/press/en/2000/20001103.gashc3615.doc.html.
19. The letter was submitted by the permanent representative of Malaysia to the United Nations to the Secretary General of the United Nations on October 3, 2000 (A/C.3/55/4). The full text of the letter is available here: https://documents-dds-ny.un.org/doc/UNDOC/GEN/N00/675/31/pdf/N0067531.pdf?OpenElement.
20. The full text of the fifth-fifth session of the General Assembly (A/55/PV.81) which took place on December 4, 2000 is available here: https://undocs.org/A/55/PV.81.
21. In discussions surrounding the third draft of the resolution, which took place in December 2004, Mr. Al Sulaiti, the new Qatari representative to the UN, articulated his country's support for the resolution to condemn crimes that are committed in the name of honor. The Qatari representative expressed his "regret" that the committee had chosen to include a statement on "sexual and reproductive health" in spite of the request made by some states to have that removed from the resolution. The Qatari representative registered his country's decision to "dissociate" themselves from the resolution (A/59/PV.74, p. 7-8). See for full text: https://undocs.org/en/A/59/PV.74.
22. The full text of the remarks which were given at the fifty-fifth session of the General Assembly (A/55/PV.81) are available here: https://undocs.org/A/55/PV.81.
23. Manjoo's full report was submitted to the United Nations Human Rights Council in 2012 (A/HRC/20/16): https://undocs.org/A/HRC/20/16.
24. Kogacioglu acknowledges the difficulties surrounding the term, arguing that "honor crimes stand at the intersection of multiple political and social dynamics" and that "the debate on honor crimes unfolds in dialogue with debates on other 'problematic non-Western practices' such as female genital mutilation, sati, arranged marriages, and dowry murders" (2004, 119).
25. In their analysis, Sev'er and Yurdakul make distinctions between expressions of honor such as *izzet, seref, unur,* and *namus,* which they identify as a "type of sexual honor that presupposes physical and moral qualities that women ought to have. This type is associated with the shame of women and women's families" (2001, 973).
26. In their definition of honor-based violence, Dietrich Oberwittler and Julia Kasselt state that the honor killing is a "peculiar type of gendered domestic violence rooted in an archaic 'code of honor' still prevalent in agrarian societies in north Africa and in west and central Asia; societies that are characterized, over long historical periods, by scarce natural resources, strong collectivist traditions, and the lack of a state monopoly of power" (2014, 665).
27. Aasiya Hassan (Zubair) was gruesomely murdered by her husband in 2009 in Buffalo, New York. For an analysis of media coverage of Aasiya Hassan's murder, see Zareena Grewal's "Death by Culture? How Not to Talk about Islam and Domestic Violence" (2009). Also, see Hammer's *Peaceful Families: American Muslim Efforts Against Domestic Violence* (2019).

28. In a recent study on ending honor killing violence, Robert Paul Churchill cites a slightly different version of the HRW definition, which states that honor killings are "acts of vengeance, usually deaths, committed by male family members against female family members who are held to have brought dishonour upon the family" (qtd in Churchill 2018, 4). Churchill uses this definition in his analysis of the distinct features of the honor killing because he considers it "free of implicit judgement, a factor that could undermine objectivity and defeat efforts to engage in rational, respectful dialogue with persons in areas in which the honour killings occur" (5). To make the argument regarding neutrality a viable one, Churchill focuses only on the language that is used by HRW and ignores the occasion of its utterance at the UN and its transnational circulations.
29. See "Defining 'Honour' Crimes and 'Honour' Killings" (2011), available through the UN Women's Virtual Knowledge Centre to End Violence Against Women and Girls: https://www.endvawnow.org/en/articles/731-defining-honourcrimes-and-honour-killings.html.
30. The World Health Organization defines intimate partner violence as "any behaviour within an intimate relationship that causes physical, psychological or sexual harm to those in the relationship." See "Understanding and Addressing Violence Against Women," available here: https://apps.who.int/iris/bitstream/handle/10665/77432/WHO_RHR_12.36_eng.pdf. While the definition is expansive and includes physical, emotional, sexual, and psychological forms of violence, emphasis is placed on "male intimate partners or ex-partners."
31. See, for example, Uni Wikan (2008) and Phyllis Chesler (2009). See also popular opinion pieces on the distinctions between honor-based violence and violence against women such as Barbara Kay's article "Honour Killing Is Not 'Domestic' Violence," from the *National Post* (July 29, 2009).
32. In her groundbreaking article on differences and similarities between Western and Eastern legal systems in relation to the prosecution of the honor crime, Lama Abu Odeh showcases how there exists in these seemingly different legal systems a "tolerance in both places of an increasing variety of violence against women" (1997, 290–91). Abu Odeh's work exposes the fallacies of Western legal superiority and the assumption of greater protection of women under Western legal codes and stipulations.
33. A manifestation of the concept of "reward" is at work, for example, in some courts' admissibility and consideration of the "gay panic defense" in prosecuting the murder of gay men. In an article on the importance of battling the gay panic defense in criminal courts, Cynthia Lee explains the legal strategy as such: "When a heterosexual man kills a gay man and faces a murder charge, a common defense strategy is to use the concept of 'gay panic' to explain the killing. There is no officially recognized 'gay panic' defense but many use the term to refer to defense strategies that rely on the notion that a criminal defendant should be excused or justified if his violent actions were in response to a (homo)sexual advance" (2008, 475). Lee's article explains why and how this "defense" has currency in US criminal courts.
34. The Shafia murders took place on June 30, 2009, when the bodies of three sisters, Zainab (19), Sahar (17), and Geeti (13), and their stepmother, Rona Amir Mohammed (50), were found in the Kingston Mills of the Rideau Canal. It was later discovered that the girls' father and mother, along with a younger brother, had helped in committing the murder, and they were all found guilty for their role in this quadruple homicide. The murder caused a national frenzy, with many calling for the reform of the Canadian immigration system. I have written elsewhere on these murders in "Gendered Violence, Cultural Otherness, and Honour Crimes in Canadian National Logics" (2013).
35. Together with Nahla Abdo, Mojab edited one of the first collections on honor-based violence. Titled *Violence in the Name of Honor: Theoretical and Political Challenges* (2004), the collection brings together a number of essays from scholars and activists who seek to define the honor crime and provide critical analysis of strategies to confront it.

36. The binary of racism versus culturalism pervades many of the discussions that relate to forms of violence like honor killings. Sherene Razack discusses the conundrums of feminist analysis of sexual violence in South Asian communities in her article "A Violent Culture or Culturalized Violence? Feminist Narratives of Sexual Violence Against South Asian Women" (2003). In her essay, Razack comes to the conclusion that feminists of color who speak on gender and sexual violence in their communities cannot avoid the issue of culture. As she states, "Since South Asian women run headlong into the orientalist narrative whenever cultural practices such as arranged marriages are discussed, an effective strategy might be to aggressively rather than defensively confront it" (102). Razack worries that a deculturalized approach to violence "can seldom pack a sufficient enough punch to knock out the orientalist fantasy" that often shapes how violence against women in people of color communities is narrated (95).
37. In his work on the rhetorics surrounding child victims of abuse, Joel Best argues that the way social problems get framed often impacts how they are confronted and what types of responses they evoke. Best writes, "Social problems claims-making is rarely static; claims evolve over a problem's history" (1990, 65). Best uncovers the social, political, and rhetorical processes that help shape not only what forms of violence become recognizable as child abuse but also what is reported on and what laws and social policies are crafted to confront the phenomenon.

NOTES TO CHAPTER 1

1. Articles abound about Aqsa Parvez's murder in Canadian newspapers, including the *Toronto Star*, the *Globe and Mail*, and the *National Post*. The murder was covered across a range of liberal and conservative publications. See Allen and Freisen (2010); Humphreys, O'Toole, and Wallace (2010); and Mitchell (2010).
2. The codification of multiculturalism into the realm of law and policy worked to bring diversity into the fold of the state. The Canadian government's adoption of this policy allowed the state to manage difference under the guise of benign recognition and tolerance. This approach helped Canada present itself as a welcoming state for persons from nondominant backgrounds or as a "multicultural mosaic" in which difference is celebrated. As scholars have shown, the embrace of Canadian multiculturalism as a national priority was premised on the obscuring of Canada's settler colonial past and present and its recasting of its immigration system as generous and open. For work on Canadian multiculturalism and a critique of how this policy works, see Himani Bannerji's *The Dark Side of the Nation: Essays on Multiculturalism, Nationalism, and Gender* (2000). For a focus on language and construction of identity, see Eve Haque's *Multiculturalism Within a Bilingual Framework: Language, Race, and Belonging in Canada* (2012) and Sunera Thobani's *Exalted Subjects: Studies in the Making and Race and Nation in Canada* (2007).
3. See Reimers (2007) for the coverage of Fadime Sahindal's 2002 murder in the Swedish press. Reimers offers a discourse analysis of media responses to the murder, arguing that "the newspapers represented Fadime Sahindal as a martyr for the Swedish way of living, which is signified by equality, modernity, freedom, and enlightenment. This representation was founded on, and thereby reiterated, cultural racism, sexism, and class prejudice" (252). Reimers's careful analysis of these representations shows the difficulties of utilizing the honor killing trope in presenting such murders. Her works serve to "illustrate how difficult it is to address violence motivated by conceptions of family honor without confirming oppressive and discriminatory social norms and notions" (252). Weber (2013) also provides insights into media representations of murders of Muslim women in Germany.

4. Mona Eltahawy (2008) argues that Muslim women who integrate too well into Western societies are punished by murder and that "knee-jerk defensiveness" prevents Muslims from acknowledging the occurrence of these crimes. Sheema Khan (2010) similarly has argued that Muslims living in multicultural states like Canada are holding on to customs and traditions that are harmful to women.
5. The Urban Alliance on Race Relations remains active today. Their website is available here: https://urbanalliance.ca/.
6. The debate over the politics of naming honor-based violence as an exceptional form of violence undergirded by unique understandings and deployments of patriarchy is long and ongoing. Feminist scholars writing on violence have shown why these crimes must be understood as distinct and separate from a broader continuum of patriarchal and domestic violence because of their nature and because of the legal and cultural sanctioning that such crimes receive. This chapter does not engage these debates in detail (see the introduction) but focuses instead on the discourses generated about these crimes and how these narratives travel within and through transnational spheres and their co-optations.
7. When asked about the controversy caused by the publication of her article and whether she regretted her use of the term *honor killing* to describe Aqsa Parvez's murder, Rogan said the following: "No, not at all. I think the story's critics make a willful and profoundly irrational attempt to distinguish the crime from its context. Let me explain it this way: if someone is walking down the street and killed in the course of a crime, that's a terrible thing. But if three guys in a pickup truck with a Confederate flag stop a black man, drive him into the woods and hang him, we know something very different has happened, and we have a word for that. Lynching means something very specific. Similarly, a hate crime is a very specific charge. It surprised me that people were so afraid to describe Aqsa's death as an honour killing. It's irrational to think that we can't call something what it is because that community can't sustain that kind of criticism. Ultimately, I think that's very infantilizing. If the Muslim community can't sustain the kind of criticism that other communities go through, then there's no hope for moving forward" (*Toronto Life* 2010).
8. Another important effort in contesting the murder of Aqsa Parvez is the launching of the *Aqsa Zine* by a collective of Muslim youth in Toronto. The youth organized a zine that includes essays, art, and poetry in remembrance of Aqsa's life. Their work sought to place the murder beyond the dominant honor killing discourse. As the organizers state, "We recognize her murder as physical form of patriarchal violence, and the response to her murder from public institutions as Islamophobic, racist, and patriarchal." See https://localwiki.org/toronto/AQSA_Zine and https://zeedesigns.wixsite.com/aqsazineonline.
9. As Rita Dhamoon notes, "Even though the concept of culture provides convenience in talking about grouped ways of thinking, feeling, and action, it simply does not provide an adequate means to contextually explore the processes by which identities and relations are constituted and reconstituted" (2010, 359). In other words, culture's strength rests precisely in the convenience or the ease with which it is wielded and the multiplicity of uses it can elicit. Himani Bannerji reminds us in her critique of Canadian multiculturalism that culture is a "reductionism that hides the social relations of domination that continually create 'difference' as inferior and thus signifies continuing relations of antagonism" (2000, 97).
10. The story of the failure of multiculturalism is a recurrent feature in much of the coverage of honor-based violence that takes place in Western contexts. See, for example, the work of Katherine Pratt Ewing in *Stolen Honor* (2008). In feminist theory, the issue of multiculturalism and its tolerance toward bad "cultural behavior" has been theorized in a number of texts. See, for example, Sarah Bracke and Nadia Fadil's "'Is the Headscarf Oppressive or Emancipatory?' Field Notes from the Multicultural Debate" (2012).
11. For an analysis that moves beyond veiling and not veiling as binaristic choices, see Nadia Fadil's "Not-/Unveiling as an Ethical Practice" (2011). Fadil's article troubles the binary of

veiling versus unveiling and maps how Muslim women negotiate different practices in relation to the different spaces and roles they occupy in society.

12. In *Do Muslim Women Need Saving?* Abu-Lughod explores how certain forms of gender violence, including the honor crime in particular, become "objects of earnest and widespread concern" (2013, 140). She demonstrates how these acts become an index for "Muslim women's rights" and how they circulate across local and global scales to cathect activist and reader response, produce moral outrage, and encourage action on behalf of battered, abused, or murdered Muslim women. As such, honor crimes become "pawns in political battles" that signify well beyond the borders and geographies of one nation-state and that are seized upon to draw civilizational lines (139).
13. Tarek Fatah is a Muslim Canadian journalist. He writes for conservative Canadian journals such as the *National Post* and often pens articles against what he views as the threat of encroachment of Islamic fundamentalism in Canada. For an important discussion regarding the role of Muslim experts such as Tarek Fatah in Canada, see Krista Melanie Riley's (2009) analysis of the accumulation of national capital through the reification of categories of "good" and "bad" Muslims and the articulation of concern for endangered Muslim women.
14. Park 51 was a project proposed by developer Sharif El-Gamal, a Muslim American, who was invested in taking over the former Burlington Coat Factory building in lower Manhattan. Together with Imam Feisal Abdul Rauf, he sought to build a center, similar to the YMCA, for Muslim communities. Although the proposed project was intended as a community center that included a prayer space, it was often misrepresented as a mosque in popular media. The project was stopped when a controversy erupted in summer 2010 over the suitability of building a mosque in close proximity to the hallowed area known as "Ground Zero." The objection to the center's construction brought to the fore the levels of anti-Muslim discourse routinely normalized in popular discussions. See Derek Ruez's "'Partitioning the Sensible' at Park 51: Rancière, Islamophobia, and Common Politics" (2012).
15. In response to the conference, the Arab American Institute scheduled a concurrent event titled "Rejecting Islamophobia: A Community Stand Against Hate." For a discussion of the conference and the debates it stirred, see Jonathan Oosting's "Rejecting Islamophobia: Town Hall Counters 'Jessica Mokdad Human Rights Conference' in Dearborn" (2012).
16. For more information on the wall, see https://usa.jnf.org/about-jnf/news/press-releases/2008/pr_jnf-establishes-wall-of.html.

NOTES TO CHAPTER 2

1. In *Spectacular Rhetorics,* Wendy Hesford draws on the work of Ulrich Baer on memory, witnessing, and photography to argue that photographs bear a trace of the ungovernable in them. This trace is materialized when the picture or image interacts with the various narratives that a viewer may project onto it. But the ungovernable part of viewership is configured not necessarily as a loss but as a potential that is held within future projections. As Hesford states, "There is a trace of the ungovernable in every photograph. Trauma, like the past, is an unstable reference; so is the photograph" (2011, 98).
2. The Palestinian National Authority (PNA) was established after the signing of the Oslo agreement in 1994 between Israel and the Palestinian Liberation Organization (PLO). It is also known as the Palestinian Authority or the PA. As the presumptive representative of the Palestinian people, the Palestinian Authority operates as a pseudo-government and pseudo-state; it is dependent on foreign aid for its existence and survival, and its sovereignty is superseded by the occupying authority of the Israeli state.

3. The Occupied Palestinian Territories (OPT) is the designation for the areas of West Bank, East Jerusalem, and the Gaza Strip which have been under Israeli occupation since 1967. The OPT is the area that the PA hoped to establish the future Palestinian state, and this area excludes Israeli settlements, the Jordan Valley, and the roads that connect Palestinian villages within the West Bank.
4. The National Committee to Combat Violence Against Women was formed in 2008 by the Palestinian Council of Ministries and is led by the Ministry of Women's Affairs (MoWA). Its members include representatives from a number of official state ministries, the General Secretariat of the General Union of Palestinian Women, and the NGO Forum to Combat Violence Against Women (*Al-Muntada* Coalition). See the *National Strategy* for a full membership list.
5. The Palestinian Basic Law functions as the temporary constitution of the Palestinian Authority. See http://www.palestinianbasiclaw.org/basic-law/2003-amended-basic-law.
6. The Arabic version of the report is available here: http://www.pcbs.gov.ps/Downloads/book1268.pdf.
7. See Lena Odgaard's (2014) analysis of the protests against the rising number of murders.
8. Various spellings of Aya's last name proliferate on the internet. I have used "Baradiyah" as it is the spelling most commonly used in English-language articles about her.
9. Many media accounts detail the horrific murder across local, regional, and international press. In the Arabic press, numerous articles were published in the local Palestinian newspapers, including several articles that appear on the pages of *MaanNews*. See http://www.maannews.net/Content.aspx?id=385985 and http://www.maannews.net/Content.aspx?id=387164. *Dunya Al Watan* also published an article about the murder: https://www.alwatanvoice.com/arabic/news/2011/05/17/176686.html. Coverage in regional Arab press includes an article in *Laha Magazine and Al Imirat al Yawm*. In the *Guardian*, Harriet Sherwood's "Death in the West Bank: The Story of an 'Honour' Killing" (2011) provides important details about the case and also connects it to the local activism that ensued in its aftermath.
10. The organization, whose Arabic name means *change*, launched the campaign to raise awareness about the killing of Palestinian women. The campaign sheds light on the continued abuse and marginalization and harming of women worldwide and in Palestine. To access the organization's website, see https://mappingher.ps/?page_id=8.
11. See Ebtihal Mahadeen's "Doctors and Sheikhs: 'Truths' in Virginity Discourse in Jordanian Media" (2013) and "'The Martyr of Dawn': Femicide in Jordanian Media" (2017).
12. On the workings of patriarchy and gossip in honor-related crimes in Palestine, see Manar Hassan's "The Politics of Honor: Patriarchy, the State and the Murder of Women in the Name of Family Honor" (2002). See also Nadera Shalhboub-Kevorkian's "Reexamining Femicide: Breaking the Silence and Crossing 'Scientific' Borders" (2003) for a discussion of the relationship between gossip against female kin and male reputation. On the discourse of gossip and shame and its workings in sanctioning honor-related violence, see Amani M. Awwad's "Gossip, Scandal, Shame and Honor Killing: A Case for Social Constructionism and Hegemonic Discourse" (2001).
13. Coverage of honor-related violence, in the Palestinian context, often reproduces the idea of deserved versus undeserved violence by questioning whether girls and women who are victims of violence upheld moral and sexual codes (including virginity) before their murders.
14. Website available here: https://mappingher.ps/?page_id=8.
15. On its website, the organization describes its goals thus: "fostering democracy and upholding human rights, taking action to prevent the destruction of the global ecosystem, advancing equality between women and men, securing peace through conflict prevention in crisis zones, and defending the freedom of individuals against excessive state and economic power—these are the objectives that drive the ideas and actions of the Heinrich Böll

Foundation." See https://www.boell.de/en/foundation/who-we-are for more information on the organization.

16. See, for example, the article in *Maan News* on Aya's murder: http://www.maannews.net/Content.aspx?id=385985.
17. On March 18, 2019, the State of Palestine acceded to the 1989 Second Optional Protocol to the International Covenant on Civil and Political Rights (ICCPR), which aims to abolish the death penalty. From its founding in 1993 till 2017, there have been forty-one executions in Palestine (thirty-nine of which took place in Gaza). The death penalty has not been used against men who murder women, and the calls for the imposition of such a penalty reflect the entrenchment of a punitive and carceral view in relation to fighting violence against women in Palestinian society, a matter I return to in my discussion of the Jordanian legal context.
18. In the Palestinian context, the use of the discourse of martyrdom is primarily applied to men, women, and children who die or are killed as a result of Israeli occupation. The use of this language to speak about Aya's murder constitutes a significant break from the dominant discourse surrounding martyrdom in Palestine and signifies the honorable place that Aya occupies in remembrance discourses in Palestine. The bestowing of this status on Aya is directly related to her favorable reputation and the general societal agreement that she had not broken any sexual or moral codes prior to her murder.
19. The full televised interview, which took place on May 16, 2011, is available here: https://www.youtube.com/watch?v=HDTKrLEqFqE. Analysis of this interview is available from *Maan News* here: http://maannews.net/Content.aspx?id=387453.
20. Two legal systems exist in the West Bank and Gaza. In the West Bank, the Jordanian Penal Code of 1960 is in effect and governs the lives of Palestinians who live there. In Gaza, the Egyptian Penal Code is in effect. This dual system creates complicated results in terms of people's ability to navigate between these codes.
21. I return to a discussion of these laws and efforts to upend and change them in more detail in the following chapter. It is important here to note that, contrary to his stated intention to put a stop to honor-related violence, a legal aide to Abbas would reveal that the announced changes were mainly to "garner public opinion" and that the president had no intention of changing the law since it would cause administrative and legal challenges (qtd in Al-Ghussein and Patchett 2012).
22. The campaign was launched by a Palestinian women's group called *Sabaya Hai'rat* and Al-Muntada. The coalition of Palestinian men and women worked together to lobby the president against gender violence, using media to solicit broad societal appeal for their work and working to expose the lack of appropriate government response and action on this issue.
23. See Dalia Hatuqa's "'Paradigm Shift': Palestinians Join Treaties" (2014).
24. The Palestinian Authority ratified the convention without placing any reservations on any of its articles. Most Arab countries have placed reservations on aspects of the CEDAW agreement. For more information on this, see S. El-Masri's "Challenges Facing CEDAW in the Middle East and North Africa" (2011) and Elizabeth Ann Mayer's "Internationalizing the Conversation on Women's Rights: Arab Countries Face the CEDAW Committee" (2004).
25. As Noura Erakat makes clear, the Palestinian statehood bid was a strategic maneuver meant to help rescue the Palestinian Authority's reputation, which had suffered serious setbacks. While it had the potential to enable the Palestinian Authority to make Israel accountable to international law and its own juridical standards, the Palestinian Authority repeatedly failed to do so, opting instead to return to bilateral talks in 2013. See *Justice for Some: Law and the Question of Palestine* (2019).
26. In 2018, for example, the Palestinian Authority entered a five-year agreement with the Government of Canada and five UN agencies, including UN Women, UNFPA, UN Habitat, and UNODC, to launch "Haya: Eliminating Violence Against Women in the West Bank

and Gaza (2018–2022)." The program aimed to address harmful practices and causes of violence in Palestinian society by helping the Palestinian Authority develop comprehensive "prevention, protection, and response systems" (see UNFPA 2018). The project's reported budget is 17 million CAD.

27. In 2015 UN Women posted a job search for a national consultant to provide a midterm review of the Palestinian National Strategy to Combat Violence Against Women. https://jobs.undp.org/cj_view_job.cfm?cur_job_id=61905.
28. See the Israeli Central Bureau of Statistics.
29. The "Green Line" refers to the *de facto* borders of the Israeli state drawn in the Armistice Agreement of 1949 between Israel, Jordan, Egypt, Lebanon, and Syria. This designation separates the geographies of Palestine between 1948 (referring to villages and towns that now exist within Israel, or within the "green line") and 1967 Palestine (referring to the West Bank and Gaza, areas that were occupied by Israel in 1967).
30. Shira Robinson's *Citizen Strangers: Palestinians and the Birth of Israel's Liberal State* (2013) offers a clear and historical study of the formation of the Israeli state and the granting of an exclusionary form of citizenship to the Palestinian minority living in Israel. For discussion of the racialized system of rights and rightlessness structuring life for Palestinian citizens of Israel, see Shourideh C. Molavi's *Stateless Citizenship: The Palestinian-Arab Citizens of Israel* (2013). For a focused analysis of the gendered aspect of differential citizenship in Israel and its impact on women, see Nahla Abdo's *Women in Israel: Race, Gender and Citizenship* (2011).
31. See Rouhana and Sabbagh-Khoury (2015).
32. See Yiftachel and Yacoubi, who note that "within the context of a Jewish settler society, the Arabs of Lod [*sic*] are both discriminated against as Palestinians in a Jewish state, and excluded as residents in their own city, which declares itself 'mixed.' This setting is common to settler societies, where conflict with the indigenous population is constructed as a pivotal axis for the formation of essentialized collective identities and geographies" (2003, 689).
33. The town is known as Lyd and Lod in Hebrew, as Lydda in Greek-Latin, and as Al-Lyd in Arabic.
34. Bisan Abu Ghanem was murdered in a drive-by shooting. Six people were convicted of involvement in planning her murder. Two of her sisters were also murdered under similar conditions. More information on her murder can be found in Glazer (2019) and Salaime (2014).
35. Sharon D. Lang notes that while in theory Israeli law "makes no distinction or concession in cases of murder motivated by sharaf," there is an understanding that Israeli authorities may have provided more lenient sentences to perpetrators of honor-based violence (2005, 72). As Lang explains, "The articulated rationale for community sentences in family sharaf killing cases is that the Israelis are trying to be flexible when it comes to Arab cultural or religious beliefs; they are trying to be cultural relativists" (73).
36. The second Palestinian intifada began in 2000.
37. In an important article on the history of DAM, Ted Swedenburg (2013) reminds readers that DAM began their career as part of the Israeli rap scene and that the band's earlier musical contributions focused in large part on issues like narcotics and the sales of drugs in Palestinian towns like Lyd. Swedenburg offers a cautionary note against efforts to claim DAM as a resistance band that ignore their ability to speak to multiple issues and audiences, a facet of their identity as performers that is captured in their very name, which is translatable to English, Hebrew, and Arabic.
38. See Maira's *Jil Oslo: Palestinian Hip Hop, Youth Culture, and the Youth Movement* and Maira (2008).
39. Eqeiq (2010) makes the point that DAM's music emphasizes the indigenous status of Palestinians with Israeli citizenship in order to distinguish between their position and the

position of the refugee or resident. This particular claim subverts liberal Zionist discourse surrounding the Palestinian identity of the over two million Palestinians who hold Israeli citizenship and who are often described as "Arab-Israelis."

40. In an article that focuses on "indigenous hip hop," Kyle Mays argues that indigenous artists have taken up the genre in order to "challenge settler colonialism, white supremacy, and heteropatriarchy, among other things" (2019, 461). DAM's work can be understood through the framework Mays provides.
41. All videos for these songs are available on the band's website: https://www.damofficialband.com/media.
42. In 2015 DAM launched a campaign called #Who_You_R that challenged sexism in Palestinian and Arab society. On Twitter, the group asked fans to send pictures of themselves challenging traditional gender roles. See Tom Barnes (2015) for coverage of the campaign.
43. The full transcript and translation of the lyrics are available on DAM's website: https://genius.com/Dam-if-id-go-back-in-time-lyrics. I use this version of the text throughout this chapter. Please note also that the band sometimes uses "If I'd Go Back In Time" in English translations of the song.
44. The choice of the brother as his sister's murderer is not accidental. Studies show that once a decision to kill a woman is made, families may choose the younger brother as the perpetrator of the crime. The reasons for this relate to the recognition that the legal system may offer a younger perpetrator a more lenient sentence for the crime. See Glazer (2019) for testimonies from Palestinian men who have murdered their sisters about why they were selected and what this has meant for their later recognition of their guilt.
45. In an interview with Ali Abunimah (2012) from *Electronic Intifada,* DAM band member Tamer Nafar explained that the band hoped that the video of the song would resonate with "the leaders in the Middle East so they can fix the law. Murder is murder, it doesn't matter what is the cause." In the same article, Abunimah reports that at an event to launch the song, Suhell Nafar explained that "the song is not a specific incident but it describes the phenomena of honor killing in general."
46. To be clear, collaborations between Palestinians and NGOs are not in and of themselves suspect or in question. In the context of a post-Oslo world order, such collaborations inform every aspect of Palestinian life as nongovernment funding continues to be used to produce all types of projects, many of them essential to Palestinian life and livelihood.
47. See, for example, the anthropological debate in the 1990s around cultural relativism and female genital cutting. Walley (1997) reminds us that the controversies surrounding the range of practices that she labels "female genital operations" were intimately tied to concerns about human rights and cultural rights in light of increased migration to Europe and the US. Significantly, the debates indexed broader anxieties over the meaning and viability of multicultural societies and nation-states. See also the debate between Joseph Massad and Helem, stirred by the publication of Massad's article on the "gay international," and the response to it, from Ghassan Makarem (2009). Another reflection on the tensions between activists and academics is presented in Abu Odeh (2015).

NOTES TO CHAPTER 3

1. The ban put into place impacted applicants from eight states: Venezuela, North Korea, Iran, Iraq, Syria, Yemen, Somalia, and Libya. In the later versions of the ban, signed by President Trump on March 7, 2017, Iraq was removed from this list in response to worries that this would impact Iraqi interpreters who had served with the US Army. This version also exempted citizens of these states if they were legal US permanent residents (or green card holders) and if they held valid US visas. See de Vogue, Diamond, and Liptak (2017)

for more information. The newer iterations of the ban also removed Chad and Sudan from the list.

2. See "Purpose" section of the order.
3. See 8 USC 1182: "Inadmissible aliens." Full text available here: http://uscode.house.gov/view.xhtml?req=granuleid:USC-prelim-title8-section1182&num=0&edition=prelim.
4. Scholars have shown how the policies instituted by Trump constitute a continuation rather than a break with past legal practices. See Bill Ong Hing (2018) and Robert S. Chang (2018).
5. For analysis of the nationwide protests that took place in response to the ban's issuance in popular media and press, see Lauren Gambino et al. in the *Guardian* (2017), Andrew Buncombe in the *Independent* (2017), Andy Newman for the *New York Times* (2017), and Kelly Lunde in *Al Jazeera* (2017).
6. The "no ban on stolen land" campaign started by indigenous activists on social media questioned the right of the settler state to prevent people from entering this country, showcasing the links between theft of indigenous lands and the closure and bordering up of the US state. See Lenard Monkman (2017) for more information.
7. The full text of the recording is available in *State v. Isa 1993* (No. 74479). I have chosen not to reproduce it in here to avoid reducing Tina's life to the last and macabre scene of her murder. While I believe it is important to remember and document the terror and violence that women like Tina Isa experience, I do not wish to do so in a way that contributes to the further sensationalism that surrounds this case and the murder of women.
8. During the trial, Maria Isa would later request that her case be tried separately from her husband's. Maria Isa's request was based on the argument that her role in the murder was diminished, as she did not kill her daughter but assisted in the murder.
9. In *State v. Isa* (1993), the prosecutor reported that the conflict between Tina and her parents was due to her relationship with a Black man, which they disapproved of.
10. The cultural defense is the use of "culture" as a mitigating excuse for murder in a criminal court. Defendants utilize "culture" as an explanatory framework for violent acts that they commit, seeking reduced sentences from judges sympathetic to their patriarchal worldviews. As Melissa Demian shows in an important article on the anthropology of the cultural defense, it is a "technique of explication" that "tends to privilege the cultural rights of men over the rights of women and children to life, liberty, or bodily integrity" (2008, 433). For a legal perspective on the problems with this defense, see Volpp (2000). For a discussion of its resonance in Canadian courts, see Pascale Fournier, Pascal McDougall, and Anna R. Deker's "Dishonour, Provocation and Culture: In the Beholder's Eye?" (2012). See also Sirma Bilge's "Behind the 'Culture' Lens: Judicial Representations of Violence Against Women" (2006).
11. The organization was also known as the Fatah Revolutionary Council.
12. The act authorized the secretary of state (in consultation with the secretary of the treasury and the attorney general) to designate an organization as a terrorist organization if it is believed to engage in terrorist activities that are threatening to the interests of the state or to the security of its citizens. For the full text of the act, see https://www.congress.gov/bill/104th-congress/senate-bill/735.
13. According to the FBI, the organization's targets include "the United States, the United Kingdom, France, Israel, moderate Palestinians, the PLO, and various Arab countries." This information is reported in the FBI's "Background Information on Designated Foreign Terrorist Organizations," available on the FBI's archive page: https://2009-2017.state.gov/documents/organization/31946.pdf.
14. The men's houses were wiretapped in accordance with Title 50 of US code on "Electronic Surveillance." Full text of the law is available here: https://www.govinfo.gov/content/pkg/USCODE-2011-title50/pdf/USCODE-2011-title50-chap36-subchapI-sec1801.pdf.

15. The four men indicted for racketeering charges were Zein Isa, Saif Nijmeh, Luie Nijmeh, and Tawfiq Musa.
16. None of the reports that discuss Zein Isa's involvement with ANO provide information on the political context that leads to the rise of this group or their plans to target the Israeli embassy. Instead, Zein Isa's religious identity is blamed for his political association with this organization, and reports portray the organization's hatred for the State of Israel as driven by anti-Semitism.
17. Zein Isa died in prison as a result of health complications in 1997. Tina's mother, Maria Isa, died in prison in 2014. See *Associated Press* (2014).
18. Volpp's scholarship has been central to efforts to draw attention to culturalized framings of gender violence, and Volpp is one of a small number of scholars who have paid critical attention to Tina Isa's murder and its public framings. In 1995 Ellen Francis Harris published a book about the murder, *Guarding the Secrets: Palestinian Terrorism and a Father's Murder of his too-American Daughter*. Harris amasses a wealth of information about Tina Isa's murder, the investigation of her father and his terrorist accomplices, and the criminal proceedings and trials in both courts.
19. Volpp argues that citizenship is composed of four interconnected discourses: "citizenship as legal status, citizenship as rights, citizenship as political activity, and citizenship as identity/solidarity" (2002, 578). Even though one might have acquired citizenship and may be guaranteed legal status, exclusion from the other categories of citizenship that enable community and kin-making are possible, especially for foreign-born citizens who are of minoritized and racialized backgrounds.
20. The murder of Tina Isa never really disappears from public view. In recent years, it has existed primarily in the virtual archives of right-wing news sites. On the websites of news outlets like *Fox News,* Brietbart.com, Jihadwatch.org, and danielpipes.org, Tina Isa's murder is cited as one of the earliest accounts of honor-related murders in the US. Its occurrence evidences the threat that immigrants—and by extension migration as a whole—pose to the country. In a 2018 article, Brigitte Gabriel, a notorious anti-Muslim activist and founder of Act for America, an agency that bills itself as the largest grassroots national security organization in the US, wrote at length about the murder of Tina Isa to stoke right-wing rhetoric about the dangers of open borders and relaxed migration policies which would lead to eventual *Sharia* invasion and takeover of the US. See Brigitte Gabriel's *Rise: In Defense of Judeo-Christian Values and Freedom.*
21. This point is further borne out in the fact that Zein Isa's home was wiretapped for two years before the murder. This means that the FBI had targeted him and his family because of suspicion of his involvement with the organization well before the murder took place.
22. Feminist scholarship has long maintained that the domestic sphere and the family unit are not spaces of safety for women and that the privacy of the domestic often makes it difficult to gauge and confront violence against women and children and vulnerable people that takes place in the homestead. In her work on the feminist fight against sexual violence, Kristin Bumiller shows how the recognition of the prevalence of violence within the structure of the heteronormative family unit shattered any illusions of the family as a safe space (2008).
23. The full text of the strategy is available here: https://2009-2017.state.gov/documents/organization/196468.pdf.
24. The text of the executive order is available here: https://obamawhitehouse.archives.gov/the-press-office/2012/08/10/executive-order-preventing-and-responding-violence-against-women-and-gir.
25. For the full text of the order, see https://www.federalregister.gov/documents/2012/08/16/2012-20259/preventing-and-responding-to-violence-against-women-and-girls-globally.
26. S.2279-International Violence Against Women Act of 2007 is available here: https://www.congress.gov/bill/110th-congress/senate-bill/2279. The bill has undergone various revi-

sions, and the latest version issued under President Trump's rule removes references to President Obama's strategy.

27. See Corinne L. Mason's "Global Violence Against Women as a National Security 'Emergency'" (2013). Mason argues that the intertwining of US foreign policy and security interests becomes readily apparent when we review the development of the I-VAWA policy and Hillary Clinton's record on fighting violence against women. She suggests that an analysis of both may help show how they "have the potential to be used as a tool to justify global interventions on the grounds of US national security emergencies" (57). Mason is careful to note that such a critique does not entail a complete "disapproval" of state feminism or a dismissal of the need for global policies for fighting gender-based violence (57).
28. See *The Council on Women and Girls: Violence Against Women Accomplishments* (June 2016): https://obamawhitehouse.archives.gov/sites/whitehouse.gov/files/documents/Women%20and%20Girls_VAW.pdf.
29. In her 2010 speech for TEDWomen, Hillary Clinton stated that "the subjugation of women is . . . a threat to the common security of our world and to the national security of our country." See the full speech here: https://obamawhitehouse.archives.gov/sites/whitehouse.gov/files/documents/Women%20and%20Girls_VAW.pdf.
30. See Jacqui True's *The Political Economy of Violence Against Women* (2012).
31. See 60/15 69/150 "Intensifying Global Efforts for the Elimination of Female Genital Mutilations" at https://www.un.org/en/ga/search/view_doc.asp?symbol=A/RES/69/150.
32. https://www.law.cornell.edu/uscode/text/18/116.
33. See S. 1919—Girls Protection Act of 2011, available here: https://www.congress.gov/bill/112th-congress/senate-bill/1919 and *National Defense Authorization Act for Fiscal Year 2013*. Public Law 112-329 (January 2, 2013): https://www.congress.gov/bill/112th-congress/senate-bill/1919.
34. See https://travel.state.gov/content/travel/en/us-visas/visa-information-resources/fact-sheet-on-female-genital-mutilation-or-cutting.html and also the report submitted by the Government Accountability Office.
35. See Enrolled Senate Bill No.337: http://www.legislature.mi.gov/documents/2017-2018/billenrolled/Senate/pdf/2017-SNB-0337.pdf.
36. See the report submitted to the Honorable Harry Reid by the US Government Accountability Office of 2016: https://www.gao.gov/assets/680/678098.pdf.
37. For a chronology of all litigation against the three versions of the executive order, see https://www.nafsa.org/professional-resources/browse-by-interest/executive-order-travel-ban-nafsa-resources.
38. The full text of Ferguson's case is available here: https://www.uscourts.gov/cameras-courts/state-washington-vs-donald-j-trump-et-al.
39. For the full text of Judge Robart's ruling, see https://www.documentcloud.org/documents/3446391-Robart-Order.html.
40. For information on the waiver program, see https://www.cbp.gov/travel/international-visitors/visa-waiver-program/visa-waiver-program-improvement-and-terrorist-travel-prevention-act-faq/. To de-exceptionalize Trump's order requires its placement in longer historical iterations of migration control. The link between Trump's order and Obama's waiver program is made in Laleh Khalili's "With Muslim Ban, Trump and Bannon Wanted Chaos, But Not Resistance" (2017).
41. As Volpp (2019) states, the first version of the executive order has two references to honor killings. In the purpose section, the order places the word *honor* in quotation marks. In the second reference to honor killings, the quotation marks are suddenly dropped. The naming is again altered in the March 6, 2017, version, when the crime is referred to as "so-called 'honor killings'" in the reporting section. For the full version of the text, see https://www.whitehouse.gov/presidential-actions/executive-order-protecting-nation-foreign-terrorist-entry-united-states-2/. Volpp connects the changing language surrounding honor killings

in the text of the order to its critical reception and the administration's attempts to deflect the charge of anti-Muslim bias by removing, or at least somewhat mitigating, this rhetorical evidence from the final version of the order.

42. See the Department of Homeland Security's website here: https://www.dhs.gov/topic/preventing-terrorism-overview.
43. See "Fact Sheet: Protecting the Nation from Foreign Terrorist Entry to the United States" at https://www.dhs.gov/news/2017/01/29/protecting-nation-foreign-terrorist-entry-united-states.
44. Interest in tracking the number of honor-related murders that have occurred in the US precedes the government-issued mandate to do so. In 2014, Westat, an organization dedicated to "improving lives through research," helped publish a report on "honor violence" in the US (Helba, Bernstein, Leonard, and Bauer 2014). The report, which was funded in part by the Department of Justice, exists in full online on the government website of the National Criminal Justice Reference Service (NCJRS). See Volpp (2019) for a detailed discussion of the methodological limits of this study.
45. The full text of Abu-Lughod's declaration is available here: https://www.muslimadvocates.org/files/DeclarationBanAdvancesStereotypesAgainstMuslims.pdf.
46. See Brief of Social Science Scholars as Amici Curiae in Support of Respondents no. Nos. 16-1436, 16-1540, available here: https://www.muslimadvocates.org/files/MuslimAdvocates_SCOTUSAmicusBriefonMuslimBan_FILED.pdf.

NOTES TO CHAPTER 4

1. The king's decision to form the committee is available in Arabic here: http://www.moj.gov.jo/DetailsPage/MOJ/NewsDetails.aspx?ID=669.
2. The full text of the report is available in Arabic here: http://www.moj.gov.jo/DetailsPage/MOJ/NewsDetails.aspx?ID=756.
3. The full text of these laws and their most current amendments are available in Arabic from the website of the Ministry of Justice in Jordan here: http://www.moj.gov.jo/EchoBusV3.0/SystemAssets/5d38ea27-5819-443e-a380-b65c7e1f5b56.pdf.
4. See Abu Odeh (1997), Warrick (2009), and Sonbol (2003) for comparative analyses of these laws that also place them within longer legal genealogies and histories.
5. Ziba Mir-Hosseini (2007) has made a distinction between the study of text (primarily the study of jurisprudence or legislation) and the operations of the text in legal and court cases. This distinction is crucial. While Mir-Hosseini focuses on the latter in her work, my study does not attend to the ways in which the law becomes interpreted or applied by judges in real-life cases or to how clerks, working the court and judiciary systems, and the police come to understand the law and apply it.
6. Judith Tucker (2018) distinguishes between different modes of legal analysis that currently exist in the literature on Arab families and the law: exegetical approaches, sociological approaches, etatist approaches, culturalist approaches, discursive approaches, and feminist approaches. In reading the text of the law and its relationship to feminist activism, my work exists in the nexus between discursive and feminist analytic legal approaches and the etatist approach "which highlights the place of law in the governmentality of modern states, both colonial and postcolonial" (399).
7. Much of the work of documenting cases of gender-based violence in Jordan has been done by the Sisterhood Is Global Institute Jordan (also known as SIGI or *Tadamon*), a civil society organization in Jordan that collects information on gender violence and its occurrence and collectively organizes against it. The organization has called on the Jordanian government to create a national database of these crimes. See http://www.sigi-jordan.org/

for more information on the organization's demands. Other information about the current rates of honor crimes in Kingdom are available from Human Rights Watch; see Adam Coogle (2016).

8. A discussion of the early role played by Princess Basma in leading some of these organizations and the government oversight over women's issues and control of the feminist agenda is available in Sherry L. Lowrance (1998).
9. For an important analysis of the Arab "first lady phenomenon," see Mayssoun Sukarieh (2015). Sukarieh offers a critical reading of the discourse of empowerment and modernization shaping public reception of two Arab first ladies, Queen Rania and Asma Assad, the wife of Bashar Assad, over a period that stretches from 1990 to the outbreak of the Arab uprisings in 2010.
10. The Jordanian Nationality Law does not grant women and men the same rights; Jordanian women married to non-Jordanian men are unable to pass their citizenship to their children. When her reign began, the queen spoke publicly about issues of equality in citizenship rights. As a result of public pushback, her efforts were quickly deflected in favor of a less politicized agenda around women's rights, one that was aligned more comfortably with the modernization efforts of the state and its neoliberal economic agenda.
11. Importantly, these advances in women's rights have often come at the expense of the most alienated members of Jordanian society, including the large segment of Palestinians living within Jordan and other refugee and minoritized communities who are continuously left out of such reform efforts.
12. Two contemporary movements that complicate or challenge this framing are the *hirak* movement for day-wage worker rights and compensation and the campaign for equal citizenship rights called "My Mother Is Jordanian and Her Nationality Is My Right." See Sara Ababneh (2016) for a detailed and ethnographic analysis of the *hirak* movement and its ability to engender women's participation.
13. Jordan established a woman quota in parliamentary elections in 2003 which allotted six seats to women in accordance with changes to the Election Law of 2001. See Abeer Bashier Dababneh (2012). *Khulu'* was first introduced into law in 2001 and later amended in 2011.
14. The battle over the legal age of marriage continues in Jordan. In 2019 the Jordanian Parliament overwhelmingly voted to reject raising the marriage age from fifteen to sixteen. See Sawsan Tabazah (2019).
15. The quest for equal citizenship rights for Jordanian women who are married to non-Jordanian men has been an ongoing site of contestation. Jordan continues to define this issue as a sovereignty matter, but there is broad recognition that what is at stake in the state's refusal to grant citizenship rights to women is the large number of Jordanian women citizens who are married to non-Jordanian men of Palestinian origin and the fear, on the part of the state, that granting citizenship to the children of these marriages would alter the national makeup of the country and tip it in favor of a Palestinian majority. In 2011 a cable sent by the Charge d'Affaires at the American Embassy in Amman in 2008 was released by Wikileaks. Titled "Jordanian Identity Politics Trump Gender Concerns on Citizenship Law Changes," the cable made note of this issue, recognizing that "while the issue is on its surface a gender concern, it is more fundamentally about identity politics in Jordan" (qtd in Malkawi 2011).
16. Since his ascension to the throne, King Abdullah has released seven discussion papers. In each one, he relays his vision for social, economic, and political change in Jordanian society. The sixth discussion paper is available at https://rhc.jo/en/media/sixth-discussion-paper-rule-law-and-civil-state.
17. In Jordan, power is divided between three branches of government: the executive branch, which is represented by the king; the legislative branch, which consists of the appointed members of the Senate (*majlis al-a'yan*) and the elected members of the House of Representatives or Parliament (*majlis al-nuwwab*); and the judicial branch, which includes the

civil, religious, and special courts. The king has absolute power over all three branches. Legal changes are initiated at the level of the House of Representatives, which has the capacity to accept, amend, or reject any proposed legal changes before they are passed on to the Senate and from there to the king for final approval before they become law. The judiciary's independence is enshrined in the Jordanian Constitution of 1952, which states that judges are "subject to no authority but that of the law." See http://www.kinghussein.gov.jo/government4.html.

18. Stefanie Eileen Nanes (2003) suggests that the campaign against honor-based violence began in Jordan as early as 1999. The focus of the initial campaign was article 340, which activists rightly argued provided legal cover for the murder of women.
19. See Warrick (2005, 2009) for detailed analysis of the workings of the law and its conception of gender-based violence. See also Sonbol (2003), Abu Odeh (1997, 2010), and Faqir (2001).
20. In *Islam in Liberalism,* Joseph Massad argues that "most laws on the books that discriminate against women in formerly colonized Muslim-majority countries, including nationality law, as we saw, are derived from Western liberal and secular colonial and national laws" (2015, 206).
21. Alongside the legal system and *Sharia* law exists customary or tribal law. Tribal law functions outside of and/or apart from the formal legal system, allowing tribes to resolve conflicts internally and through the *jaha* or tribal system of mediation. See Linda L. Layne (1994) and Ann Furr and Muwafaq Al-Serhan (2008). See also Amira El-Azhary Sonbol's (2003) discussion of tribal law and "*diyya* settlements" in cases of murder. An examination of tribal resolutions of gender violence is outside the scope of this study.
22. As Amira Sonbol states in her work on Jordan and the law, the Jordanian state primarily utilized the Hanafi *madhhab,* but "when it came to laws of guardianship, they mixed between the Hanafi and Maliki *madhahib*" (2003, 37).
23. Husseini has played a key and leading role in bringing societal attention to the occurrence of crimes of honor in Jordan; she has dedicated many articles to exposing these crimes and received much attention for her work, including being selected for the 1998 Reebok Human Rights Award. In 2009 Husseini published a book about her efforts to bring honor crimes to Jordanian and international attention. The book, *Murder in the Name of Honour: The True Story of One Woman's Heroic Fight Against an Unbelievable Crime,* is a mix between memoir and essay-style chapters, outlining the author's commitment to fighting the "global phenomenon" (xiii) of honor crimes and her desire to "live as part of a system in which crimes are seen for what they are, freed of the double standards that mask their heinous nature, and punished with a severity that matches the crime" (xiv).
24. The campaign's website is available here: http://www.women.jo/.
25. The film can be accessed here: https://www.youtube.com/watch?v=belzQYQEUyA&t=1s.
26. The *mahr* is traditionally an amount of money paid to the bride in cash, property, or gold. In some cases, the *mahr* is paid fully or partially prior to the consummation of the marriage.
27. This move mirrors what scholars writing on gender violence in the US have uncovered about the connections between feminist antiviolence campaigns and women's organizing and the state. For example, Kristin Bumiller (2008) carefully shows how feminist efforts to curb violence against women became aligned with the neoliberal state. Bumiller's important study explores how, for over four decades, feminist campaigns against gender and sexual violence were able to transform public discourse around this phenomenon and how a feminist agenda shaped national action against the broad and frequent occurrence of gender violence in US society. Bumiller links campaigns against gender violence to core feminist agendas regarding the promotion of freedom, equality, and autonomy. Bumiller provides a historical genealogy of the alliance between feminist movements to end violence and state institutions and practices, demonstrating how the twinning of the

feminist agenda with state concern to curb violent crime coincided with the rise of the neoliberal state. Through this alliance, gender violence was transformed "into a social, medical, and legal problem" (13). By relegating women's safety and health to the power of the state, feminist efforts to curb violence against women became increasingly reliant on the juridical and "carceral capacities of the state" to protect women from the occurrence of violence in their lives (2). Similarly, Emily L. Thuma has also demonstrated how the 1994 passage of the Violence Against Women Act (VAWA), which enabled a "crack down on individual perpetrators of violence against women[,] became a critical lever of legitimacy for expanding the carceral state" (2019, 7). Thuma's argument demonstrates the ways in which certain forms of feminist antiviolence activism challenged the criminalization and statist approach adopted by "feminist advocacy for criminal justice–based approaches" (7). These works, while focused on the US context, help place the turn toward the state within transnational histories of antiviolence campaigns that wed justice to the realm of the legal and the carceral.

28. Elizabeth Bernstein has explored how feminist agendas to curb violence against women "have become intricately interwoven with punitive agendas in contemporary US (and by extension, global) politics" (2012, 235). Bernstein's work focuses on the efforts of anti-trafficking movements in the US, showing how they propelled border control practices, stricter immigration law, and the expansion of the prison industrial complex. Bernstein names this phenomenon the "carceral turn" in feminist movements, which emanates from a broader shift toward the governance of crime through more extensive and pervasive forms of punishment. Bernstein shows how feminist antitrafficking activism shifted from a focus on the economic, political, and structural conditions that allowed for the abuse of women's sexual labor to the "sexual violation" itself (242). This shift, as she notes, was essential for transforming antitrafficking activism "into a legal framework with powerful material and symbolic effects" (242).
29. The 2017 repeal of article 308 and the amendment to article 98 coincided with the Parliament's adoption of the Law on the Rights of Persons with Disabilities, which prohibits discrimination against people with disabilities and imposes limits on pretrial detentions, except in cases associated with security and intelligence. In addition to adoption of this important law, the reforms were accompanied by the passing of harsher penalties for a number of crimes, including acts of terrorism, crimes against legal persons or property, crimes against public officials, and electronic crimes (*Jordan Times* 2017).
30. See Dena's interview in this video by Rosie-Lyse Thompson and Shanshan Chen: http://news.trust.org/item/20170816090413-sc4e7/.
31. It is important here to highlight the groundbreaking research conducted by the journalistic website *7iber*, which has released detailed, carefully researched, and well-documented investigative journalism on the phenomenon of protective custody as well as on honor-based violence in Jordan. Some of this work is available here: https://www.7iber.com/2014/12/honor-crimes/.
32. See Rimaz Musa's work here: https://www.7iber.com/2015/02/administrative-detention-governer/?utm_source=yarpp&utm_medium=post&utm_campaign=related.
33. In December 2019 I had the opportunity to meet Eva Abu Halaweh, who generously shared her wealth of knowledge and information about the creation of *Dar Amneh* and helped shed light on its formation and the concerted efforts of Jordanian women activists in its setup. I am deeply grateful for her willingness to help me better understand Jordanian efforts to combat gender violence and their various intricacies and complexities with respect to the women's movement and to legal reform in the country.

WORKS CITED

Ababneh, Sara. 2016. "Troubling the Political: Women in the Jordanian Day-Waged Labor Movement." *International Journal of Middle East Studies* 48, no. 1: 87–112.

Abdo, Nahla. *Women in Israel: Race, Gender and Citizenship*. London: Zed Books, 2011.

Abunimah, Ali. 2012. "Watch: New DAM Hip Hop Track with Video Co-directed by Jackie Salloum Targets Violence Against Women." *Electronic Intifada*, November 6, 2012. https://electronicintifada.net/blogs/ali-abunimah/watch-new-dam-hip-hop-track-video-co-directed-jackie-salloum-targets-violence.

Abu Odeh, Lama. 1997. "Comparatively Speaking: The Honor of the East and the Passion of the West." *Utah Law Review* 2: 287–307.

Abu Odeh, Lama. 2010. "Honor Killings and the Construction of Gender in Arab Societies." *The American Journal of Comparative Law* 58, no. 4: 911–52.

Abu Odeh, Lama. 2011. "Crimes of Honor and the Construction of Gender in Arab Societies." *Comparative Law Review* 2, no. 1: 1–47.

Abu Odeh, Lama. 2015. "Holier Than Thou? The Anti-imperialist versus the Local Activist." *Open Democracy*, May 4, 2015. https://www.opendemocracy.net/en/5050/holier-than-thou-antiimperialist-versus-local-activist/.

Abu-Lughod, Lila. 1998. "Introduction: Feminist Longings and Postcolonial Conditions." In *Remaking Women: Feminism and Modernity in the Middle East*, edited by Lila Abu-Lughod. Princeton: Princeton University Press. 3–32.

Abu-Lughod, Laila. 2002. "Do Muslim Women Really Need Saving? Anthropological Reflections on Cultural Relativism and Its Others." *American Anthropologist* 104, no. 3: 783–90.

Abu-Lughod, Laila. 2009. "Dialectics of Women's Empowerment: The International Circuitry of the *Arab Human Development Report 2005*." *International Journal of Middle East Studies* 41: 83–103.

Abu-Lughod, Lila. 2011. "Seductions of the 'Honor Crime.'" *differences* 22, no. 1: 17–63.

Abu-Lughod, Lila. 2013. *Do Muslim Women Need Saving?* Cambridge, MA: Harvard University Press.

Abu Lughod, Lila, and Maya Mikdashi. 2012a. "Tradition and the Anti-Politics Machine: DAM Seduced by the 'Honor Crime.'" *Jadaliyya,* November 23, 2012. http://www.jadaliyya.com/Details/27467/Tradition-and-the-Anti-Politics-Machine-DAM-Seduced-by-the-%E2%80%9CHonor-Crime%E2%80%9D.

Abu Lughod, Lila, and Maya Mikdashi. 2012b. "Honoring Solidarity During Contentious Debates . . . A Letter to DAM from Lila Abu Lughod and Maya Mikdashi." *Jadaliyya.* December 26, 2012. http://www.jadaliyya.com/Details/27700/Honoring-Solidarity-During-Contentious-Debates—A-Letter-to-DAM-From-Lila-Abu-Lughod-and-Maya-Mikdashi.

Abueish, Tamara. 2019. "Palestinian Officials Confirm Israa Ghareeb Died from Physical Assault Wounds." *Al Arabiya,* September 12, 2019. https://english.alarabiya.net/en/features/2019/09/04/-We-are-all-Israa-Ghareeb-Death-of-Palestinian-woman-sparks-public-outrage-.

Adely, Fida J. 2009. "Educating Women for Development: The *Arab Human Right Report 2005* and the Problem with Women's Choices." *International Journal of Middle East Studies* 41: 105–22.

Ahmed, Leila. 1992. *Women and Gender in Islam: Historical Roots of a Modern Debate.* New Haven, CT: Yale University Press.

Ahmed, Leila. 2011. "Treacherous Sympathy with Muslim Women." *Qantara.de,* August 18, 2011. https://en.qantara.de/content/feminism-colonialism-and-islamophobia-treacherous-sympathy-with-muslim-women.

Al Emam, Dana. 2016. "Administrative Detention of Women for Protection Is 'Illegal,' Activists Say." *Jordan Times,* November 1, 2016. http://jordantimes.com/news/local/administrative-detention-women-protection-illegal%E2%80%99-activists-say.

Al Samman, Hanadi. 2017. "Invading Muslim Bodies in the Era of Trump." *Journal of Middle East Women's Studies* 13, no. 3: 483–85.

Al Tahat, Jassar. 2017. "'I Was More of a Victim of Article 308 Than My Rapist': Lawmaker Says House Legal Committee Supports Removal Of Notorious Provision." *Jordan Times,* May 14, 2017. https://search-proquest-com.libezproxy2.syr.edu/docview/1898657244?accountid=14214.

Al-Ali, Nadje. 2016. "How to Talk about Gender-Based Violence?" *Kohl: A Journal for Body and Gender Research* 2, no. 1 (Summer): 7–11.

Al-Ali. Nadje. 2018. "Sexual violence in Iraq: Challenges for Transnational Feminist Politics." *European Journal of Women's Studies* 25, no. 1: 10–27.

Al-Atiyat, Ibtesam. 2012. "Harvests of the Golden Decades: Contemporary Women's Activism in Jordan." In *Mapping Arab Women's Movements: A Century of Transformations from Within,* edited by Pernille Alrenfeldt and Nawar Al-Hassan Golley. Cairo, Egypt: The American University in Cairo Press. 133–70.

Al-Atiyat, Ibtesam. 2019. "Repealing Jordan's Rape Article 308." *Confluences Méditerranée* 110: 99–111.

Al-Ghussein, Soraya, and Hannah Patchett. 2012. "Abbas Aide: No Plans to Outlaw 'Honor Killing.'" *Ma'an News Agency,* December 24, 2012. https://www.marsad.ps/en/2012/12/25/abbas-aide-no-plans-to-outlaw-honor-killing/.

Alcoff, Linda Martín. 2018. *Race and Resistance: Understanding the Complexities of Sexual Violation.* Cambridge: Polity Press.

Allen, Kate, and Joe Freisen. 2010. "Father, Brother Plead Guilty to So-Called 'Honour Killing'" *Globe and Mail*, June 15, 2010. https://www.theglobeandmail.com/news/toronto/father-brother-plead-guilty-to-so-called-honour-killing/article1367964/

Alvarado, Monsy. 2018. "'Vacation Cutting': ICE Agents at Newark Airport Seek to Deter Female Genital Mutilation." *NorthJersey.com*, June 24, 2018. https://www.northjersey.com/story/news/2018/06/24/newark-airport-ice-agents-seek-deter-female-genital-cutting/669029002/.

Anderson, R. Reeves et al. 2017. "Brief of Social Sciences Scholars as *Amici Curiae* in Support of Respondents." September 18, 2017. https://www.scotusblog.com/wp-content/uploads/2017/09/16_1436_16_1540_bsac_Social_Science_Scholars.pdf.

Arab Renaissance for Democracy and Development (ARDD). 2017. *Draft Legislative Changes to Article 308: Discrimination Against Women Continues.* May 16, 2017: 1–8.

Asaad, Soheir. 2019. "Tali'at: Our Struggle to Reclaim Politics." Translated by Jehan Bseiso and Yamila Hussein Shannan. *Mada Masr*, December 16, 2019. https://www.madamasr.com/en/2019/12/16/opinion/u/taliat-our-struggle-to-reclaim-politics/.

Associated Press. 1991. "Parents Sentenced to Death in Killing of Daughter." December 19, 1991. https://www.apnews.com/9c9cfd91e6aefcf02cafaf3995192a99.

Awwad, Amani M. 2001. "Gossip, Scandal, Shame and Honor Killing: A Case for Social Constructionism and Hegemonic Discourse." *Social Thought & Research* 24, no. 1/2: 39–52.

Baker, Jo, and Elna Søndergaard. 2014. "Conditions for Women in Detention in Jordan: Needs, Vulnerabilities, and Good Practices." *Dignity Publication*. https://dignity.dk/wp-content/uploads/publication_series_no9.pdf.

Bannerji, Himani. 2000. *The Dark Side of the Nation: Essays on Multiculturalism, Nationalism, and Gender.* Toronto: Canadian Scholars' Press.

Barnard, Ann, and Alan Feuer. 2010. "Outraged, and Outrageous." *New York Times*, October 8, 2010. https://www.nytimes.com/2010/10/10/nyregion/10geller.html.

Barnes, Tom. 2015. "These Palestinian Rappers Are Tearing Down Sexism in the Best Way Possible." *MIC*, April 20, 2015. https://www.mic.com/articles/115940/these-palestinian-rappers-are-tearing-down-sexism-in-the-best-way-possible.

Barrett, Devlin and Dan Frosch. 2017. "Federal Judge Temporarily Halts Trump Order on Immigration, Refugees." *The Wall Street Journal*, February 4, 2017. https://www.wsj.com/articles/legal-feud-over-trump-immigration-order-turns-to-visa-revocations-1486153216.

Bartolucci, Valentina. 2012. "Terrorism Rhetoric Under the Bush Administration: Discourses and Effects." *Journal of Language and Politics*. 11, no. 4: 562–582.

Baxter, Diane. 2007. "Honor Thy Sister: Selfhood, Gender, and Agency in Palestinian Culture." *Anthropological Quarterly* 80, no. 3 (Summer): 737–75.

Begum, Rothna. 2019. "When It Mattered, PALESTINIAN LAW FAILED Israa Ghrayeb. It's High Time That Changed." *The New Arab*, September 18, 2019. https://www.alaraby.co.uk/english/Comment/2019/9/18/The-lethal-cost-of-being-a-woman-in-Palestine.

Bernstein, Elizabeth. 2012. "Carceral Politics as Gender Justice? The 'Traffic in Women' and Neoliberal Circuits of Crime, Sex, and Rights." *Theory and Society* 41, no. 3 (May): 233–59.

Bernstein, Elizabeth. 2018. *Brokered Subjects: Sex, Trafficking, and the Politics of Freedom.* Chicago: Chicago University Press.

Best, Joel. 1990. *Threatened Children: Rhetoric and Concern about Child-Victims.* Chicago: University of Chicago Press.

Bever, Lindsey. 2015. "Pamela Geller, the Incendiary Organizer of Texas 'Prophet Muhammad Cartoon Contest.'" *Washington Post*, May 4, 2015. https://www.washingtonpost.com/news/

morning-mix/wp/2015/05/04/why-a-woman-named-pamela-geller-organized-a-prophet-muhammad-cartoon-contest/.

Bierman, Noah. 2019. "What's Behind All Those Executive Orders Trump Loves to Sign? Not Much." *Los Angeles Times,* March 27, 2019. https://www.latimes.com/politics/la-na-pol-trump-executive-orders-ineffective-20190327-story.html.

Bilge, Sirma. 2006. "Behind the 'Culture' Lens: Judicial Representations of Violence Against Women" *Canadian Woman Studies* 25, no. 1/2 (Winter): 173–80.

Borjas, George J. 2016. "The Case for Extreme Immigrant Vetting." *Politico Magazine,* August 17, 2016. https://www.politico.com/magazine/story/2016/08/donald-trump-2016-immigration-vetting-214171.

Bracke, Sarah, and Nadia Fadil. 2012. "'Is the Headscarf Oppressive or Emancipatory?' Field Notes from the Multicultural Debate." *Religion and Gender* 2, no.1: 36–56.

Brand, Laurie A. 1999. "The Effects of the Peace Process on Political Liberalization in Jordan." *Journal of Palestine Studies* 28, no. 2 (Winter): 52–67.

Brand, Laurie A. 2003. "Jordan: Women and the Struggle for Political Opening." In *Women and Globalization in Arab the Middle East: Gender, Economy, and Society,* edited by Eleanor Abdella Doumata and Marsha Pripstein Posusney. Boulder: Lynne Rienner. 143–68.

Bumiller, Kristin. 2008. *In an Abusive State: How Neoliberalism Appropriated the Feminist Movement Against Sexual Violence.* Durham, NC: Duke University Press.

Buncombe, Andrew. 2017. "Donald Trump's Muslim Ban Inspires Mass Protests Across the United States Involving Millions of Americans." *Independent,* January 30, 2017. https://www.independent.co.uk/news/world/americas/donald-trump-muslim-ban-protests-us-refugee-immigration-policy-syria-iran-iraq-demonstrations-a7553476.html.

Canadian Council of Muslim Women. 2012. "CCMW Position on Femicide [not Honour Killing]." January 1, 2012. https://static1.squarespace.com/static/5b43ad2bf407b4a036d27f06/t/5c5e13c1eb39311832e6eb7a/1549669313993/ccmw_position_femicide_not_honour_killing.pdf.

CARE USA et al. 2017. "Dear President Trump." March 13, 2017. https://www.amnestyusa.org/pdfs/eo_gbv_letter.pdf.

CBC News. 2010. "Father, Son Plead Guilty to Aqsa Parvez Murder." June 15, 2010. https://www.cbc.ca/news/canada/toronto/father-son-plead-guilty-to-aqsa-parvez-murder-1.905089.

Chesler, Phyllis. 2009 "Are Honor Killings Simply Domestic Violence?" *The Middle East Quarterly* 26, no. 2 (September): 61–69. https://www.meforum.org/2067/are-honor-killings-simply-domestic-violence.

Chowdhury, Elora Halim. 2011. *Transnationalism Reversed: Women Organizing Against Gendered Violence in Bangladesh.* Albany, NY: State University of New York Press.

Churchill, Robert Paul. 2018. *Women in the Crossfire: Understanding and Ending Honor Killing.* Oxford: Oxford University Press.

Clark, Janine A. 2006. "The Conditions of Islamist Moderation: Unpacking Cross-Ideological Cooperation in Jordan." *International Journal of Middle East Studies* 38, no. 4: 539–60.

Clark, Janine A. and Amy E. Young. 2008. "Islamism and Family Law Reform in Morocco and Jordan." *Mediterranean Politics* 13, no.3: 333–52.

Clinton, Hillary. 2011. "It's Time to Get Tough on Violence Against Women." *Guardian,* December 10, 2011. https://www.theguardian.com/commentisfree/2011/dec/10/violence-women-hillary-clinton.

Clough, Patricia Ticineto, and Craig Willse. 2010. "Gendered Security/National Security: Political Branding and Population Racism." *Social Text,* 28, no. 4 (105): 45–63.

Connors, Jane. 2005. "United Nations Approaches to 'Crimes of Honour.'" In *'Honour': Crimes, Paradigms, and Violence Against Women,* edited by Lynn Welchman and Sara Hossain. London: Zed Books. 22–41.

Coogle, Adam. 2016. "Recorded 'Honor' Killings on the Rise in Jordan." *Human Rights Watch,* October 27, 2016. https://www.hrw.org/news/2016/10/27/recorded-honor-killings-rise-jordan.

Cooney, Mark. 2014. "Death by Family: Honor Violence as Punishment." *Punishment and Society* 16, no. 4: 406–27.

Cuthbert, Olivia. 2017. "Protesters Say Jordanian Law Dealing With 'Honour' Crimes Is a "License to Kill." *Open Democracy,* March 16, 2017. https://www.opendemocracy.net/en/north-africa-west-asia/protesters-say-jordanian-law-dealing-with-honour-crimes-is-license-to/.

Dababneh, Abeer Bashier. 2012. "Jordanian Women's Political Participation: Legislative Status and Structural Challenges." *European Journal of Social Sciences,* 27, no. 2: 213–21.

De Bode, Lisa. 2014. "Ayaan Hirsi Ali Film Ignites Row over Islam, Censorship." *Al Jazeera America,* April 14, 2014. http://america.aljazeera.com/articles/2014/4/15/ayaan-hirsi-ali-honordiariesbrandeisuniversity.html.

De Vogue, Ariane, Jeremy Diamond, and Kevin Liptak. 2017. "US President Donald Trump Signs New Travel Ban, Exempts Iraq." *CNN,* March 7, 2017. https://www.cnn.com/2017/03/06/politics/trump-travel-ban-iraq/index.html.

Demian, Melissa. 2008. "Fictions of Intention in the 'Cultural Defense.'" *American Anthropologist* 110, no. 4 (December): 432–42.

Dhamoon, Rita. 2006. "Shifting from 'Culture' to 'Cultural': Critical Theorizing of Identity/Difference Politics." *Constellations* 13, no. 3: 354–73.

Dingo, Rebecca. 2012. *Networking Arguments: Rhetoric, Transnational Feminism, and Public Policy Writing.* Pittsburgh: University of Pittsburgh Press.

Dukureh, Jaha. 2015. "Millions of Women Risk Female Genital Mutilation. Will Obama Defend Them?" *Common Dreams.* July 25, 2015. https://www.commondreams.org/views/2015/07/25/millions-women-risk-female-genital-mutilation-will-obama-defend-them.

Eisner, Manuel, and Lana Ghuneim. 2013. "Honor Killing Attitudes amongst Adolescents in Amman, Jordan." *Aggressive Behavior* 39: 405–17.

El-Masri, Samar. 2012. "Challenges facing CEDAW in the Middle East and North Africa." *The International Journal of Human Rights* 16, no. 7: 931–46.

El Muhtaseb, Lamis, Nathan J. Brown, and Abdul-Wahab Kayyali. 2016. "Arguing about Family Law in Jordan: Disconnected Spheres?" *International Journal of Middle East Studies* 48, no. 4: 721–41.

Ellis, Jonathan. 2015. "Film Provokes Censorship, Tolerance Debate at USD." *Argus Leader,* March 27, 2015. https://www.argusleader.com/story/jonathanellis/2015/03/27/censorship-tolerance-debate-at-usd/70542856/.

Eltahawy, Mona. 2008. "Caught in the Clash of Civilizations." *New York Times,* January 18, 2008. https://www.nytimes.com/2008/01/18/opinion/18iht-edelta.1.9323537.html.

Eqeiq, Amal. 2010. "Louder Than the Blue ID: Palestinian Hip-Hop in Israel." In *Displaced at Home: Ethnicity and Gender among Palestinians in Israel,* edited by Rhoda Ann Kanaaneh and Isis Nusair. Albany: State University of New York Press. 53–74.

Erakat, Noura. 2019. *Justice for Some: Law and the Question of Palestine.* Stanford: Stanford University Press.

Ewing, Katherine Pratt. 2008. *Stolen Honor: Stigmatizing Muslim Men in Berlin.* Stanford: Stanford University Press.

Ewing, Katherine Pratt. 2013. "From German Bus Stop to Academy Award Nomination: The Honor Killing as Simulacrum." In *Gender, Violence, and Human Security: Critical Feminist Perspectives,* edited by Aili Mari Tripp, Myra Marx Ferree, and Christina Ewig. New York: New York University Press. 163–90.

Exec. Order No. 13,769, 82 Fed. Reg. 8,977 (Jan. 27, 2017). "Executive Order Protecting the Nation from Foreign Terrorist Entry into the United States." https://www.whitehouse.gov/presidential-actions/executive-order-protecting-nation-foreign-terrorist-entry-united-states/.

Fadil, Nadia. 2011. "Not-/Unveiling as an Ethical Practice." *Feminist Review* 98, no. 1: 83–109.

Faqir, Fadia. 2001. "Intrafamily Femicide in Defence of Honour: The Case of Jordan." *Third World Quarterly* 22, no. 1: 65–82.

Farris, Sara R. 2017. *In the Name of Women's Rights: The Rise of Femonationalism.* Durham: Duke University Press.

Ferguson, James. 1994. *The Anti-Politics Machine: "Development," Depoliticization, and Bureaucratic Power in Lesotho.* Minnesota: University of Minnesota Press.

Ferguson, Peter. 2017. "The State of Jordanian Women's Organizations—Five Years beyond the Arab Spring." *Politics and Governance* 5, no. 2: 59–86.

Forliti, Amy. 2018. "Ruling in Michigan Genital Mutilation Case Shocks Women's Advocates." *Chicago Sun Times,* November 23, 2018. https://chicago.suntimes.com/2018/11/23/18438711/ruling-in-michigan-genital-mutilation-case-shocks-women-s-advocates.

Fournier, Pascale, Pascal McDougall, and Anna R. Deker. 2012. "Dishonour, Provocation and Culture: In the Beholder's Eye?" *Canadian Criminal Law Review* 16, no. 2: 161–93.

Furr, Ann, and Muwafaq Al-Serhan. 2008. "Tribal Customary Law in Jordan." *South Carolina Journal of Law and Business* 4, no. 2: 17–34.

Gabriel, Brigitte. 2018. *Rise: In Defense of Judeo-Christian Values and Freedom.* Lake Mary, Florida: Charisma House Book Group, 2018.

Galusca, Roxana. 2012. "Slave Hunters, Brothel Busters, and Feminist Interventions: Investigative Journalists as Anti-Sex-Trafficking Humanitarians." *Feminist Formations* 24, no. 2: 1–24.

Gambino, Lauren, Sabrina Siddiqui, Paul Owen, and Edward Helmore. 2017. "Thousands Protest Against Trump Travel Ban in Cities and Airports Nationwide." *Guardian,* January 29, 2017. https://www.theguardian.com/us-news/2017/jan/29/protest-trump-travel-ban-muslims-airports.

Geller, Pamela. 2009. "Honoring the Victims of Honor Killings." *American Thinker,* June 11, 2009. http://www.americanthinker.com/articles/2009/06/honoring_the_victims_of_honor.html.

Geller, Pamela. 2011. "Pamela Geller, Big Government: Stand Against Honor Killing August 24th in Jerusalem: Dedication of Aqsa Parvez Grove." *Geller Report,* May 31, 2011. http://pamelageller.com/2011/05/pamela-geller-big-government-august-24th-in-jerusalem-dedication-of-aqsa-parvez-grove.html/.

Geller, Pamela. 2012. "Arab-Americans Stand Up for Honor Killings." *WND,* May 8, 2012. http://www.wnd.com/2012/05/arab-americans-stand-up-for-honor-killing/.

Genette, Gerard. 1997. *Paratexts: Thresholds of Interpretation.* Cambridge: Cambridge University Press.

Gill, Aisha K. 2010. "Reconfiguring 'Honour'-Based Violence as a Form of Gendered Violence." In *Honour, Violence, Women and Islam,* edited by Mohammad Mazher Idriss and Tahir Abbas. New York: Routledge. 218–31.

Gill, Aisha K. 2018. "Social and Cultural Implications of 'Honor'-Based Violence." In *International Human Rights of Women,* edited by Niamh Reilly. Singapore: Springer. 1–16.

Glazer, Hilo. 2019. "'I Didn't Hesitate for a Second': What Drives a Young Man to Murder His Sister." *Haaretz,* February 23, 2019. https://www.haaretz.com/israel-news/.premium.MAGAZINE-i-didn-t-hesitate-for-a-second-what-drives-a-young-man-to-murder-his-sister-1.6956850.

Glenister, Jade. 2016. "Good Intentions: Can the 'Protective Custody' of Women Amount to Torture?" *The Equal Rights Review* 16: 13–37.

Gökariksel, Banu. 2017. "The Body Politics of Trump's 'Muslim Ban.'" *Journal of Middle East Women's Studies* 13, no. 3: 469–71.

Goldberg, Howard, Paul Stupp, Ekwutosi Okoroh, Ghenet Besera, David Goodman, and Isabella Danel. 2016. "Female Genital Mutilation/Cutting in the United States: Updated Estimates of Women and Girls at Risk, 2012." *Public Health Reports* 131, no. 2 (March/April): 340–47.

Gorman, Cynthia S. 2019. "Feminist Legal Archeology, Domestic Violence and the Raced-Gendered Juridical Boundaries of U.S. Asylum Law." *EPA: Economy and Space* 51, no. 5: 1050–67.

Grewal, Inderpal. 2005. *Transnational America: Feminisms, Diasporas, Neoliberalisms.* Durham: Duke University Press.

Grewal, Inderpal. 2013. "Outsourcing Patriarchy: Feminist Encounters, Transnational Mediations and the Crime of 'Honour Killings.'" *International Feminist Journal of Politics* 15, no. 1: 1–19.

Grewal, Inderpal, and Caren Kaplan. 2001. "Global Identities: Theorizing Transnational Studies of Sexuality." *GLQ: A Journal of Lesbian and Gay Studies* 7, no. 4: 663–79.

Grewal, Zareena. 2009. "Death by Culture? How *Not* to Talk about Islam and Domestic Violence." *Institute for Social Policy and Understanding,* July 2009. https://www.ispu.org/death-by-culture-how-not-to-talk-about-islam-and-domestic-violence/.

Hammami, Rema. 2019. "Follow the Numbers: Global Governmentality and the Violence Against Women Agenda in Occupied Palestine." In *Governance Feminism: Notes from the Field,* edited by Janet Halley, Prabha Kotiswaran, Rachel Rebouché, and Hila Shamir. Minneapolis: University of Minnesota Press. 479–504.

Hammer, Juliane. 2013. "(Muslim) Women's Bodies, Islamophobia, and American Politics." *Bulletin for the Study of Religion* 42, no. 1: 29–36.

Hammer, Juliane. 2019. *Peaceful Families: American Muslim Efforts Against Domestic Violence.* Princeton: Princeton University Press.

Haque, Eve. 2010. "Homegrown, Muslim and Other: Tolerance, Secularism and the Limits of Multiculturalism." *Social Identities* 16, no. 1: 79–101.

Haque, Eve. 2012. *Multiculturalism Within a Bilingual Framework: Language, Race, and Belonging in Canada.* Toronto: University of Toronto Press.

Harkov, Lahav. 2016. "40 Arab Women Murdered in Ramle and Lod in Past 30 Years." *Jerusalem Post,* October 6, 2016. https://www.jpost.com/israel-news/40-arab-women-murdered-in-ramle-and-lod-in-past-30-years-469571.

Harris, Ellen Frances. *Guarding the Secrets: Palestinian Terrorism and a Father's Murder of his too-American Daughter.* New York, Scribner, 1995.

Hassan, Manar. 2002. "The Politics of Honor: Patriarchy, the State and the Murder of Women in the Name of Family Honor." *Journal of Israeli History* 21, nos. 1–2: 1–37.

Hasso, Frances. 2005. *Resistance, Repression, and Gender Politics in Occupied Palestine and Jordan.* Syracuse: Syracuse University Press.

Hasso, Frances. 2014. "Bargaining with the Devil: States and Intimate Life." *Journal of Middle East Women's Studies*10, no. 2 (Spring): 107–34.

Hatem, Mervat. 2005. "In the Shadow of the State: Changing Definitions of Arab Women's 'Developmental' Citizenship Rights." *Journal of Middle East Women's Studies* 1, no. 3 (Fall): 20–45.

Hatuqa, Dalia. 2014. "'Paradigm Shift': Palestinians Join Treaties." *Al Jazeera,* April 22, 2014 https://www.aljazeera.com/news/2014/04/22/paradigm-shift-palestinians-join-treaties/.

Hawari, Yara. 2019. "Israa Gharib's Murder Has Nothing to Do with Honour." *Al Jazeera,* September 4, 2019. https://www.aljazeera.com/opinions/2019/9/4/israa-gharibs-murder-has-nothing-to-do-with-honour/.

Hayes, Chris. 2019. "Trump Attacked Obama for Using Executive Powers on Immigration, Now Plans to Do the Same Thing." *USA Today,* February 14, 2019. https://www.usatoday.com/story/news/politics/2019/02/14/donald-trump-2014-president-shouldnt-use-executive-authority/2875541002/.

Hayoun, Masoud. 2013. "Moroccan Teen, Forced to Marry Her Rapist, Commits Suicide." *Aljazeera America,* November 22, 2013. http://america.aljazeera.com/articles/2013/11/22/moroccan-teen-marriedtoherrapistcommitssuicide.html.

Helba, Cynthia, Matthew Bernstein, Mariel Leonard, and Erin Bauer. 2014. "Report on Exploratory Study into Honor Violence Measurement Methods." *Westat.* November 26, 2014. https://www.ncjrs.gov/pdffiles1/bjs/grants/248879.pdf.

Heller, Jeffrey. 2011. "Glenn Beck Rallies for Israel Near Jerusalem Holy Sites." *Reuters,* August 24, 2011. https://www.reuters.com/article/us-israel-beck/glenn-beck-rallies-for-israel-near-jerusalem-holy-sites-idUSTRE77N5WL20110824.

Henry, Michelle, and Bob Mitchell. 2007. "Muslim Teen Was Abused, Friends Say." *Toronto Star,* December 12, 2007. https://www.thestar.com/news/gta/2007/12/12/muslim_teen_was_abused_friends_say.html.

Hesford, Wendy. 2011. *Spectacular Rhetorics: Human Rights Visions, Recognitions, Feminisms.* Durham, NC: Duke University Press.

Hing, Bill Ong. 2009. "Institutional Racism, ICE Raids, and Immigration Reform." *University of San Francisco Law Review* 44, no. 2: 307–52.

Hing, Bill Ong. 2018. "Entering the Trump Ice Age: Contextualizing the New Enforcement Regime." *Texas A&M Law Review* 5, no. 2: 253–321.

Human Rights Watch. 2001. "Item 12—Integration of the Human Rights of Women and the Gender Perspective: Violence Against Women and 'Honor' Crimes." April 5, 2001. https://www.hrw.org/news/2001/04/05/item-12-integration-human-rights-women-and-gender-perspective-violence-against-women.

Human Rights Watch. 2004. "Honoring the Killers: Justice Denied for 'Honor' Crimes in Jordan." *Human Rights Watch* 16, no. 1, https://www.hrw.org/reports/2004/jordan0404/jordan0404.pdf.

Human Rights Watch. 2009. "Guests of the Governor: Administrative Detention Undermines the Rule of Law in Jordan." May 26, 2009. https://www.hrw.org/report/2009/05/26/guests-governor/administrative-detention-undermines-rule-law-jordan.

Human Rights Watch. 2017a. "Jordan: A Strong Move for Justice Reform." March 14, 2017. https://www.hrw.org/news/2017/03/14/jordan-strong-move-justice-reform.

Human Rights Watch. 2017b. "Jordan: Parliament Passes Human Rights Reforms." October 4, 2017. https://www.hrw.org/news/2017/10/04/jordan-parliament-passes-human-rights-reforms.

Humphreys, Adrian, Meghan O'Toole, and Kenyon Wallace. 2010. "Aqsa Parvez's Father, Brother Plead Guilty in Death." *Global News,* June 15, 2010. https://globalnews.ca/news/91493/aqsa-parvezs-father-brother-plead-guilty-in-death/.

Husseini, Rana. 2000. "Crimes of Honor." *Al-Raida* 17, no. 89 (Spring): 19–21.

Husseini, Rana. 2009. *Murder in the Name of Honor: The True Story of One Woman's Heroic Fight Against an Unbelievable Crime.* Oxford: One World, 2009.

Husseini, Rana. 2015. "57% of Sexual Assault Survivors Hesitate to Report It—Study." *Jordan Times,* October 13, 2015. https://www.jordantimes.com/news/local/57-sexual-assault-survivors-hesitate-report-it-%E2%80%94-study.

Husseini, Rana. 2016a. "Activists Urge Justice for Torture Victims." *Jordan Times,* October 25, 2016. http://www.jordantimes.com/news/local/activists-urge-justice-torture-victims.

Husseini, Rana. 2016b. "Honour Crimes Anti-Islamic—Fatwa." *Jordan Times,* December 1, 2016. http://jordantimes.com/news/local/honour-crimes-anti-islamic-%E2%80%94-fatwa.

Husseini, Rana. 2016c. "New Projected Shelter to House Women Under Threat Over 'Family Honour'." *Jordan Times,* December 3, 2016. https://www.jordantimes.com/news/local/new-projected-shelter-house-women-under-threat-over-family-honour%E2%80%99.

Husseini, Rana. 2017a. "Jordanian Court Sets Precedent, Toughens Sentence for 'Honor' Killing." *Al Bawaba,* March 22, 2017. https://www.albawaba.com/news/jordanian-court-sets-precedent-toughens-sentence-%E2%80%98honor%E2%80%99-killing-953540.

Husseini, Rana. 2017b. "Debate Continues as Article 308 on Way to Lower House's Vote." *Jordan Times,* May 31, 2017. https://jordantimes.com/news/local/debate-continues-article-308-way-lower-houses-vote..

Husseini, Rana. 2017c. "Jordan Delivers 'Real Change' on Important Human Rights—HRW." *Jordan Times,* October 5, 2017. https://www.jordantimes.com/news/local/jordan-delivers-real-change-important-human-rights-%E2%80%94-hrw.

Husseini, Rana. 2018. "Women in 'Protective Custody' to Be Moved to Guesthouses by End of Month—Lattouf." *Jordan Times,* May 6, 2018. http://www.jordantimes.com/news/local/women-protective-custody%E2%80%99-be-moved-guesthouses-end-month-%E2%80%94-lattouf.

Hyndman, Jennifer. 2007. "Feminist Geopolitics Revisited: Body Counts in Iraq." *The Professional Geographer* 59, no. 1: 35-46.

Jabiri, Afaf. 2016. *Gendered Politics and Law in Jordan: Guardianship over Women.* London: Palgrave Macmillan.

Jehl, Douglas. 1993. "4 Palestinians are Charged in Plot Linked to Terrorist Group." *New York Times,* April 2, 1993. https://www.nytimes.com/1993/04/02/us/4-us-palestinians-are-indicted-in-plot-linked-to-terrorist-group.html.

Jiwani, Yasmin. 2006. *Discourses of Denial: Mediations of Race, Gender, and Violence.* Vancouver: University of British Columbia Press.

Jiwani, Yasmin. 2014. "Posthumous Rescue: The Shafia Young Women as Worthy Victims." *Girlhood Studies* 7, no. 1 (Summer 2014): 27–45.

Joachim, Jutta M. 2007. *Agenda Setting, the UN, and NGOs: Gender Violence and Reproductive Rights.* Washington, DC: Georgetown University Press.

Jordan Times. 2016. "King Orders Setting Up Judicial Reform Panel." *Jordan Times.* October 19, 2016. https://www.jordantimes.com/news/local/king-orders-setting-judicial-reform-panel.

Jordan Times. 2017a. "King Urges Strict, Swift Implementation of Judicial Reform Plan." February 26, 2017. https://www.jordantimes.com/news/local/king-urges-strict-swift-implementation-judicial-reform-plan.

Jordan Times. 2017b. "Senate Approves Changes to Penal Code." *Jordan Times*, August 2, 2017. http://www.jordantimes.com/news/local/senate-approves-changes-penal-code.

Kanji, Azeezah, Khadijah Kanji, Naila Butt, Alia Hogben, Salha Jeizan, and Shahina Siddiqui. 2014. "'Honor Diaries': Breaking Silence on Violence or Reinforcing Stereotypes?" *Rabble*, April 17, 2014. https://rabble.ca/news/2014/04/honor-diaries-breaking-silence-on-violence-or-reinforcing-stereotypes.

Kay, Barbara. 2009. "Honour Killing is Not 'Domestic' Violence." *The National Post*, July 29, 2009. http://barbarakay.ca/articles/view/378.

Kay, Jonathan. 2007. "The Death of Aqsa Parvez." *National Post*, December 11, 2007. http://www.irfi.org/articles/articles_1701_1750/the_death_of_aqsa_parvez.htm.

Kay, Jonathan. 2011. "Canadian Imams Take a Praiseworthy Stand on Honour Killings." *National Post*, December 9, 2011. https://nationalpost.com/opinion/jonathan-kay-canadian-imams-take-a-praiseworthy-stand-on-honour-killings.

Khalili, Laleh. 2017. "With Muslim Ban, Trump and Bannon Wanted Chaos, but Not Resistance." Truthout, January 31, 2017. https://truthout.org/articles/sowing-mayhem-to-reap-power-the-sinister-strategy-behind-trump-s-muslim-ban/.

Khan, Sheema. 2010. "The Shame of Honour Crimes." *Globe and Mail*, July 21, 2010. https://www.theglobeandmail.com/opinion/the-shame-of-honour-crimes/article1387126/.

Khan, Sheema. 2014. "We Can End Honour Killings, But Not with Films by Anti-Muslim Zealots." *Globe and Mail*, April 16, 2014. https://www.theglobeandmail.com/opinion/we-can-end-honour-killings-but-not-with-films-by-anti-muslim-zealots/article18036639/.

Khouri, Norma. 2003. *Honor Lost: Love And Death In Modern-Day Jordan*. New York: Atria Books.

Khoury, Jack. 2018. "Report: Murder Rate among Israeli Non-Jews Far Outstrips Jewish Rate." *Haaretz*, February 12, 2018. https://www.haaretz.com/israel-news/report-murder-rate-among-israeli-non-jews-far-outstrips-jewish-rate-1.5809175.

King Abdullah II. 2016a. "Sixth Discussion Paper: Rule of Law and Civil State." *King Abdullah II Official Website*, October 16, 2016. https://rhcjoenglish.wordpress.com/.

King Abdullah II. 2016b. "Letter to Zaid Rifa'i Entrusting Him with Leading a Royal Committee to Develop Judiciary and Strengthen the Rule of Law." *King Abdullah II Official Website*, October 18, 2016. https://kingabdullah.jo/en/letters/letter-zaid-rifai-entrusting-him-leading-royal-committee-develop-judiciary-and-strengthen.

King, Diane E. 2008. "The Personal Is Patrilineal: *Namus* as Sovereignty." *Identities: Global Studies in Culture and Power* 15, no. 3: 317–42.

Kogacioglu, Dicle. 2004. "The Tradition Effect: Framing Honor Crimes in Turkey." *differences: A Journal of Feminist Cultural Studies* 15, no. 2: 118–50.

Krajicek, David K. 2013. "Justice Story: 'Die, My Daughter, Die!' An Old-World 'Honor Killing' in Modern St. Louis." *New York Daily News*, November 10, 2013. https://www.nydailynews.com/news/justice-story/justice-story-honor-killing-article-1.1510125.

Kumar, Deepa. 2012. *Islamophobia and the Politics of Empire*. Chicago: Haymarket.

Lang, Sharon D. 2005. *Sharaf Politics: Honor and Peacemaking in Israeli-Palestinian Society*. London: Routledge.

Layne, Linda L. 1994. *Home and Homeland: The Dialogics of Tribal and National Identities in Jordan*. Princeton, NJ: Princeton University Press.

Lee, Cynthia. 2008. "The Gay Panic Defense." *U.C. Davis Law Review* 42: 471–566.

Lidman, Melanie. 2016. "Using the Term 'Honor Killings' Leads to Many More Victims, Israeli Arab Activists Warn." *Times of Israel,* October 14, 2016. https://www.timesofisrael.com/using-the-term-honor-killings-leads-to-many-more-victims-israeli-arab-activists-warn/.

Lis, Jonathan. 2010. "Israel Arab MK: No Murders Should Ever Be Called 'Honor Killing.'" *Haaretz,* November 10, 2010. https://www.haaretz.com/1.5137697.

Lowrance, Sherry L. 1998. "After Beijing: Political Liberalization and the Women's Movement in Jordan." *Middle Eastern Studies* 34, no. 3: 83–102.

Lucas, Russell. 2008. "Side Effects of Regime Building in Jordan: The State and the Nation." *Civil Wars* 10, no. 3 (September): 281–93.

Luck, Taylor. 2018. "In Jordan, 'House of Safety' Offers Hope and Freedom to At-Risk Women." *Christian Science Monitor,* September 14, 2018. https://www.csmonitor.com/World/Middle-East/2018/0914/In-Jordan-house-of-safety-offers-hope-and-freedom-to-at-risk-women.

Lunde, Kelly. 2017. "US Protests Grow Against Donald Trump's Immigration Ban." *Al Jazeera,* January 29, 2017. https://www.aljazeera.com/news/2017/01/protests-grow-trump-immigrant-ban-order-170129194912379.html.

Maayeh, Suha. 2016. "Jordan Says 'Honour Killing' Is Against Islam." *The National,* December 3, 2016. https://www.thenational.ae/world/jordan-says-honour-killing-is-against-islam-1.203182.

Mahadeen, Ebtihal. 2013. "Doctors and Sheikhs: 'Truth' in Virginity Discourse in Jordanian Media." *Journal of International Women's Studies* 14, no. 4: 80–94.

Mahadeen, Ebtihal. 2017. "'The Martyr of Dawn': Femicide in Jordanian Media." *Crime, Media, Culture* 13, no. 1: 41–54.

Mahmood, Saba. 2011. *Politics of Piety: The Islamic Revival and the Feminist Subject.* Princeton, NJ: Princeton University Press.

Maira, Sunaina. 2008. "We Ain't Missing: Palestinian Hip Hop—A Transnational Youth Movement." *CR: The New Centennial Review* 8, no. 2 (Fall): 161–92.

Maira, Sunaina. 2013. *Jil Oslo: Palestinian Hip Hop, Youth Culture, and the Youth Movement.* Washington, DC: Tadween.

Makarem, Ghassan. 2009. "We Are Not Agents of the West: Ghassan Makarem Replies to Joseph Massad." *Reset Doc,* December 14, 2009. https://www.resetdoc.org/story/we-are-not-agents-of-the-west/.

Malkawi, Banan. 2011. "US Embassy Cable: Jordan's Citizenship Law 'More about Identity Politics, Not Gender Concerns." *Ammon News,* March 1, 2011. http://en.ammonnews.net/article.aspx?articleNO=11296#.XUxkWKl7lRo.

Marcus, Isabel. 1994. "Reframing 'Domestic Violence': Terrorism in the Home." In *The Public Nature of Private Violence: The Discovery of Domestic Violence,* edited by Martha Albertson Fineman and Roxanne Mykitiuk. New York: Routledge. 11–35.

Marshood, Hala. 2019. "Tali'at: Putting Feminism at the Center of Palestinian Liberation." *MadaMasr,* October 16, 2019. https://madamasr.com/en/2019/10/26/opinion/u/taliat-putting-feminism-at-the-center-of-palestinian-liberation/.

Marshood, Hala, and Riya Alsanah. 2020. "Tal'at: A Feminist Movement That Is Redefining Liberation and Reimagining Palestine." *Mondoweiss,* February 25, 2020. https://mondoweiss.net/2020/02/talat-a-feminist-movement-that-is-redefining-liberation-and-reimagining-palestine/.

Mason, Corinne L. 2013. "Global Violence Against Women as a National Security 'Emergency.'" *Feminist Formations* 25, no. 2 (Summer): 55–80.

Mason, Corinne L. 2017. *Manufacturing Urgency: The Development Industry and Violence Against Women.* Regina, Saskatchewan: University of Regina Press.

Massad, Joseph A. 2001. *Colonial Effects: The Making of National Identity in Jordan.* New York: Columbia University Press.

Massad, Joseph A. 2009. "'I Criticize Gay Internationalists, Not Gays': Joseph Massad Counter-replies to Ghassan Makarem." *Reset Doc,* December 14, 2009. https://www.resetdoc.org/story/i-criticize-gay-internationalists-not-gays/.

Massad, Joseph A. 2015. *Islam in Liberalism.* Chicago: University of Chicago Press.

Mather, Mark, and Charlotte Feldman-Jacobs. 2016. "Women and Girls at Risk of Female Genital Mutilation/Cutting in the United States." *PRB,* February 5, 2016. https://www.prb.org/us-fgmc/.

Mayell, Hillary. 2002. "Thousands of Women Killed for Family 'Honor.'" *National Geographic,* February 12, 2002. https://www.nationalgeographic.com/culture/2002/02/thousands-of-women-killed-for-family-honor/.

Mayer, Elizabeth Ann. "Internationalizing the Conversation on Women's Rights: Arab Countries Face the CEDAW Committee." In *Islamic Law and the Challenges of Modernity,* edited by Yvonne Yazbeck Haddad, Barbara Freyer Stowasser. Walnut Creek: Altamira Press, 2004. 133–60.

Mays, Kyle T. 2019. "Decolonial Hip Hop: Indigenous Hip Hop and the Disruption of Settler Colonialism." *Cultural Studies* 33, no. 3: 460–79.

McAlister, Melani. 2001. *Epic Encounters: Culture, Media, and U.S. Interests in the Middle East, 1945–2000.* Berkeley: University of California Press.

McKinnon, Sara. 2014. "Text-Based Approaches to Qualitative Research An Overview of Methods, Process, and Ethics." In *The International Encyclopedia of Media Studies,* 1st edition, edited by Angharad N. Valdivia. Hoboken: John Wiley & Sons, 1–19.

McKinnon, Sara L. 2016a. "Gender Violence as Global Phenomenon: Refugees, Genital Surgeries, and Neocolonial Projects of the United States." *Cultural Studies; Critical Methodologies* 16, no. 4: 414–26.

McKinnon, Sara L. 2016b. *Gendered Asylum: Race and Violence in U.S. Law and Politics.* Urbana, Chicago, and Springfield: University of Illinois Press.

McQuigge, Michelle. 2011. "Muslim Clerics Band Together to Denounce 'Honour Killings.'" *The Star,* December 9, 2011. https://www.thestar.com/news/canada/2011/12/09/muslim_clerics_band_together_to_denounce_honour_killings.html.

McVeigh, Karen. 2018. "'US Is Moving Backwards': Female Genital Mutilation Ruling A Blow To Girls At Risk." *The Guardian.* November 22, 2018. https://www.theguardian.com/society/2018/nov/22/us-is-moving-backwards-female-genital-mutilation-ruling-a-blow-to-girls-at-risk.

Meetoo, Veena, and Heidi Safia Mirza. 2007. "'There Is Nothing 'Honourable' about Honour Killings': Gender, Violence and the Limits of Multiculturalism." *Women's Studies International Forum* 30, no. 3: 187–200.

Melhem, Ahmad. 2014. "Palestinian Activists Press Abbas to Outlaw Honor Crimes." *Al-Monitor,* March 12, 2014. https://www.al-monitor.com/pulse/originals/2014/03/palestine-honor-crime-women-abuse-law-abbas.html.

Merry, Sally Engle. 2006. *Human Rights and Gender Violence: Translating International Law into Local Justice.* Chicago: University of Chicago Press.

Merry, Sally Engle. 2016. *The Seductions of Quantification: Measuring Human Rights, Gender Violence, and Sex Trafficking.* Chicago: University of Chicago Press.

Middle East Monitor. 2018. "Palestinian Poverty Level Almost Double Israel Average." December 31, 2018. https://www.middleeastmonitor.com/20181231-palestinian-poverty-level-almost-double-israel-average/.

Milani, Leila. 2017. "Violence Against Women and 'Honor Killings' Are Used as Justification in Executive Order." *Futures without Violence,* March 23, 2017. https://www.futureswithoutviolence.org/violence-against-women-and-honor-killings-are-used-as-justification-in-executive-order/.

Mir-Hosseini, Ziba. 2007. "How the Door of Ijtihad Was Opened and Closed: A Comparative Analysis of Recent Family Law Reforms in Iran and Morocco." *Washington and Lee Law Review* 64, no. 4: 1499–1511.

Mitchell, Bob. 2010. "Town Remembers Slain Teen." *The Star,* January 6, 2010. https://www.thestar.com/news/ontario/2010/01/06/town_remembers_slain_teen.html.

Mitchell, Bob, and Noor Javed. 2010. "'I Killed My Daughter . . . With My Hands.'" *The Star,* June 16, 2010. https://www.thestar.com/news/crime/2010/06/16/i_killed_my_daughter__with_my_hands.html.

Mohanty, Chandra Talpade. 1988. "Under Western Eyes: Feminist Scholarship and Colonial Discourses." *Feminist Review* no. 30 (Autumn): 61–88.

Mojab, Shahrzad. 2012. "The Politics of Culture, Racism, and Nationalism in Honour Killing." *Canadian Law Review* 16, no. 2: 115–34.

Mojab, Shahrzad, and Nahla Abdo, eds. 2004. *Violence in the Name of Honour: Theoretical and Political Challenges.* Istanbul: Istanbul Bilgi University Press.

Molavi, Shourideh C. *Stateless Citizenship: The Palestinian-Arab Citizens of Israel.* Leiden: Brill, 2011.

Monkman, Lenard. 2017. "'No Ban on Stolen Land,' Say Indigenous Activists in U.S." *CBC,* February 2, 2017. https://www.cbc.ca/news/indigenous/indigenous-activists-immigration-ban-1.3960814.

Moss, David. 2005. *Cultivating Development: An Ethnography of Aid Policy and Practice.* London; Ann Arbor, MI: Pluto Press.

Musa, Rimaz. 2015. "الحاكم بأمر «الشرف»: مقابلة مع المتصرف حجازي عساف" ["The Governor of 'Honor': An Interview with Governor Hijazi Assad."] *7iber,* February 11, 2015. https://www.7iber.com/2015/02/administrative-detention-governer/?utm_source=.

Muslim Advocates. 2017. "'Honor Killings' and the Muslim Ban: How President Trump's Executive Orders Are Premised on Animus and Negative Stereotypes Against Muslims." Issue Brief, September 2017. https://muslimadvocates.org/files/IssueBrief_HonorKillingsandMuslimBan.pdf.

Naber, Nadine. 2019. "Here We Go Again: Saving Muslim Women and Queers in the Age of Trump." *Mada Masr,* April 18, 2019. https://madamasr.com/en/2019/04/18/feature/society/here-we-go-again-saving-muslim-women-and-queers-in-the-age-of-trump/.

Naber, Nadine, and Junaid Rana. 2019. "The Trouble with 21st Century Anti-Muslim Racism." *Jadaliyya,* June 19, 2019. https://www.jadaliyya.com/Details/39830/The-21st-Century-Problem-of-Anti-Muslim-Racism.

Nafar, Tamer, Suhell Nafar, and Mahmood Jrery. 2012. "DAM Responds: On Tradition and the Anti-Politics of the Machine." *Jadaliyya,* December 26, 2012. http://www.jadaliyya.com/Details/27683/DAM-Responds-On-Tradition-and-the-Anti-Politics-of-the-Machine.

Nagar, Richa. 2014. *Muddying the Waters: Coauthoring Feminisms across Scholarship and Activism.* Urbana: University of Illinois.

Nanes, Stefanie Eileen. 2003. "Fighting Honor Crimes: Evidence of Civil Society in Jordan." *The Middle East Journal* 57, no. 1 (Winter): 112–29.

Narayan, Uma. 1997. *Dislocating Cultures: Identities, Traditions, and Third World Feminism.* New York: Routledge.

National Committee to Combat Violence Against Women. 2011. Ministry of Women's Affairs, the Palestinian National Authority. January 17, 2011. *National Strategy to Combat Violence Against Women 2011 - 2019.* https://www.unwomen.org/~/media/headquarters/media/stories/en/palestinianauthoritynationalstrategytocombatpdf.pdf?v=1&d=20140917T101042.

National Post. 2007. "The Meaning of Aqsa Parvez." December 12, 2007, p. A26.

Nesheiwat, Christina. 2012. "DAM Explores the Unmapped in Their New Album 'Dabke on the Moon.'" *Jadaliyya,* December 19, 2012. http://www.jadaliyya.com/Details/27653/DAM-Explores-the-Unmapped-in-Their-New-Album-Dabke-on-the-Moon.

Neuman, Gerald. 2017. "Neither Facially Legitimate Nor Bona Fide—Why the Very Text of the Travel Ban Shows It's Unconstitutional." *Just Security,* June 9, 2017. https://www.justsecurity.org/41953/facially-legitimate-bona-fide-why-unconstitutional-travel-ban/.

Newman, Andy. 2017. "Highlights: Reaction to Trump's Travel Ban." *New York Times,* January 29, 2017. https://www.nytimes.com/2017/01/29/nyregion/trump-travel-ban-protests-briefing.html.

Oberwittler, Dietrich, and Julia Kasselt. 2014. "Honour Killings." In *The Oxford Handbook of Gender, Sex, and Crime,* edited by Rosemary Gartner and Bill McCarthy. Oxford: Oxford University Press. 652–70.

Odgaard, Lena. 2014. "Upsurge in Palestinian 'Honour Killings.'" *Al Jazeera,* March 25, 2014. https://www.aljazeera.com/features/2014/3/25/upsurge-in-palestinian-honour-killings.

Olwan, Dana M. 2013. "Gendered Violence, Cultural Otherness, and Honour Crimes in Canadian National Logics." *Canadian Journal of Sociology* 38, no. 4: 533–56.

Olwan, Dana M. 2014. "'No Place in Canada': Triumphant Discourses, Murdered Women and the 'Honour Crime.'" In *'Honour' Killing and Violence: Theory, Policy, and Practice,* edited by Aisha Gill, Carolyn Strange, and Karl Roberts. London: Palgrave Macmillan. 218–36.

Olwan, Dana M. 2019. "Pinkwashing the 'Honor Crime': Murdered Muslim Women and the Politics of Posthumous Solidarities." *Signs* 44, no. 4: 905–30.

Oosting, Jonathan. 2012. "Rejecting Islamophobia: Town hall counters 'Jessica Mokdad Human Rights Conference' in Dearborn." *M Live Michigan,* April 27, 2012. https://www.mlive.com/news/detroit/2012/04/rejecting_islamophobia_town_ha.html.

Ostrow, Ronald J. 1993. "U.S. Indicts Four Tied to Terrorist Abu Nidal Group." *Los Angeles Times,* April 2, 1993. https://www.latimes.com/archives/la-xpm-1993-04-02-mn-18130-story.html.

Pain, Rachel. 2014. "Everyday Terrorism: Connecting Domestic Violence and Global Terrorism." *Progress in Human Geography* 38, no. 4: 531–50.

Pain, Rachel, and Lynn Staeheli. 2014. "Introduction: Intimacy-Geopolitics and Violence." *Area* 46, no. 4: 344–60.

Palestinian Central Bureau of Statistics. 2006. *Domestic Violence Survey (December, 2005–January, 2006): Main Findings.* June 2006. Ramallah, Palestine. https://www.cepal.org/mujer/noticias/paginas/7/42837/domestic_violence_Palestine.pdf.

PC, Zoe. 2019. "Palestinian Women to March Against Gender-Based Violence." *People's Dispatch,* September 25, 2019. https://peoplesdispatch.org/2019/09/25/palestinian-women-to-march-against-gender-based-violence/.

Perry, Marc D. 2008. "Global Black Self-Fashioning: Hip Hop as Diasporic Space." *Identities: Global Studies in Culture and Power*15, no. 6: 635–64.

Perry, Nicholas J. 2004. "The Numerous Federal Legal Definitions of Terrorism: The Problem of Too Many Grails." *Journal of Legislation* 30, no. 2: 249–74.

Petra News Agency. 2017. "King Receives Report on Judiciary Reform." *Jordan News Agency,* February 26, 2017.

Politico Staff. 2016. "Full Text: Donald Trump's Speech on Fighting Terrorism." *Politico,* August 15, 2016. https://www.politico.com/story/2016/08/donald-trump-terrorism-speech-227025.

Pratt, Nicola. 2015. "A History of Women's Activism in Jordan: 1946–1989." *7iber,* May 26, 2015. https://www.7iber.com/society/a-history-of-womens-activism-in-jordan-1946-1989/.

Prieto, Ana V. Ibáñez. 2018. "Women Groups Hail Opening of Shelter for Abused Women." *Jordan Times,* August 2, 2018. http://www.jordantimes.com/news/local/women-groups-hail-opening-shelter-abused-women.

Prusher, Ilene. 2014. "Film Wages 'Interfaith Campaign' Against Abuse of Muslim Women." *Haaretz,* March 26, 2014. https://www.haaretz.com/honor-diaries-for-muslim-women-1.5339100.

Puar, Jasbir. 2007. *Terrorist Assemblages: Homonationalism in Queer Times.* Durham, NC: Duke University Press.

Puar, Jasbir K., and Amit Rai. 2003. "Monster, Terrorist, Fag: The War on Terrorism and the Production of Docile Patriots." *Social Text* 20, no. 3 (Fall): 117–48.

Razack, Sherene. 1998. *Looking White People in the Eye: Gender, Race, and Culture in the Courtrooms and Classrooms.* Toronto: Toronto University Press.

Razack, Sherene. 2003. "A Violent Culture or Culturalized Violence? Feminist Narratives of Sexual Violence Against South Asian Women." *Studies in Practical Philosophy* 3, no. 1: 80–104.

Razack, Sherene. 2008. *Casting Out: The Eviction of Muslims from Western Law and Politics.* Toronto: University of Toronto Press.

Reene, Alex. 2017. "Has Donald Trump Signed More Executive Orders in His First 100 Days Than Past Presidents?" *ABC,* April 25, 2017. https://www.abc10.com/article/news/local/has-donald-trump-signed-more-executive-orders-in-his-first-100-days-than-past-presidents/103-433762172.

Reimers, Eva. 2007. "Representations of an Honor Killing: Intersections of Discourses on Culture, Gender, Equality, Social Class, and Nationality." *Feminist Media Studies* 7, no. 3: 239–55.

Reuters. 2007. "Father Says Killed Daughter in Canadian Hijab Case." December 11, 2007. https://www.reuters.com/article/us-crime-hijab/father-says-killed-daughter-in-canadian-hijab-case-idUSN1151774720071211.

Riley, Krista Melanie. 2009. "How to Accumulate National Capital: The Case of the 'Good' Muslim." *Global Media Journal* 2, no. 2: 57–71.

Robinson, Bill. 2009. "Bench Dedicated for Honor-Killing Victim." *Niagara This Week,* September 1, 2009, p. 24.

Robinson, Glenn E. 1998. "Defensive Democratization in Jordan." *International Journal of Middle East Studies* 30, no. 3 (August): 387–410.

Robinson, Shira. *Citizen Strangers: Palestinians and the Birth of Israel's Liberal Settler State.* Stanford: Stanford University Press, 2013.

Rogan, Mary. 2008. "Girl, Interrupted." *Toronto Life,* December 42: 52–59.

Rosella, Louie. 2017. "Mississauga Dad who killed Teenage Daughter Dies in Prison." *Mississauga News,* March 2, 2017. https://www.simcoe.com/news-story/7167867-mississauga-dad-who-killed-teenage-daughter-dies-in-prison/.

Rouhana, Nadim N., and Areej Sabbagh-Khoury. 2015. "Settler-Colonial Citizenship: Conceptualizing the Relationship between Israel and Its Palestinian Citizens." *Settler Colonial Studies* 5, no. 3: 205–25.

Ruez, Derek. 2013. "'Partitioning the Sensible' at Park 51: Rancière, Islamophobia, and Common Politics." *Antipode* 45, no. 5: 1128–47.

Safieh, Randa. 2013. "Identity, Diaspora, and Resistance Palestinian Hip-Hop." In *Palestinian Music and Song: Expression and Resistance Since 1900,* edited by Moslih Kanaaneh, Stig-Magnus Thorsén, Heather Bursheh, and David A. McDonald. Bloomington: Indiana University Press. 69–81.

Saiya, Nilay, Tasneem Zaihra, and Joshua Fidler. 2017. "Testing the Hillary Doctrine: Women's Rights and Anti-American Terrorism." *Political Research Quarterly* 70, no. 2 (June): 421–32.

Salaime, Samah. 2014. "Who Will Put an End to the Murder of Arab Women in Israel?" *+972,* November 4, 2014. https://972mag.com/who-will-put-an-end-to-the-murder-of-arab-women-in-israel/98400/.

Salaime, Samah. 2015. "New Name for an Old Crime: Police Get Creative with 'Honor Killings.'" *+972,* January 2, 2015. https://972mag.com/new-name-for-an-old-crime-israeli-police-get-creative-with-honor-killings/100852/.

Schwedler, Jillian. 2012. "The Political Geography of Protest in Neoliberal Jordan." *Middle East Critique* 20, no. 3: 259–70.

Semati, Mehdi. 2010. "Islamophobia, Culture and Race in the Age of Empire." *Cultural Studies* 24, no. 2: 256–75.

Sengupta, Somini. 2017. "One by One, Marry-Your-Rapist Laws Are Falling in the Middle East." *New York Times,* July 22, 2017. https://www.nytimes.com/2017/07/22/world/middleeast/marry-your-rapist-laws-middle-east.html.

Sensoy, Özlem, and Elizabeth Marshall. 2010. "Missionary Girl Power: Saving the 'Third World' One Girl at a Time." *Gender and Education* 22, no. 3: 295–311.

Sev'er, Aysan, and Gökçeçiçek Yurdakul. 2001. "Culture of Honor, Culture of Change: A Feminist Analysis of Honor Killings in Rural Turkey." *Violence Against Women* 7, no. 9: 964–98.

Shalev, Ben. 2012. "It's More Than a Hip-hop and a Jump to the Moon for This Arab-Israeli Band." *Haaretz,* December 7, 2012. https://www.haaretz.com/.premium-arab-israeli-hip-hop-band-shoots-for-the-moon-1.5300170.

Shalhoub-Kevorkian, Nadera. 2003. "Reexamining Femicide: Breaking the Silence and Crossing 'Scientific Borders." *Signs* 28, no. 2 (Winter): 581–608.

Shalhoub-Kevorkian, Nadera, and Suhad Daher-Nashif. 2012. "The Politics of Killing Women in Colonized Contexts." *Jadaliyya,* December 17, 2012. http://www.jadaliyya.com/Details/27636/The-Politics-of-Killing-Women-in-Colonized-Contexts.

Shalhoub-Kevorkian, Nadera, and Suhad Daher-Nashif. 2013. "Femicide and Colonization: Between the Politics of Exclusion and the Culture of Control." *Violence Against Women* 19, no. 3: 295–315.

Shalhoub-Kevorkian, Nadera, Sarah Ihmoud, and Suhad Daher-Nashif. 2014. "Sexual Violence, Women's Bodies, and Israeli Settler Colonialism." *Jadaliyya,* November 17, 2014. https://www.jadaliyya.com/Details/31481.

Shepherd, Laura. 2008. *Gender, Violence and Security: Discourse as Practice.* London: Zed Books.

Sherwood, Harriet. "Death in the West Bank: The Story of An 'Honour' Killing." *The Guardian,* June 30, 2011. https://www.theguardian.com/world/2011/jun/30/honour-killing-west-bank-palestine.

Sonbol, Amira El Azhar. 2003. *Women of Jordan: Islam, Labor, and the Law.* Syracuse, NY: Syracuse University Press.

Sparks, Grace. 2018. "Americans Have Been Split on Trump's Travel Ban for a While." *CNN*, June 26, 2018. https://www.cnn.com/2018/06/26/politics/travel-ban-polling/index.html.

Spencer, Robert. 2010. "Canadian Town Embarrassed That It Sort of Stood Up Against Honor Killing." *Jihad Watch*, January 6, 2010. https://www.jihadwatch.org/2010/01/canada-town-embarrassed-that-it-sort-of-stood-up-against-honor-killing.

Spivak, Gayatri. 1988. "Can the Subaltern Speak?" In *Marxism and the Interpretation of Culture*, edited by Cary Nelson and Lawrence Grossberg. Urbana: University of Illinois Press. 271–313.

Staeheli, Lynn A., and Eleonore Kofman. 2004. "Mapping Gender, Making Politics: Toward Feminist Political Geographies." In *Mapping Women, Making Politics: Feminist Perspectives on Political Geography*, edited by Lynn A. Staeheli, Eleonore Kofman, and Linda J. Peake. New York: Routledge. 1–14.

Stampnitzky, Lisa. 2013. *Disciplining Terror: How Experts Invented 'Terrorism.'* Cambridge: Cambridge University Press.

Stern, Mark Joseph. 2017. "Why Judge Robart Blocked the Muslim Ban." *Slate*, February 4, 2017. https://slate.com/news-and-politics/2017/02/why-judge-robart-blocked-trumps-muslim-ban.html.

Suchland, Jennifer. 2015. *Economics of Violence: Transnational Feminism Postsocialism, and the Politics of Sex Trafficking*. Durham, NC: Duke University Press.

Sukarieh, Mayssoun. 2015. "The First Lady Phenomenon: Elites, States, and the Contradictory Politics of Women's Empowerment in the Neoliberal Arab World." *Comparative Studies of South Asia, Africa and the Middle East* 35, no. 3: 575–87.

Sultany, Nimer. 2012. "The Making of an Underclass: The Palestinian Citizens in Israel." *Israel Studies Review* 27, no. 2: 190–200.

Swedenburg, Ted. 2013. "Palestinian Rap: Against the Struggle Paradigm." In *Popular Culture in the Middle East and North Africa: A Postcolonial Outlook*, edited by Walid El Hamamsy and Mounira Soliman. New York: Routledge. 17–32.

Sweis, Rania. 2012. "Women's Rights at a Standstill in Jordan." *New York Times*, November 7, 2012. https://www.nytimes.com/2012/11/08/world/middleeast/womens-rights-at-a-standstill-in-jordan.html.

Tahhan, Zena. 2017. "Meet the Woman who Pushed to Repeal Jordan's Rape Law." *Al Jazeera*, August 4, 2017. https://www.aljazeera.com/features/2017/08/04/meet-the-woman-who-pushed-to-repeal-jordans-rape-law/?gb=true.

Terman, Rochelle. 2010. "To Specify or Single Out: Should We Use the Term 'Honor Killing'?" *Muslim World Journal of Human Rights* 7, no. 1: 1–39.

Terman, Rochelle. 2016. "Islamophobia, Feminism, and the Politics of Critique." *Theory, Culture, and Society* 33, no. 2: 77–102.

The White House. 2012. "Fact Sheet: Preventing and Responding to Violence Against Women and Girls Globally." *The White House: President Barak Obama*. August 10, 2012. https://obamawhitehouse.archives.gov/the-press-office/2012/08/10/fact-sheet-preventing-and-responding-violence-against-women-and-girls-gl

The White House. 2015. "Remarks by President Obama to the Kenyan People." *The White House: President Barak Obama*. July 26, 2015. https://obamawhitehouse.archives.gov/the-press-office/2015/07/26/remarks-president-obama-kenyan-people.

The White House. 2016. "Statement by the President on the International Day of Zero Tolerance for Female Genital Mutilation/Cutting." February 5, 2016. https://obamawhitehouse.archives.gov/the-press-office/2016/02/05/statement-president-international-day-zero-tolerance-female-genital.

Thobani, Sunera. 2007a. *Exalted Subjects: Studies in the Making of Race and Nation in Canada.* Toronto: University of Toronto Press.

Thobani, Sunera. 2007b. "White Wars: Western Feminisms and the 'War on Terror.'" *Feminist Theory* 8, no. 2: 169–85.

Thobani, Sunera. 2015. "Sovereignty, Culture, Rights: The Racial Politics of Gendered Violence in Canada." *Borderlands* 14, no. 1: 1–26.

Thoet, Alison. 2018. "Why the U.S. Ban on Female Genital Mutilation Was Ruled Unconstitutional." *PBS News Hour,* December 3, 2018. https://www.pbs.org/newshour/nation/why-the-u-s-ban-on-female-genital-mutilation-was-ruled-unconstitutional.

Thompson, Rosie-Lyse. 2017. "Jordanian Women Imprisoned in Name of Family Honor." *Reuters,* August 16, 2017. https://www.reuters.com/article/us-jordan-women-prison/jordanian-women-imprisoned-in-name-of-family-honor-idUSKCN1AW0IO.

Thomsen, Jacqueline. 2019. "Supreme Court Rules Against Trump on Census Citizenship Question." *The Hill,* June 27, 2019. https://thehill.com/regulation/court-battles/450641-supreme-court-rules-against-trump-administration-over-census.

Thuma, Emily L. 2019. *All Our Trials: Prisons, Policing, and the Feminist Fight to End Violence.* Urbana: University of Illinois Press.

Ticktin, Miriam. 2008. "Sexual Violence as the Language of Border Control: Where French Feminist and Anti-immigrant Rhetoric Meet." *Signs* 33, no. 4: 863–89.

Toronto Life. "Revisiting Aqsa Parvez: Q&A with Mary Rogan." *Toronto Life,* June 21, 2010. https://torontolife.com/city/revisiting-aqsa-parvez-qa-with-mary-rogan/.

Townsend, Mark. 2017. "Rape and Slavery Was Lure for UK Isis Recruits with History of Sexual Violence." *Guardian,* October 7, 2017. https://www.theguardian.com/world/2017/oct/07/isis-rape-slavery-british-recruits-islamic-state.

Treen, Joe. 1992. "'Die, My Daughter, Die!'" *People,* January 20, 1992. https://people.com/archive/die-my-daughter-die-vol-37-no-2/.

Treuthart, Mary Pat. 2016. "Feminist-in-Chief? Examining President Obama's Executive Orders on Women's Rights Issues." *Chicago-Kent Law Review* 91, no. 1: 171–206.

True, Jacqui. *The Political Economy of Violence Against Women.* New York: New York University Press, 2012.

Tucker, Judith E. 2018. "Arab Families and Islamic Law." In *Arab Family Studies: Critical Reviews,* edited by Suad Joseph. Syracuse, NY: Syracuse University Press. 399–415.

United Nations Development Programme. 2006. *Arab Human Development Report 2005: Towards the Rise of Women in the Arab World.* http://hdr.undp.org/sites/default/files/rbas_ahdr2005_en.pdf.

United Nations Economic and Social Council. 1999. *Violence Against Women in the Family.* Report of the Special Rapporteur on violence against women, its causes and consequences, Ms. Radhika Coomaraswamy, submitted in accordance with Commission on Human Rights resolution 1995/85." E/CN.4/1999/68. March 10, 1999. https://www.refworld.org/docid/3d6ce3cc0.html.

United Nations Economic and Social Council. 2002. *Cultural Practices in the Family that are Violent Towards Women.* E/CN.4/2002/83. January 31, 2002. https://documents-dds-ny.un.org/doc/UNDOC/GEN/G02/104/28/pdf/G0210428.pdf?OpenElement.

United Nations General Assembly. 1993. "Declaration on the Elimination of Violence against Women." 48/4. https://www.ohchr.org/Documents/ProfessionalInterest/eliminationvaw.pdf.

United Nations General Assembly. 2000a. "Letter dated 3 October 2000 from the Permanent Representative of Malaysia to the United Nations addressed to theSecretary General."

A/C.3/55/4. October, 4, 2000. https://documents-dds-ny.un.org/doc/UNDOC/GEN/N00/675/31/pdf/N0067531.pdf?OpenElement.

United Nations General Assembly. 2000b. "Third Committee Adopts Two Draft Resolutions on Crimes Against Women – Urging Elimination of 'Honor Crime' and All Forms of Violence." GA/SHC/3615. November 3, 2000. https://www.un.org/press/en/2000/20001103.gashc3615.doc.html.

United Nations General Assembly. 2000c. "81st. Plenary Meeting." A/55/PV.81. December 4, 2000. https://documents-dds-ny.un.org/doc/UNDOC/GEN/N00/779/61/pdf/N0077961.pdf?OpenElement.

United Nations General Assembly. 2001. "Working Towards the Elimination of Crimes Against Women Committed in the Name of Honour." A/RES/55/6. January 31, 2001. https://documents-dds-ny.un.org/doc/UNDOC/GEN/N00/563/35/PDF/N0056335.pdf?OpenElement.

United Nations General Assembly. 2003. "Working Towards the Elimination of Crimes Against Women Committed in the Name of Honour." A/Res/57/179. January 30, 2003. https://www.refworld.org/docid/3f4352da4.html.

United Nations General Assembly. 2004. "Working towards the Elimination of Crimes Against Women and Girls Committed in The Name of Honour." A/Res/59/165. February 10, 2005. https://undocs.org/en/A/RES/59/165.

United Nations General Assembly. 2012. "Report of the Special Rapporteur on violence against women, its causes and consequences, Rashida Manjoo." A/HRC/20/16. May 23, 2012. https://documents-dds-ny.un.org/doc/UNDOC/GEN/G12/136/00/pdf/G1213600.pdf?OpenElement.

United Nations Human Rights Committee. 2017. "Human Rights Committee examines the report of Jordan." October 20, 2017. https://www.ohchr.org/en/NewsEvents/Pages/DisplayNews.aspx?NewsID=22269&LangID=E.

United Nations Population Fund (UNFPA). 2000. "Lives Together, Worlds Apart: Men and Women in a Time of Change." *The State of the World Population 2000*. https://www.unfpa.org/publications/state-world-population-2000.

United Nations Population Fund (UNFPA). 2012. "'Cultural Tradition' is No Excuse for Female Genital Mutilation/Cutting." February, 17, 2012. https://www.unfpa.org/news/cultural-tradition-no-excuse-female-genital-mutilationcutting.

United Nations Population Fund (UNFPA). 2018. "Ministry of Women's Affairs and Government of Canada Launch a Flagship Programme to Eliminate Violence Against Women in the West Bank and Gaza." May 7, 2018. https://palestine.unfpa.org/en/news/ministry-womens-affairs-and-government-canada-launch-flagship-programme-eliminate-violence.

United States District Court, Eastern District of Missouri. Proffer of Information and Affidavit of Special Agent James C. Van Rhein, Jr., 1993. https://static1.squarespace.com/static/57f993ee46c3c42b615156b5/t/5c80aba1419202f922e86c62/1551936422710/zeinisa-affidavit.pdf.

UN Women. 2011. "Defining 'Honour' Crimes and 'Honour' Killings." February 26, 2011. https://www.endvawnow.org/en/articles/731-defining-honourcrimes-and-honour-killings.html.

UN Women. 2012. "Palestinian Hip Hop Group DAM Raises Awareness of 'Honour Killings' through a Powerful Music Video." November 9, 2012. http://www.unwomen.org/en/news/stories/2012/11/palestinian-hip-hop-group-dam-raises-awareness-of-honour-killings-through-a-powerful-music-video.

Urban Alliance. 2008. "Media Advisory." November 7, 2008. https://urbanalliance.files.wordpress.com/2012/10/aqsa-parvez.pdf.

US Code, Title 18, § 116. 2013. Female genital mutilation. United States Code, Supplement 5, Title 18 - CRIMES AND CRIMINAL PROCEDURE. Section 116.

US Immigration and Customs Enforcement. 2017. "ICE pilots FGM outreach program at JFK airport." July 12, 2017. https://www.ice.gov/news/releases/ice-pilots-fgm-outreach-program-jfk-airport.

US Immigration and Customs Enforcement. 2018. "ICE Brings Fight Against Female Genital Mutilation to Washington's International Air Hub." June 15, 2018. https://www.ice.gov/news/releases/ice-brings-fight-against-female-genital-mutilation-washingtons-international-air-hub.

US Department of State—Bureau of Consular Affairs. n.d. "U.S. Government Fact Sheet on Female Genital Mutilation or Cutting (FGM/C)." https://travel.state.gov/content/travel/en/us-visas/visa-information-resources/fact-sheet-on-female-genital-mutilation-or-cutting.html.

US Department of State. 2019. "United States Strategy to Prevent and Respond to Gender-Based Violence Globally (GBV Strategy)." March 11, 2019. https://www.state.gov/u-s-strategy-to-prevent-and-respond-to-gender-based-violence-globally-gbv-strategy/.

Valentine, David. 2003. "'The Calculus of Pain': Violence, Anthropological Ethics, and the Category Transgender." *Ethnos* 68, no. 1: 27–48.

Volpp, Leti. 2000. "Blaming Culture for Bad Behavior." *Yale Journal of Law & the Humanities* 2, no. 1: 89–116.

Volpp, Leti. 2002. "The Citizen and the Terrorist." *UCLA Law Review* 49, no. 1575: 561–86.

Volpp, Leti. 2006. "Disappearing Acts: On Gendered Violence, Pathological Cultures, and Civil Society." *PMLA* 121, no. 5: 1631–38.

Volpp, Leti. 2011. "Framing Cultural Difference: Immigrant Women and Discourses of Tradition." *differences* 22, no. 1: 90–110.

Volpp, Leti. 2017. "Trump's Mentions of 'Honor Killings' Betray the Truth of His 'Muslim Ban.'" *The Hill*, February 22, 2017. https://thehill.com/blogs/pundits-blog/immigration/320632-trumps-mention-of-honor-killings-betray-the-truth-of-his.

Volpp, Leti. 2019. "Protecting the Nation from Honor Killings: The Construction of a Problem Symposium: Constitutional Law in the Trump Era." *Constitutional Commentary* 34, article 1167: 133–69.

Walley, Christine J. 1997. "Searching for 'Voices': Feminism, Anthropology, and the Global Debate over Female Genital Operations." *Cultural Anthropology* 12, no. 3 (August): 405–38.

Wamsley, Laurel. 2017. "Michigan Laws Will Increase Penalties for Performing Female Genital Mutilation." *NPR*. July 12, 2017. https://www.kcur.org/2017-07-12/michigan-laws-will-increase-penalties-for-performing-female-genital-mutilation.

Warmington, Joe. 2008. "Dared to Be Different; Strangled teen Aqsa Parvez Rests in Numbered Gravesite." *Toronto Sun*, December 8, 2008: 4.

Warrick, Catherine. 2005. "The Vanishing Victim: Criminal Law and Gender in Jordan." *Law and Society Review* 39, no. 2: 315–48.

Warrick, Catherine. 2009. *Law in the Service of Legitimacy: Gender and Politics in Jordan*. New York: Routledge.

Weber, Beverly M. 2013. *Violence and Gender in the "New" Europe*. London: Palgrave Macmillan.

Weber, Cynthia. 2017. "The Trump Presidency, Episode 1: Simulating Sovereignty." *Theory and Event* 20, no. 1 (January Supplement): 132–42.

Webster-Kogan, Ilana. 2018. "Modalities of Space, Time, and Voice in Palestinian Hip-Hop Narratives." In *Traveling Towards Home: Mobilities and Homemaking*, edited by Nicola Frost and Tom Selwyn. Oxford: Berghan Books. 105–26.

Weinglass, Simona. 2015. "The Deadly War on Women That Israel Refuses to Talk About." *Times of Israel,* August 30, 2015. https://www.timesofisrael.com/the-deadly-war-on-women-that-israel-refuses-to-talk-about/.

Welch, Michael. 2004. "Trampling Human Rights in the War on Terror: Implications to the Sociology of Denial." *Critical Criminology* 12, no. 1: 1–20.

Welchman, Lynn, and Sarah Hossain, eds. 2005. *'Honour': Crimes, Paradigms, and Violence Against Women.* London: Zed Books.

Whitlock, Gillian. 2004. "Tainted Testimony: The Khouri Affair." *Australian Literary Studies* 21, no. 4: 165–77.

Whitlock, Gillian. 2007. *Soft Weapons: Autobiography in Transit.* Chicago: Chicago University Press.

Wikan, Unni. 2008. *In Honor of Fadime: Murder and Shame.* Chicago: Chicago University Press.

Wiktorowicz, Quintan. 2000. "Civil Society as Social Control: State Power in Jordan." *Comparative Politics* 33, no. 1: 43–61.

Worthington, Rogers. 1993. "A Family Tragedy or Terrorists' Scheme?" *Chicago Tribune,* June 13, 1993. https://www.chicagotribune.com/news/ct-xpm-1993-06-13-9306130207-story.html.

Wright, Melissa W. 2008. "Gender and Geography: Knowledge and Activism across the Intimately Global." *Progress in Human Geography* 33, no. 3: 379–86.

Yiftachel, Oren and Haim Yacoubi. 2003. "Urban Ethnocracy: Ethnicization and The Production of Space In An Israeli 'Mixed City.'" *Environment and Planning D: Society and Space,* no. 21: 673-693.

Zine, Jasmin. 2009. "Unsettling the Nation: Gender, Race and Muslim Cultural Politics in Canada." *Studies in Ethnicities and Nationalism* 9, no. 1: 146–63.

Ziya, Afiya Shehrbano. 2019. "Can Rescue Narratives Save Lives? Honor Killing in Pakistan." *Signs* 44, no. 2: 355–78.

Zoroya, Gregg. 2016. "'Honor Killings': 5 Things to Know." *USA Today,* June 9, 2016. https://www.usatoday.com/story/news/world/2016/06/09/honor-killings-united-nations-pakistan/85642786/.

INDEX